*New Casebooks*

# TESS OF THE D'URBERVILLES

# New Casebooks

*New Casebooks*

# TESS OF THE D'URBERVILLES

THOMAS HARDY

EDITED BY PETER WIDDOWSON

MACMILLAN

First published 1993 by
MACMILLAN PRESS LTD
Houndmills, Basingstoke, Hampshire RG21 6XS
and London
Companies and representatives
throughout the world

ISBN 0–333–54584–2 hardcover
ISBN 0–333–54585–0 paperback

A catalogue record for this book is available
from the British Library.

12  11  10  9  8  7  6  5  4  3
04  03  02  01  00  99  98  97  96  95

Printed in Hong Kong

**Hardy: The Tragic Novels: R. P. Draper**

This title is available in the original *Casebook Series*, offering
criticism inspired by the text throughout its history. The *New
Casebooks* series is developed from the original *Casebooks Series*,
edited by A. E. Dyson.

For a full listing of the *Casebook Series*, please write to the
Customer Services Department, Macmillan Distribution Ltd,
Houndmills, Basingstoke, Hampshire RG21 2EY.

To the memory of my parents
Ernest and Mary Widdowson,
with love and gratitude

# Contents

# Acknowledgements

I have a real debt of gratitude to the library staff on the Enfield site of Middlesex University – and particularly Val Weinstein and Geraldine Parkes – for their unremitting zeal and helpfulness. I am also deeply grateful to Jean Tonini, secretary to the School of English at the same institution, who has typed and retyped when others would have drawn the line. Without her the present volume would have been forever unfinished.

The editor and publishers wish to thank the following for permission to use copyright material:

John Barrell, extracts from 'Geographies of Hardy's Wessex', *Journal of Historical Geography* 8 (1982), by permission of Harcourt Brace Jovanovich Ltd;

Penny Boumelha, extract from *Thomas Hardy and Women: Sexual Ideology and Narrative Form* (1982), by permission of Harvester Wheatsheaf Ltd and The University of Wisconsin Press;

Laura Claridge, for 'Tess: A Less than Pure Woman Ambivalently Presented', *Texas Studies in Literature and Language*, 28, 3 (1986), by permission of The University of Texas Press;

Simon Gatrell, extracts from 'From *Tess* to *Jude* 1892–1984' in *Hardy the Creator: A Textual Biography* (1988). Copyright © 1988 Simon Gatrell, by permission of Oxford University Press;

John Goode, extracts from *Thomas Hardy: The Offensive Truth* (1988), by permission of Basil Blackwell Ltd;

Patricia Ingham, extracts from 'Fallen Woman as Sign, and Narrative Syntax in *Tess of the d'Urbervilles*' in *Thomas Hardy: A*

*Feminist Reading*, Feminist Readings Series (1989), by permission of Harvester Wheatsheaf Ltd and Humanities Press International, Inc.;

Jean Jacques Lecercle, extracts from 'The Violence of Style in *Tess of the d'Urbervilles*' in *Alternative Hardy*, ed. Lance St John Butler (1989), by permission of the author and Macmillan Press Ltd;

Jane Marcus, for 'A Tess for Child Molesters', *Jump Cut* (26 December 1981), 3, by permission of *Jump Cut*;

Kaja Silverman, extracts from 'History, Figuration and Female Subjectivity in *Tess of the d'Urbervilles*', *Novel*, 18, 1 (1984). Copyright © 1969 Novel Corp., by permission of Novel; a Forum on Fiction;

Charlotte Thompson, extracts from 'Language and the Shape of Reality in *Tess of the d'Urbervilles*', *English Literary History*, 50, 4 (1983), by permission of The Johns Hopkins University Press;

Peter Widdowson, extracts from '"A Tragedy of Modern Life?" Polanski's *Tess*' in *Hardy in History: A Study in Literary Sociology* (1989), by permission of Routledge;

Merryn and Raymond Williams, extracts from 'Hardy and Social Class' in *Thomas Hardy: The Writer and his Background*, ed. Norman Page (1980), Bell and Hyman, by permission of HarperCollins Publishers Ltd;

George Wootten, extracts from '*Tess of the d'Urbervilles*: towards a materialist criticism' in *Thomas Hardy: Towards a Materialist Criticism* (1985), Gill and Macmillan and Barnes and Noble Books, by permission of Gill and Macmillan Publishers.

Every effort has been made to trace all the copyright holders but if any have been inadvertently overlooked the publishers will be pleased to make the necessary arrangement at the first opportunity.

# General Editors' Preface

The purpose of this series of New Casebooks is to reveal some of the ways in which contemporary criticism has changed our understanding of commonly studied texts and writers and, indeed, of the nature of criticism itself. Central to the series is a concern with modern critical theory and its effect on current approaches to the study of literature. Each New Casebook editor has been asked to select a sequence of essays which will introduce the reader to the new critical approaches to the text or texts being discussed in the volume and also illuminate the rich interchange between critical theory and critical practice that characterises so much current writing about literature.

In this focus on modern critical thinking and practice New Casebooks aim not only to inform but also to stimulate, with volumes seeking to reflect both the controversy and the excitement of current criticism. Because much of this criticism is difficult and often employs an unfamiliar critical language, editors have been asked to give the reader as much help as they feel is appropriate, but without simplifying the essays or the issues they raise. Again, editors have been asked to supply a list of further reading which will enable readers to follow up issues raised by the essays in the volume.

The project of New Casebooks, then, is to bring together in an illuminating way those critics who best illustrate the ways in which contemporary criticism has established new methods of analysing texts and who have reinvigorated the important debate about how we 'read' literature. The hope is, of course, that New Casebooks will not only open up this debate to a wider audience, but will also encourage students to extend their own ideas, and think afresh about their responses to the texts they are studying.

*John Peck and Martin Coyle*
*University of Wales, Cardiff*

# Introduction: 'Tess of the d'Urbervilles' Faithfully Presented By

*PETER WIDDOWSON*

Anyone who has read *Tess of the d'Urbervilles* (and certainly any modern criticism about it) will be in no doubt that the novel is emphatically visual in many of its effects. There are those famous set-piece 'descriptions' of rural Wessex (not quite Dorset, let us remember); the inescapably scenic moments, such as the May-dance at Marlott as the novel opens or sunrise at Stonehenge towards the end, which render talk about Hardy's proto-cinematic techniques more than merely chic; and the narrative's obsessive voyeuristic gazing at Tess herself (especially that famous 'mobile peony mouth'[1]) which has made so many readers *wonder* a little about Thomas Hardy. But there is also a great deal of visual imagery in the novel of a rather more self-reflexive sort – a kind of metadiscourse about looking, seeing, perception, representation, imaging. This is not new or unique to *Tess of the d'Urbervilles* of course: it is everywhere apparent in Hardy's fiction – from the subtitling of *Under the Greenwood Tree* as 'A Rural Painting of the Dutch School' to the presence (betimes) of a photographer in *A Laodicean*; from the staged artificiality of the tableaux vivants in *The Hand of Ethelberta* to the blindness of Clym in *The Return of the Native*; from the astronomer's telescope in *Two on a Tower* to striking 'moments of vision' (a phrase I shall return to) such as that in *Desperate Remedies* (Hardy's first published novel) where Cytherea Graye, watching her father and some masons at the top of a church spire – 'it was an *illuminated miniature, framed in* by the dark *margin* of the window' (my italics) – suddenly sees him fall to his death: 'he reeled off into the air, immediately disappearing downwards'.[2] And there are the typographical signs and devices scattered throughout the text of *Jude the Obscure* – a novel significantly characterised by its author in his preface to the first edition (1895) as 'a series of seemings, or personal impressions'.[3]

But self-conscious techniques of visualisation are particularly insistent in *Tess*, a novel also prefatorily described by Hardy as 'an impression'[4] – a significant word, perhaps, given his fascination with the late 'impressionist' paintings of J. M. W. Turner.[5] Chapter Two, for example, opens with a reference to a 'landscape-painter', and from there on the novel abounds with overt or covert references to pictures.[6] There is also the complex ambiguity of the narrator's point of view – towards Tess in particular. For instance:

> As she walked along today, for all her *bouncing handsome womanliness, you* could sometimes *see* her twelfth year in her cheeks, or her ninth *sparkling from her eyes*; and even her fifth would flit over the *curves of her mouth* now and then.
>
> Yet *few* knew, and *still fewer* considered this. *A small minority*, mainly strangers, would *look long at her* in casually passing by, and grow momentarily fascinated by her freshness, and wonder if *they* would ever *see* her again: but *to almost everybody* she was a *fine and picturesque* country girl, and no more.
>
> (p. 52)

My italics draw attention to the voyeurism of the passage, but the uncertainty of focus ('you . . . few . . . still fewer . . . a small minority . . . almost everybody') and the peculiar logic of the syntax in the second paragraph ('Yet . . . but . . . and no more') make it very difficult to say who sees her like this and whether the narrative is attempting to distance itself from the erotic imaging the passage in fact delivers or is fully complicit in it. Furthermore, there is the continual presentation of Tess in terms of the way she is 'seen' by others – most especially, of course, Alec and Angel – until her 'character' seems to be composed entirely of other people's images of her (a point I will return to later). And there are the many other instances where the narrative deploys strikingly visual devices and motifs, from the filmic long-shots (the farm-girls picking swedes at Flintcomb-Ash) and close-ups (Tess's mouth), to the final scene where Angel and Liza Lu, 'their eyes riveted' to the gaol's flag-pole, watch the 'black flag' unfurl which denotes that Tess has been hanged (notice how, at this point, a novel which has fetishised Tess's visual presence throughout now signals its absence by her displacement into a black flag).

It is quite possible to think, therefore, that *Tess of the d'Urbervilles* is actually in some way *about* seeing and representation. After all, Hardy himself describes it in the preface to the first edition – although we can never really trust that wary old ironist and least self-revealing of writers – as 'an *attempt to give artistic form* to a true sequence of things' (my italics). And he also claims, by way of the novel's hugely contentious subtitle ('appended', he would have us believe in a prefatory postscript of 1912, 'at the last moment' and with no premeditation), that his 'Pure Woman' is '*faithfully presented* by Thomas Hardy' (my italics). Does the phrasing here suggest just how ironically conscious he was of representation as a potent source, precisely, of *mis*representation? Had the image, as we all now know in these post-modern times, already substantively replaced 'the thing itself' for Hardy? Was he already discrediting the notion that there is an ultimate reality, or true essence, outside of history and discourse – such as 'human nature', for example, or even perhaps: *pure woman*? But a discussion of this key term in Hardy's disingenuous subtitle – and a central theme of critical commentary on Tess – must wait for a moment, although, as we shall see, the 'pure woman' and her attendant debate in fact focuses the issues of seeing and representation which I have suggested the novel so insistently raises. Certainly a good deal of the criticism which follows in this volume emphasises these issues as crucial terms in discussing *Tess of the d'Urbervilles* – an emphasis which derives principally from two very contemporary critical sources: feminism and poststructuralism. In order to explain what I mean, and also to account for the nature and composition of this New Casebook, I need to reflect briefly on the general state of recent Hardy criticism, before returning to the problems of 'seeing', (mis)representation and pure women.

What is particularly noteworthy about the present collection is the fact that all the essays come from the last decade. In other words, although the brief for these New Casebooks is to select work from the past twenty years, I found that with a few honourable exceptions which the Bibliography will identify, all the really interesting material came after 1980. It appeared that work from the 1970s, even that of high quality and sophisticated in its own terms, somehow 'belonged' to an earlier critical phase[7] – rather like those auto-mobiles which are still being made new and still function adequately, but which, when you lift the bonnet, clearly betray a prior generation of technology. I do not mean to be gratuitously dismissive, or to foster a 'whig' view of literary-critical history as continually 'pro-gressive', nor do I wish to be wilfully partial and partisan, but so much critical writing on *Tess* in the 70s, with its emphases on plot, character, 'ideas' and imagery (sometimes symbolism), does now seem *passé*, beside the point, going nowhere – except over well-trodden (some might say exhausted) ground.

What gradually becomes apparent, despite an obsessive innovativeness and self-presentation of *difference*, is that by far the greatest proportion of criticism on Hardy's fiction in the 1970s was held within the (by then) traditional parameters of critical intelligibil-ity.[8] These were fundamentally humanist-realist in origin, promoting notions of a unified human subject ('the individual', 'character') at the centre of the general scheme of things – metaphysical, natural and social ('environment') – and of the artist's prime responsibility and achievement as being to represent this relationship with veracity (or with 'realism'). This, in turn, implies, on the one hand, the existence of an external reality to be copied – a given 'real world' and 'characters' both knowable and describable – and, on the other, the possibility of deploying a language which could accurately *describe* – not mediate – that reality, one which had a precise referentiality and would 'tell things as they really are'. What lies at the heart of such an essentialist world-view is a belief that everything has an ultimate ontological reality, an irreducible essence, quite outside its material, historical or discursive circumstances (things as they *really* are). The commonest (and most ideologically potent) expression of this is the notion of 'Human Nature' – the proposition that whatever the circumstances, and with the best will in the world, human beings cannot change their basic nature, or have it changed for them: that they are, as it were, trapped by their own very human-ness. But it is, of course, this 'essential' human nature which artists are most praised for depicting, and their 'realism' is, paradoxically, at once their ability to represent the contingent reality of everyday life, *and*, by way of this, the essential unchanging reality of 'human nature' itself. In its attempt to render this essence visible by describing it in refer-ential language, realism too is essentialist.

Hardy, against the grain of much of his writing, has, from the earliest reviews, been hauled into consonance with such a world-view and such an aesthetic. Borrowing his own phrase, 'Novels of Character and Environment',[9] to praise what are generally regarded as his 'major' novels, critics have characteristically seen Hardy, 'at his best', as the tragic humanist-realist of Wessex, finding essential human nature in the lives of his rural protagonists (and in his 'rustic chorus') pitted in conflict with 'Fate' or 'Nature' (much less often with 'Society'). This, together with his descriptions of nature and his evocation of a 'passing' rural community, has been regarded as his major achievement, and accounts for the elevation into canonic texts of about eight of his fourteen novels (the six 'minor novels' fail in various ways to fit this mould[10]). Even so, Hardy presents problems, and it is noteworthy how much damage-limitation criticism has had to go in for in order to wrench this 'flawed genius' into the canon and tradition. Hardy's 'faults' are said to be: his tendency to 'melo-drama'; the excessive use of chance and coincidence in his plots; his 'pessimism'; his parading of 'ill-digested' ideas; his at times pedantic, awkward, mannered style; and, over and above all these – indeed subsuming them – his tendency to 'improbability' and 'implausibil-ity'; in other words, his failure to be 'realistic', or, to put it yet another way, to represent 'essential reality' accurately. These 'faults' and 'flaws' bedevil even his major works, where they have to be ignored or explained away, but they are the principal cause of his 'failure' in the 'minor novels'.

All too often, and however sophisticated the particular inflexions of critical inquiry in the 1970s, many of these governing co-ordinates remained unchallenged. Certainly there were innovative approaches, with a kind of high-powered humanistic formalism (emphasising imagery, symbolism, 'poetic structure' and so forth) replacing the older 'character'/'Fate'/Tragedy/rural-elegy nexus, but fundamentally similar underlying assumptions (about Hardy's humanism, about his 'flaws', and especially about his 'uneasy' relation to realism) contin-ued to determine the critical positions taken up. There was no attempt, for example, to rethink the tendency to reject large chunks of Hardy's texts simply as bad writing; no sense that viewing them through a realist lens might result in them appearing 'improbable', and that perhaps the lens was wrong; no inquiry into the nature and function of Hardy's language (except perhaps its 'poetics'); or into his 'inadequate' characterisation (because 'character' itself remains an unproblematic concept) or his contingent plotting; no thought that perhaps Hardy was an *anti*-realist, challenging and demystifying the limits and conventions of realism and humanist essentialism. But the fundamental inadequacy of most of the 1970s criticism which I have left out of the present volume is not so much its residual subscription to the conventional critical stereotypes of Hardy's fiction, but rather its failure to admit, disguised by grandiloquent evaluations and judgements, that it was inadequate to the task of dealing with the *entire textuality* of the literary works it had in hand. All novels, but Hardy's especially so, are riddled with contradictory discourses, are inscribed throughout with fault-lines thrown up by the clash of competing discursive 'plates' just below the text's surface, and it is surely the job of criticism, not to reject them as 'failures of taste', but to explore and explain the significance of the work *as a whole*. It is instructive to compare criticism from the 1970s with many of the essays reprinted here[11] which focus on the dynamically unstable textuality of Hardy's fictional writing: its plural discourses and competing styles, its irony, mannerisms and self-deconstructing artificiality, its self-conscious vocabulary and modes of address, its language of tension. But the perception of these features is the reflex, I have suggested particularly, of feminist and poststructuralist initiatives and it is to these that we will return in a moment.

However, there is one impressive piece of scholarship from the 70s which should first be acknowledged as fundamentally influential in the contemporary redirecting of attention to Hardy's textuality in relation to *Tess*: J. T. Laird's *The Shaping of Tess of the d'Urbervilles* (1975), a book which traces the evolution of the novel from its earliest stages of manuscript composition, through various editions and revisions, to the 'quasi-definitive' version of the Wessex Edition of 1912. Despite a rather unnerving self-contradiction when Laird seems to suggest, *contra* his own exhaustive proof of the instability of the text, that 'studying the author's creative processes . . . eventually leads to a surer and deeper understanding of the meaning of the definitive text',[12] his work nevertheless reveals the extent and significance of Hardy's revisions and emendations, how conscious their effects were, and how a detailed examination of the textuality of *Tess* reinforces the sense that 'representation' and notions of a 'pure woman' are bedrock issues in the novel. Many essays since 1975 have been deeply beholden to Laird in their pursuit of textual *cruces* to explain the signifying effects of *Tess*. His work has, of course, been developed and expanded since – most particularly in the monumental Oxford edition of the novel edited by Juliet Grindle and Simon Gatrell[13] – and an essay by the latter (number 12 in the present volume) further reminds us of the significance of a critical method its author calls 'textual biography' in establishing how extensively and radically Hardy revised his texts in a subversive experimental practice of writing which, as Terry Eagleton has put it, shows a 'novelist whose work . . . is always on the point of breaking through its own containing forms'.[14] In particular, here, Gatrell is able to suggest that Hardy's class consciousness was strengthening, as a determinant in the novel, during his revision of it for the one-volume edition of 1892.

But it is with the intervention of feminism and poststructuralism that Hardy criticism significantly begins to retool. From the start of his novel-writing career, critics noticed and focused upon 'Hardy's Heroines', and there are many essays entitled thus (or alternatively 'Hardy's Women'), most of which reproduce, not surprisingly, the sexual stereotyping of dominant gender ideology.[15] Feminist criticism, conversely, aims to decode the sexual/textual politics of literary texts, and has therefore been especially concerned with the representation of women; with the whole construction of gender in discourse; and with the notion of the 'male gaze', its consumption of women and its tendency to reproduce its own images and fantasies as female sexuality. In this respect, Hardy's novels are an ideal site on which to explore such issues – and not by any means, as this volume itself clearly shows, from a position of hostility to his representation of women, but rather from a recognition of the complexity and innovativeness of what he seems to be doing. Alternatively, poststructuralist criticism, most obviously in Deconstruction, has re-emphasised textuality as the primary concern of criticism – though not as evidence of the integrated wholeness of the text as great work of art so beloved of New Criticism, but on the contrary, as a fissured, riven, deranged, unstable linguistic terrain. In this case, too, Hardy's texts – and in particular their evident artificiality, self-reflexiveness about modes of perception and reproduction, and their contradictory constituent discourses – offer themselves as fertile ground for analysis.

A seminal early essay,[16] in the contexts of both text and gender, is one by John Goode called 'Woman and the Literary Text' (1976), in which he suggests that we can only see the 'political implications' of a work by attending to its 'formal identity', and that in relation to *Tess* what we witness (and are implicated in) is 'the objectification of Tess by the narrator', especially by way of making her 'the object of consumption' of Alec and Angel (and then of us as voyeuristic readers consuming with our eyes both the text and, hence, Tess herself). The effect is to make us 'the subject of her, and thus guilty of the object images whose contradictions she is subject to'. In other words, Tess is composed of all the 'object images' the novel defines her as, primarily deriving from male lookers and including the narrator/Hardy and us as readers in our collusion with those images: nubile country-girl, plump arms, erotic mouth, and so on. Goode comments that this is why, 'whatever Hardy's own ideological commitment, no frame will hold his novel in place', or, to put it another way, why the text's discourses *have to be* accepted as contradictory. These themes are extended in his later (1979) essay, 'Sue Bridehead and the New Woman', where he suggests that Sue is an 'exposing image' in the 'taking of reality apart' which *Jude the Obscure* effects – most particularly of the mystifications inherent in conventional notions of love and marriage.[17] It is as a kind of tribute, then, to Goode's pioneering and radical recognition of the textual/sexual politics and subversive anti-realism of Hardy's fiction that I close the present volume with a more recent essay of his, one described by Terry Eagleton as 'alert to Hardy's fiction . . . as transformative practice, disruption, intervention, texts which . . . often enough meditate on the act of writing as a metaphor of their preoccupations, [and which show] astonishing . . . radicalism of gender as well as class.'[18]

By far the largest proportion of essays in the present collection bear witness to the force of Goode's initiatives and to the subsequent influence of feminist and poststructuralist criticism. But before turning to them, let me briefly pick up the word 'class' from Eagleton's remarks on Goode above. Where, one might ask, given the influence over the past two decades of marxist critical theory, is all the criticism which displays a materialist/historical/sociological/ideological approach to *Tess*? Surely feminism and poststructuralism are not the only stories of the 1980s? Well, no, they're not, although it must be acknowledged that there is a striking paucity of materialist work of any quality on the novel in question and even on Hardy in general. I have, however, wanted to signal – and again pay tribute to – the fundamental (and to me fundamentally beneficial) influence of Raymond Williams on cultural theory and criticism, in the UK at least, since the Second World War. His chapter on Hardy in *The English Novel from Dickens to Lawrence* (1970, too early and too well-known to be included here[19]) remains an enlightening analysis of Hardy's *mentalité* and its product. So, too, does Merryn Williams's also early – and, in its historical orientation, significantly still barely superseded – *Thomas Hardy and Rural England* (1972). It is fitting, therefore, that this New Casebook should open with an essay from 1980 by both Williamses on 'Hardy and Social Class'. Thereafter, there is not a great deal of historical criticism of Hardy. However, John Barrell's essay reproduced here (number 11) subtly weaves an historical sense into the pervasive theme of 'perception' – in this case of how people construct their own quasi-geographical perceptual environment. George Wotton (also represented here, in essay 2) has written, to my mind, one of the most innovative, but less than well-known, books on Hardy to date. His *Thomas Hardy: Towards a Materialist Criticism* (1985) offers at once a materialist-historical account of 'Wessex', a sophisticated reading of the novels (again primarily in terms of seeing/representation), and an extensive 'critiographical'[20] deconstruction of the way Hardy has been continuously reproduced as a cultural myth in the twentieth century.

What follows logically from the last point is the recognition that the 'meaning' of Thomas Hardy lies as much in the *reproduction* of his works in history as in the essentialist notion of 'the texts themselves', and that after 1981, therefore, the presence of Roman Polanski's film *Tess* is an intertextual fact of inescapable proportions.[21] Very large numbers of people – especially the young, and most particularly those studying Hardy at the higher levels of education – would first come to 'his' work by way of the film. The dominant text, in other words, was not *Tess of the d'Urbervilles*, but Polanski's *Tess*, and especially Nastassia Kinski's brooding gaze – so like Meryl Streep's on the poster for the film (1981 too) of John Fowles's novel, *The French Lieutenant's Woman*, also set in Dorset and overtly indebted to Hardy. Hence the presence here – since to concentrate solely on text as novel would be to repudiate my premise above about 'reproduction' – of two essays on the film: one, by Jane Marcus (essay 6), springing from feminism and implicitly raising the vexed question of the 'faithfulness' of film to book; the other (mine, essay 7) an instantiation of the 're-writing' of the novel by the 're-reading' which the film necessarily represents. It is also worth noting, in a volume of essays which makes so much of the visual dimension of *Tess of the d'Urbervilles*, that to ignore the most obvious visualisation of the novel would simply be perverse.

What is happening to Hardy, as a reflex of the new critical reproduction enabled by the kinds of developments discussed above, is that he is in the process of being post-modernised – indeed this volume can itself be seen to be assisting in just that. The foregrounding of sexual politics in *Tess*, and of the tensions incident on a late-nineteenth-century male novelist writing so ambiguously about his 'pure woman' heroine, about the destructive maleness of his two heroes' relations with her (especially the – apparent – ambiguity of seduction and rape), and about marriage, separation, bigamy, extra-marital sex and childbirth, all imply a writer whose 'consciousness' is in some sense being recast in the mould of feminist thinking about sexuality and patriarchy. Penny Boumelha's book, from which essay 3 comes, was one of the first to offer a sophisticated analysis of gender ideology in Hardy; Patricia Ingham's more recent study (essay 5) replaces the issue in its formal matrix of sign and narrative syntax, thus also incorporating the textual initiatives of poststructuralism. Laura Claridge's essay (number 4) brings into relief a rather more contrary subtext, Tess as '*less* than pure woman', which seems to run counter at once to Hardy's (apparent) commitment to his heroine and to much recent criticism – following Laird and Mary Jacobus[22] – which sees Hardy, for whatever reason, as actively stacking the novel in favour of Tess's 'purity'. More obviously poststructuralist in their variously stylistic, semiotic and deconstructive analyses of the complex, riven, heteroglossic textuality of *Tess*, the essays by Charlotte Thompson, Kaja Silverman and Jean Jacques Lecercle (essays 8, 9, 10) all point to the unstable play of the signifier as the nodal experience of the novel. And John Goode's essay, concluding the volume, also promotes a radically subversive *Tess of the d'Urbervilles* in which the iterative indications throughout Hardy's work of strategic anti-realism emerge to such an extent that the novel cannot be 'contained' by any one frame, its disjunctions themselves becoming an aspect of the ideological anger it expresses. In other words, we have a text which has indeed become a disruptive 'series of seemings', one which, in its destabilising formal dynamics, 'disproportions' (Hardy's word – see below, pp. 14–15) reality by revealing how slippery language is, how 'meaning' (and hence ideology) is constructed within discourse, and, precisely therefore, how representation becomes *mis*representation. By disturbing and displacing 'reality' (together with its servant, Realism) in the defamiliarising discourse of his own texts, Hardy exposes (or, more exactly, as a post-modern creature *is made to* expose) the mystifications, naturalisations and (mis-)representations by which the dominant ideology and culture sentence us all to lives of false being.

However, before I alchemise Hardy once and for all as a post-modernist (and throw away the stone), let me more properly register – so that I can bring it into sharper focus in the following section – that in his own historical period, and certainly when he was publishing his poetry, Hardy was indeed a contemporary of the Modernists. It may be that the critical industry, already in his lifetime busily at work on him as both poet and novelist (combined, let us admit, with not a little self-fashioning[23]), had so constructed him as the great proto-Georgian poet, as the humanist-realist rural-tragedian, as Grand Old Man of English Letters, that the *modernist* in Hardy could not then or later easily be perceived. Of course, it is a critical truism to say that he is a 'transitional' writer, but I wonder now just *how* transitional, or whether Hardy was not in fact already *there*, already a modern. D. H. Lawrence recognised it in the *Study of Thomas Hardy* (1914), written as he launched into the work which was to become *The Rainbow* and *Women in Love*, and Ezra Pound hailed him as a contemporary poet; but still, it is only with hindsight and the clearing of the critical trees that the innovative anti-realism and self-conscious modernity of much of Hardy's fictional *oeuvre* comes into view. Which is why, I suggest, it has been so simple for contemporary criticism to find the ingredients in him for a transmogrification into post-modernist.

Well, you might say, who would have thought it: 'good little Thomas Hardy', the poet of Wessex and the English countryside, the great humanist tragedian of the 'Novels of Character and Environment', the elegist of a passing rural tradition, and all the rest of it, suddenly becoming subversively post-modern. But then, literary criticism never could quite handle Hardy: didn't make it to F. R. Leavis's Great Tradition; always 'flawed' by contingency, melodrama and improbability; neither securely 'Victorian' nor 'Modern'; uncertain whether he is primarily novelist or poet. But in neither genre has Hardy ever really been made to *fit* (except by a lot of critical manhandling and dismissal of recalcitrant elements), which makes one think, doesn't it, that our disruptive post-modern Hardy may, after all, be nearer the mark. It is with this in mind that I now return to my two focal themes: 'seeing'/representation and the notion of Tess as '(a) pure woman'.

\* \* \*

With characteristic ambiguity of utterance, Hardy entitled one of his later volumes of poetry *Moments of Vision* (1917). The ambiguity of the word 'vision' is readily apparent: at once the literal 'seeing/sight' (as in '20/20 vision'), the metaphysical notion of imaginative revelation ('she had a vision'), and the proleptic ability to see through or beyond the immediately determinate ('he has vision', 'her vision of the future'). The ambiguity of the cluster of inflections around 'moments', however, is rather less obvious. Of course, 'moments' are brief fractions of time, usually implying stopped fragments in the temporal process (as in 'wait a moment', 'magic moments' or 'moment of truth'), and this is certainly the upper meaning in Hardy's title: particular instances of 'vision'. But there are two other senses which also haunt the fringes of the word: first, that of serious consequence ('momentous', 'matters of pith and moment'); second, and for my purposes here more significant, that within physics which means the measure of a turning effect (as in 'the moment of a force'). So Hardy's title may imply that the instants of 'vision' are important ('moments' of great 'moment'), but also that the vision is somehow itself in motion, turning, swinging round a point, pivoting.

If we think for a (dare I say) moment of the effect of a turning vision – in the most literal sense – then we must conceive of a 'seeing' which moves round its object (consider astronauts observing Earth from their circulating spacecraft), and which can theoretically move round it through 360 degrees in any direction, that is, in three-dimensional mode. Move round your chair, *looking* at it, and you will, at various stages, see it from all sides and all angles (downwards, upwards, sideways). In other words you will be able to apprehend it as a totality, a three-dimensional object. But two things may strike you: one, if you 'stopped' the moment when you were theoretically looking straight up at it from below (chair suspended absolutely vertically above you), the 'image' from that 'moment of vision' would look remarkably unlike one's standard received image of a chair (think of the kind of trick-photography which takes familiar objects from unfamiliar angles: where a bucket, for example, taken from directly above, becomes no more than a set of concentric circles). Two, how on earth (and I use this phrase, here, not merely as a manner of speaking) would you represent, *in visual terms*, your total apprehension of the total, three-dimensional chair – the chair in all its chairness? How, indeed, would you 'see' it all, all in one moment? Two senses of 'moment' – turning and stopped instant of time – clash here in fundamental contradiction: one is, precisely, *in motion*, in time; the other, equally precisely, is still, 'stopped', out of time. Is there any way of resolving this physical impossibility? Well, yes – if we return to the other term in Hardy's title: 'vision'.

For vision, in what I have called its metaphysical senses, allows us (but especially the creative artist) to break out of the space/time trap of the third dimension, and enter that zone of relativity beyond the determinate factors of time and space. Put simply and crudely, 'vision' allows us to 'see' the future, or 'envisage' another world; it would also enable us to see, in one totalising 'moment' (in this case, *both* stopped instant *and* full circular movement) all of our chair at the same time. It is not without point, here, when approaching so visual an artist as Hardy (and indeed one who draws heavily on painting for both his terms of reference and his imagery[24]), to note that this liberation from space/time, this envisioned *simultaneity* of experience, was the principle on which the modernist painters, only a dozen years after *Jude the Obscure* (why don't we think of Hardy and Picasso as contemporaries? – Picasso was well into his 'Metamorphic' phase when Hardy died in 1928), based their dislocations of conventional (realist/mimetic) form. That is why one can see both profiles of a face simultaneously in Cubist portraits, or a violin dismantled with all its planes simultaneously displayed on the two-dimensional picture surface of a modernist still life.

'Vision', then, both as momentary revelation (what James Joyce, only ten years after *Tess*, was to call an 'epiphany') and as 'turning' or destabilising perception, is a way of breaking out of the conventional, the normative, the familiar, the naturalised fictions of 'commonsense'. Indeed it ruptures a (bourgeois) world constructed very largely by the cultural ideology of a Realism which 'tells things as they really are' and has a profound antipathy to the 'improbable' or 'implausible' – qualities which are themselves frequently the result of, precisely, 'vision' and 'the visionary'. For Hardy, vision in this binary sense ('double-vision'?) is a way of 'defamiliarising', of 'making strange' – and I strategically choose the Formalists' terms to signal once again his consanguinity with modernism – the naturalised world of conventional perceptual reality, of 'seeing things as they really are'. It is subversive in many ways, and not least in its anti-realist stance – which may help to explain the troubled history of Hardy's place in the conventional canon of English fiction and the difficulty many critics have had in comprehending the apparently schizophrenic textuality of his novels. It is worth adding here that Hardy himself was not just 'doing defamiliarisation' by chance –

as an automatic and unwilled reflex of his (unconscious) proto-modernist mind. On the contrary, he was thinking about it through-out his writing life, but especially from the 1880s onwards; and his last, highly self-reflexive and self-conscious work of fiction, 'Florence Emily Hardy's *The Life of Thomas Hardy*' (he composed it himself before his death in the 1920s[25]), is full of concepts and phrases which at once define 'vision' as what we would now call 'complex seeing' and which would, had they been written by a twentieth-century cultural theorist, have equal currency with terms like 'defamiliarisa-tion' and 'baring the device' or the Brechtian notion of 'alienation'.

Prior to the 1880s, Hardy's views show a more purely Romantic conception of the visionary function of art: 'irradiating . . . with "the light that never was" . . . a hitherto unperceived beauty . . . seen to be latent . . . by the spiritual eye'.[26] But by 1886 Hardy is reflecting: 'novel-writing as an art cannot go backward. Having reached the analytic stage it must transcend it by going still further in the same direction. Why not by rendering as visible essences, spectres, etc., the abstract thoughts of the analytic school?' And later in the same passage he proposes the use of 'abstract realisms', significantly stating that this project was actually carried out, not in a novel, but in 'the more appropriate medium' of his immense epic poetic-drama, *The Dynasts* (p. 177). What is clear, if nothing else, is that Hardy was being pressed against the limits of conventional realism. The following year, in expressing his admiration for the paintings of 'the much-decried, mad, late-Turner', he rejects 'the original realities – as optical effects, that is' in favour of the 'expression of. . . . abstract imaginings' (p. 185). Taken in conjunction with his remarks about 'impressions' and 'seemings' in the prefaces to the novels of the 1890s referred to earlier in this Introduction, it is clear that notions of 'vision', and how to realise it formally, were much on Hardy's mind. But it is in a couple of memoranda from 1890 (while he was completing *Tess*) that his most prophetically modernist utterances are made:

> Reflections on Art. Art is a changing of the actual proportions and order of things, so as to bring out more forcibly than might otherwise be done that feature in them which appeals most strongly to the idiosyncrasy of the artist.
>
> Art is a disproportioning – (i.e. distorting, throwing out of proportion) – of realities, to show more clearly the features that matter in those realities, which, if merely copied or reported inventorially, might

possibly be observed, but would more probably be overlooked. Hence 'realism' is not Art.

(pp. 228–9)

It is here, I think, that the core of Hardy's fictional aesthetic is to be found, and the informing frame of reference for a reading of *Tess*: art is a 'disproportioning' of reality/realism is not art. In other words, 'vision' (abstract imaginings), swinging round its 'moment', makes visible 'essences' (the notion of a pure woman, for example). But at the time, vision 'distorts', 'disproportions', those representations of reality ('copied or reported inventorially') which are the naturalised (mis)representations of Realism in order to expose essentialist misrepresentation for what it is (how can there, in fact, be 'a pure woman' or 'pure woman'?), and to illuminate another truth which those misrepresentations obscure: that 'reality' is only ever *discourse* – 'seemings', 'imaginings', 'impressions'.

'My art', Hardy wrote in 1886, 'is to intensify the expression of things . . . so that the heart and inner meaning is made vividly visible' (p. 177). *Tess*, that most 'vividly visible' of novels, may be an example of Hardy 'intensifying the expression' in order to bring into view precisely that 'expression' – the discourses of representation themselves – for scrutiny and demystification in order to exemplify the fact that 'expression' is its own very 'heart and inner meaning', that the 'reality' of an image *is* the image itself, that its only reality is what it constructs through representation. 'Expression' does not copy 'things as they really are', it forges images in its artifice. Tess may indeed be 'a pure woman', but *only as she is imaged*, only as the 'artificial' construct of representation – and who knows whether this is true or false: except, unless we miss the irony (for Hardy knows full well the claim is nonsense), when she is *'faithfully* presented by Thomas Hardy'.

Let us now turn, at last, to that subtitle itself, and consider it as the pivot of a 'moment' around which *Tess of the d'Urbervilles* swings in exemplification of Hardy's disproportioning art discussed above. The two main senses of the phrase 'a pure woman' are readily evident: the ethical/sexual (the use of which in relation to Tess as fornicator-murderess so incensed Hardy's Victorian critics), and the ontological/archetypal (in which she would be, were Bob Dylan her bard, 'just like a woman' in every respect). There is also the further related sense of the generic as 'ideal' – again, perhaps, in two inflexions: proto-typical and perfect. I am not primarily concerned here with the ethical sense, although for Hardy at the time it was clearly a strategic assault on the moral attitudes of his readers and their *perception* of purity. It is that other essentialist meaning that is of interest to me, and especially in relation to Hardy's concern with 'visible essences' noted above. The novel is full of phrases which indicate that he was thoroughly conscious of this second sense and probably more interested in it than the contemporary moral issue. Let me start with the two most obvious examples: at Talbothays, in the early-morning idyll with Angel, Tess is described as 'a visionary essence of woman – a whole sex condensed into one typical form' (p. 187); and later, as she approaches Flintcomb-Ash, the narrative, in an odd shift of tense and focus, presents her in this way: 'Thus Tess walks on; a figure which is part of the landscape; a field-woman pure and simple, in winter guise' (p. 355) – where the phrase 'pure and simple' *could* mean a pure, simple field-woman, but clearly actually implies the essential stereotype. (Much earlier, during the harvesting at Marlott, the narrative has already given us this generalisation: 'A field-man is a personality afield; a field-woman is a portion of the field; she has somehow *lost her own margin*, imbibed the *essence* of her surrounding, and assimilated herself with it' [pp. 137–8, my italics] – so that Tess, too, the 'field-woman pure and simple', must also be subsumed within this characterisation – or rather, *de*-characterisation.) Further, as we have seen, when Tess is first introduced in Chapter Two she is described as 'a fine and picturesque country girl, and no more' (p. 52, note that word 'picturesque'), and later again, just after the generalisation about field-women above, she is called, in an oddly contradictive phrase, 'an almost standard woman' (p. 141). Elsewhere, the narrative regularly generalises about women – for example on Tess's 'rally' after the death of her child, it muses: 'Let the truth be told – women do as a rule live through such humiliations, and regain their spirits, and again look about them with an interested eye' (p. 158) – a sentence remarkable both for its patriarchal patronising (do men – by implication of finer sensibility – not, then?) and for that revealing phrase 'an interested eye'. Again, in relation to the dairymaids' passion for Angel at Talbothays, we are told they are involuntarily overwhelmed by 'an emotion thrust on them by cruel Nature's law' and, in an even more insulting instance of chauvinistic essentialism, 'the differences which distinguished them as individuals were abstracted by this passion, and each was but a portion of one organism called sex' (p. 204) – 'pure women' indeed, and just like the field-women who have lost their 'own margin'. For Angel, of course (and for the narrator too?), Tess is archetypally this 'organism' in the famously erotic passage when she has just awoken on a summer dawn:

> She had not heard him enter, and hardly realised his presence there. She was yawning, and *he saw the red interior of her mouth* as if it had been a snake's. She had stretched one arm so high above her coiled-up cable of hair that he could see its satin delicacy above the sunburn; her face was flushed with sleep, and her eyelids hung heavy over their pupils. The brim-fulness of her nature breathed from her. It was a moment when *a woman's soul* is more incarnate than at any other time; when the most spiritual beauty bespeaks itself flesh; and sex takes the outside place in *the presentation*.
>
> (p. 231, my italics)

Is this what Hardy means by 'a pure woman' in his subtitle? But notice again, as in all these quotations, how he seems to be doing the very opposite of establishing Tess's 'character'; that, conversely, in rendering her as essence – 'a woman's soul' – he is making her an enigma, unknowable, subject only to speculation (rather as Hardy's later disciple, John Fowles, was to do with Sarah Woodruff in *The French Lieutenant's Woman*), and inimical, therefore, to the *raison d'être* of a fictional realism which finds its very heart in well-rounded 'character'.

But, of course, it is the continuous textual 'presentation' (notice Hardy's use of the word at the end of the quotation above) of Tess that makes the obsessive (and usually erotic) imaging of her as something to *look at*, as something *seen*, as a visual *object*, so inescapable. Space prevents a full account of the number of occasions her mouth (again, see the above quotation) is fetishistically focused upon – for example, 'To a young man with the least fire in him that little upward lift in the middle of her red top lip was distracting, infatuating, maddening. . . .' (p. 209). But her smile and her eyes also receive continual attention ('her rosy lips curved towards a smile' [p. 79], 'a roguish curl coming upon her mouth' [p. 247], 'her eyes enlarged, and she involuntarily smiled in his face' [p. 103]), as do her neck, her arms, her hair and general deportment ('Tess stood there in her prettily tucked-up milking gown, her hair carelessly heaped upon her head. . . .' [p. 247]). Equally heavily emphasised is the 'bouncing handsome womanliness' of her figure (see the quotation at the beginning of this introduction); even Angel at his most idealising – in the passage where he sees her as the 'visionary essence of woman' (see above, p. 16) – is still aware that there weren't many women 'so well endowed in person as she was' (p. 186), and for Alec she is of course the true *femme fatale* (not, by the by, necessarily a scheming woman or 'siren', merely 'irresistibly attractive'): 'She had an attribute which amounted to a disadvantage just now; and it was this that caused Alec d'Urberville's *eyes to rivet themselves upon her*. It was a luxuriance of aspect, a fullness of growth, which made her appear *more of a woman* than she really was' (p. 82, my emphases: note both the male gaze and the physical essentialism implied by 'more of a woman'). And later it is this voluptuousness which starts the process of deconverting Alec as preacher: 'his eyes, falling casually upon the familiar countenance and form, remained contemplating her. . . . "Don't look at me like that!" he said abruptly' (p. 388) – an inversion which must surely be the most brilliant evocation in fiction of male perfidy, for who, after all, is doing the looking? It is further worth noticing in passing that it is not just Tess who is made into a sex-object by the text: Car Darch, just before Alec has sex with Tess, is described thus: 'she had bared her plump neck, shoulders, and arms to the moonshine, under which they looked as luminous and beautiful as some Praxitelean[27] creation, in their possession of the faultless rotundities of a lusty country girl' (p. 112).

In late-twentieth-century terms, the above descriptions would surely amount to 'soft' pornography, or at least to accurate representations of the titillatory visual devices employed therein. And the text further emphasises this voyeuristic stance in its recurrent verbal and narrative objectification ('the presentation') of women in the novel. The 'club-walking' girls in Chapter Two, for instance, are taking part in 'their first *exhibition* of themselves' (p. 49, my italics here and below); the Clare brothers are 'on-lookers' at 'the *spectacle* of a bevy of girls dancing. . . .' (pp. 52–3); Tess, after her first visit to Trantridge, 'became aware of the *spectacle* she presented to their [her fellow-travellers'] surprised vision: roses at her breast; roses in her hat; roses and strawberries in her basket to the brim' (p. 84); Mrs Durbeyfield, 'bedecking' Tess for the sacrifice to Alec, is so proud of 'the girl's *appearance*' that she is led to 'step back *like a painter from his easel*, and survey her work as a whole'; and in order to let Tess 'zee' herself, she hangs 'a large black cloak [surely the black flag' of Tess's hanging] outside the casement, and so made a large reflector of the panes' (p. 90). On other occasions the text pans back from Tess and reduces her (once again de-characterising her in the process) to an insignificant dot on the landscape: 'Tess stood still upon the hemmed expanse of verdant flatness, like a fly on a billiard-table of indefinite length, and of no more consequence to the surroundings than that fly' (p. 159); 'the two girls crawl[ed] over the surface of [the 'desolate drab'] field like flies' (p. 360).

Throughout the novel, then, Tess in particular is highly visualised as an object of 'vision' in the swinging 'moment' of the text's gaze. Only on two significant occasions does she disappear from view: once, when she is hanged, with Angel and Liza-Lu's eyes 'riveted' (like Alec's on her body) to the gaol flag-pole, and she becomes merely 'a black flag' (p. 489); the other when, in the old phrase precisely, Alec commits 'the act of darkness' with her: 'The obscurity was now so great that he could see absolutely nothing but a pale nebulousness at his feet, which represented the white muslin figure he had left upon the dead leaves. Everything else was blackness alike' (pp. 118–19). It is as if, paradoxically and pointedly, the novel implies that the essence, the 'pure woman', can only be 'presented' as visualisations, only as she *appears*, but that the basic realities of her existence (sex, death) are unknowable, unrepresentable – like those innermost secrets of 'character' that no one quite comprehends or can describe in other people however well one knows them.

And let us be clear: we know almost nothing substantive about Tess's 'character', for the novel never attempts to penetrate her secret being. It may tell us things *about* her (she 'spoke two languages' [p. 58]); give us her views (about the 'blighted star', for example); and show her spirited moments of mettle (to Alec's male cliché, 'that's what every woman says', she retorts in implicit rejection of 'pure woman' essentialism: 'Did it never strike your mind that what every woman says some women may feel?' [p. 125], just as she tells Angel to 'call me Tess' when he insists, in the 'visionary essence' scene, on idealising her with names like Artemis and Demeter [p. 187]). The novel may further appear to try and characterise her state of mind – 'she looked upon herself as a figure of Guilt intruding into the haunts of innocence ... she fancied herself such an anomaly' (p. 135) – but only, we note, at a detached psychologistic distance; it may try and explain her love for Angel ('its single-mindedness, its meekness; what long-suffering it guaranteed, what honesty, what endurance, what good faith' [p. 279]), but the more the text produces phrase after defining phrase, the more a palpable sense of her love recedes – just as earlier, despite all its words, the narrative signally fails to describe her eyes: 'neither black nor blue nor grey nor violet; rather all these shades together, and a hundred others . . .

around pupils that had no bottom' (pp. 140–1). For all this 'charac-terisation', then, we really 'know' Tess very little indeed – which is presumably why so much critical argument has raged over whether she is 'passive' or not, whether she is 'pure' or not, indeed whether she is a 'fully-rounded character' at all.

Which is, I would suggest in conclusion, to beg the question. For *Tess of the d'Urbervilles* is precisely *not* a novel attempting to offer us a 'knowable' character, but rather one which exposes *char-acterisation* itself as a humanist-realist mystification (producing 'visible essences') and which parades the *mis*representation that 'characterisation' involves by subjecting to irony the falsifying essen-tialism of 'faithfully presenting a pure woman'. In her excellent essay of 1982, 'Pure Tess: Hardy on Knowing a Woman',[28] Kathleen Blake remarks that the novel 'really scrutinises the sexual typing that plays havoc with a woman's life', while George Wotton, in suggesting that we recognise 'class and gender conflicts . . . as conflicts of perception in the multifarious acts of seeing of the characters who inhabit Wessex', points out that Hardy's 'production (writing) determines consumption (reading) by casting the reader in the role of seer'.[29] In other words, we may say that Hardy's 'moments of vision' dispro-portion characterisation and character so that we can 'see' how they function. Tess as a 'character' is no more than an amalgam – often destructively contradictory – of 'images' of her as perceived by individuals and by 'society': Angel idealises her, Alec sees her as sex-object, the narrative voice fetishises her, society regards her as prod-igal, the novel 'faithfully presents' her as 'a pure woman' (with all the ironies that phrasing invokes). But Tess has no character at all: she is only what others (most especially the author) construct her as; and so she is herself merely a 'series of seemings' or 'impressions'. This, of course, gives the final ironic twist to the notion of her being '(a) pure woman', since there can be no such thing as 'essential character' when a woman is merely the construct of male socio-sexual images of her desired form (although the basic point here need not be limited to gender-stereotyping). Hardy's novel, then, well ahead of its time, seems to be dismantling the bourgeois-humanist (patriarchal and realist) notion of the unified and unitary human subject, and to be doing so by way of a discourse so self-reflexive and defamiliarising about representation, so unstable and dialogical, that it deconstructs itself even as it creates. Which is why, I believe, we can justly discover a contemporary post-modern text in *Tess of the d'Urbervilles*.

# NOTES

1. Thomas Hardy, *Tess of the d'Urbervilles* (1891), ed. David Skilton, with an Introduction by A. Alvarez, Penguin Classics edition (Harmondsworth, [1978] 1987), p. 51. All further references to the novel are to this edition, and appear as bracketed numbers in the text.

2. Thomas Hardy, *Desperate Remedies* (1871), ed. with Introduction by C. J. P. Beatty, New Wessex edition (London, 1975), pp. 46–7.

3. Thomas Hardy, *Jude the Obscure* (1896), ed. with Introduction by Terry Eagleton (and notes by P. N. Furbank), New Wessex edition (London, 1974), p. 23.

4. 'Author's Preface to the Fifth and Later Editions' (1892), *Tess*, Penguin Classics, p. 38. Hardy, in the same sentence here, also quotes Schiller on 'representation' and 'poetical representations'.

5. See Florence Emily Hardy, *The Life of Thomas Hardy 1840–1928* (London, [1962] 1975), p. 185, for a typical memorandum (Jan. 1887) on this subject during the period of the composition of *Tess*.

6. For extensive treatment of this subject, and of Turner in particular, see Chapter 8 especially, 'Patterns of Light and Dark in *Tess of the d'Urbervilles*', in J. B. Bullen, *The Expressive Eye: Fiction and Perception in the Work of Thomas Hardy* (Oxford, 1986).

7. This 'phase' is perhaps exemplified at its best by R. P. Draper's earlier Casebook, *Hardy: the Tragic Novels* (London, 1975), and by Albert J. LaValley's *Twentieth-Century Interpretations of Tess of the d'Urbervilles* (Englewood Cliffs, NJ, 1969).

8. For an extended analysis of these by the present author, see Peter Widdowson, *Hardy in History: a study in literary sociology* (London, 1989), especially Chapter 1, 'The Critical Constitution of "Thomas Hardy"'.

9. This singularly pre-emptive and subsequently ubiquitous phrase in Hardy criticism appears in Hardy's 'General Preface' to the Wessex Edition of his works in 1912 (which is reproduced in each volume of the Penguin and 'New Wessex' editions of his novels). It occurs when he is 'classifying', and, in effect, hierarchically evaluating, his fictional oeuvre – with the ones so described clearly privileged.

10. Widdowson, *Hardy in History*, pp. 44–55 especially, for a discussion of critical treatment of the 'minor novels'.

11. And with those, for example, collected in more recent volumes, such as Harold Bloom (ed.), *Modern Critical Interpretations of Thomas Hardy*

(New York, 1987), and Lance St John Butler (ed.), *Alternative Hardy* (London, 1989).

12. J. T. Laird, *The Shaping of Tess of the d'Urbervilles* (Oxford, 1975), p. 4. For a slightly fuller critique of Laird's stance, see Widdowson, *Hardy in History*, pp. 30–1. There is a further essay by Laird on the textual development of *Tess*, 'New Light on the Evolution of *Tess of the d'Urbervilles*', in *Review of English Studies*, 31: 124 (Winter 1980), 414–35.

13. Thomas Hardy, *Tess of the d'Urbervilles*, ed. Juliet Grindle and Simon Gatrell, the 'Clarendon Edition' (Oxford, 1983).

14. In the 'Editor's Preface' to John Goode, *Thomas Hardy: The Offensive Truth* (Oxford, 1988), p. vii.

15. For a fuller account and analysis of this, see in particular Chapter 13, 'The Production of Meaning: "Hardy's Women" and the Eternal Feminine' (part of which is reproduced as essay 2 in the present volume), in George Wotton, *Thomas Hardy: Towards a Materialist Criticism* (Goldenbridge, 1985).

16. In Juliet Mitchell and Ann Oakley (eds), *The Rights and Wrongs of Women* (Harmondsworth, 1976). The following quotations, *passim*, are from pp. 255, 253, 254. Two other influential essays on the textuality/sexuality nexus, not included in the present volume because of space and the exposure they have already received, are: Mary Jacobus, 'Tess: The Making of a Pure Woman', in Susan Lipshitz (ed.), *Tearing the Veil: Essays on Femininity* (London, 1978) which first appeared in *Critical Quarterly*, 26 (October 1976); and J. Hillis Miller, 'Fiction as Repetition: *Tess of the d'Urbervilles*', in Alan Warren Friedman (ed.), *Forms of Modern British Fiction* (Austin, 1975). This was reprinted, in revised form, as the chapter, '*Tess of the d'Urbervilles*: Repetition as Immanent Design', in Hillis Miller's *Fiction and Repetition: Seven English Novels* (Cambridge, 1982), and again, with Jacobus above, in Bloom (ed.), *Modern Critical Interpretations* (see Note 11 above).

17. In Mary Jacobus (ed.), *Women's Writing and Writing about Women* (Beckenham, 1979). See especially, pp. 100, 107–8.

18. 'Editor's Preface' to Goode, *Thomas Hardy*, p. vii (see Note 14 above).

19. *The English Novel* was first published in 1970 by Chatto and Windus, and was reprinted by Paladin Books in 1974. The section on Hardy was reproduced, virtually in its entirety, as Chapter 18, 'Wessex and the Border', of Williams's *The Country and the City* (London, 1973).

20. The notion of a 'critiography' is developed in the first part of Widdowson, *Hardy in History* (see Note 8 above). Appropriating a notion of historiography for criticism, it basically means the study of the pro-

cesses by which a text from the past is reproduced for us in the present: how it is shaped and moulded by the (critical) attention paid to it over time, so that when we get it, it is already heavily inscribed with meanings and evaluations and is not, therefore, 'primary material' or 'the text itself' in any useful sense at all.

21. Released in 1979 in France and elsewhere in 1981, it was produced by Claude Berri and Timothy Burrill, with screenplay by Gerard Brach, Polanski and John Brownjohn, and stars Nastassia Kinski, Peter Firth and Leigh Lawson.

22. See above, Notes 12 and 16 for details. Laird's book is referred to in the footnotes of the 1976 *Critical Quarterly* version of Jacobus's essay.

23. I have already implied this in Note 9 above, in reference to Hardy's own categorisation of his novels in the 'General Preface' of 1912. But we also have to remember that he himself, in fact, wrote Florence Emily Hardy's supposed biography of him, *The Life of Thomas Hardy 1840–1928*, in the years immediately preceding his death, and so effectively composed his own 'life' as he wished it to be perceived. An account of this characteristically self-protective subterfuge is to be found in the first chapter of Robert Gittings's *Young Thomas Hardy* (Harmondsworth, [1975] 1978).

24. See Bullen, *The Expressive Eye* (Note 6 above), for full discussion of this.

25. See above, Note 23.

26. *The Life of Thomas Hardy*, p. 114 (see Note 5 above). All further references appear as bracketed numbers in the text.

27. Praxiteles was a fourth-century BC Greek sculptor whose work celebrated sensuality (for example, in depicting naked gods for the first time).

28. The essay appeared first in *Studies in English Literature*, 22; 4 (Autumn 1982), 689–705, but has been reprinted in Bloom (ed.), *Modern Critical Interpretations* (see Note 11 above).

29. Wotton, *Thomas Hardy*, p. 4 (see Note 15 above).

# 1

# Hardy and Social Class

*MERRYN AND RAYMOND WILLIAMS*

## I

The language of class is the language of capitalist society, and contains at once its clarities, its complexities, its confusions and its contradictions. Instituted as a specific terminology in the late eighteenth century and intensively developed in the nineteenth century, it is readily associated, historically, with the development of industrial society; agricultural or rural society is often seen as marginal to or even exempted from it. Yet the class system, defined by differential relations to the means of production, is at least as clear in agriculture as in industry, and in fact is historically earlier. By the eighteenth century, nearly half of the cultivated land was owned by some five thousand families. Nearly a quarter of the cultivated land was owned by four hundred families, in a population of between seven and eight million people. In 1873, when Hardy was writing his first novels, four-fifths of the land of the United Kingdom was owned by less than 7000 persons.[1] The characteristic structure of social and economic relationships in agriculture, steadily extending its dominance from the late sixteenth to the early twentieth centuries, was a class of landowners, a class of tenant farmers and a class of landless labourers. These are the clarities.

The first confusion is inherent in the language of class. This replaced the earlier language of estate, order and rank. Essentially the change was due to the relatively increased mobility and the new sources of wealth of capitalist society. Class is an indicator of social position but primarily through the indices of adult economic activity.

Estate, rank and order, always more rigid categories, had indicated social position through birth and inheritance. Necessarily, of course, there is a substantial overlap between the earlier and the later categories. What was ordinarily inherited was not only a rank but property. Acquisition of property or wealth often brought formal rank in its train. On the other side of the fence, to lose wealth or property was to lose the significance of rank. The consequent confusion of categories is very marked in English society from at latest 1550; in the nineteenth and twentieth centuries it is still both a voluntary and an involuntary confusion. Hardy, as it happens, illustrates part of this process very clearly, in direct relation to the confusion itself. In *Tess*, the d'Urbervilles are a declined, indeed extinguished, family of 'rank'. Their local descendants have become the Durbeyfields. The family of Alec d'Urberville has made its money in trade and bought its way into landed property and the resumed title. The action of *Tess* makes it clear that the consequent confusion between the inheritance of categories (the 'rank', the 'family name') and both the actual physical inheritance and the decisive contemporary social relationships is profoundly damaging. For the real social classes are in flesh and blood; the inherited rank name is, either way, an ideology. More generally, however, there was a rough fit between the language of rank and the language of class: a rough fit because in general it was both assured and contrived. The decisive economic relationships carried the presence or absence of rank through the inheritance of property or of propertylessness, and where they did not they were, by a characteristic English process, eventually brought into broad alignment. This confusion persists.

Yet beyond it there is a complexity, based in the actual history. The rural structure of landlord, tenant and labourer – the matrix of capitalist agriculture – was indeed dominant but it was not exclusive. There were two substantial complications. First, there was the persistence of a class of smallholders and 'family farmers': in 1873 numerically as many as the tenant farmers, though characteristically on the smaller units, on the poorer land, or on both. The pressures of capitalist agriculture – the increasingly organised market economy, the rising level of capital investment in improved agricultural methods, the rising level of viability in size of units with the increase in mechanisation – were intensely felt by this class and, as through the whole eighteenth and early nineteenth centuries, were continually diminishing its relative importance. Secondly, from an older kind of village economy and in part distinct from, in part overlapping with, the smallholders and family farmers, there was what Hardy called, in direct comparison with the agricultural labourers,

> an interesting and better-informed class . . . including the carpenter, the smith, the shoemaker, the huckster, together with nondescript workers other than farm labourers; a set of people who owed a certain stability of aim and conduct to the fact of their being life-holders . . . copyholders, or occasionally small freeholders.
>
> (ch. 51)

It is significant that, describing this class in *Tess*, Hardy says that the village had 'formerly' contained it. It would not be the case that by the late nineteenth century all these individuals and trades had disappeared, but they were under very great pressure, from two directions: first, internally, in the dominance of orthodox capitalist agriculture (lifeholders, entitled to their cottages for the duration of three lives, were now increasingly dispossessed when the last life ended; Hardy describes such cases in *The Woodlanders* and *Tess*); second, externally, in the development of a manufacturing urban economy, which steadily cut out the more localised craftsmen. It is in these senses that capitalist social relations, while not exclusive, were dominant: that they exerted pressure on all who did not belong to or fit in with them, dispossessing, undercutting or effectively pauperising a majority of this residual class. This in its turn interacted with the altered relative economic position of agriculture, in the now industrialised and free-trading (food importing) national economy, to produce a relative 'rural depopulation'. There was prolonged and substantial emigration to the cities and industrial towns, and to the dominions, the colonies and the New World. Within this vast process, in which the residual complexity of the English rural social structure was being sharply reduced, Hardy especially regretted the disappearance of the relatively independent and intermediate class. As he put it, again in *Tess*:

> Cottagers who were not directly employed on the land were looked upon with disfavour, and the banishment of some starved the trade of others, who were thus obliged to follow. These families, who had formed the backbone of the village life in the past, who were the depositaries of the village traditions, had to seek refuge in the large centres; the process, humorously designated by statisticians as 'the tendency of the rural population towards the large towns', being really the tendency of water to flow uphill when forced by machinery.
>
> (ch. 51)

Here a social and economic change is seen also as a cultural change, but not only (although crucially) as the expulsion of the carriers of traditional village culture. What was happening was also a political change, for it was from this relatively independent and intermediate class that, as it happened, most of the early trade-union leaders and organisers had come. Describing and analysing their displacement, Hardy was looking forward as well as back. 'Every one of these banished people', he wrote, 'imbibes a sworn enmity to the existing order of things.'[2]

## II

Thomas Hardy was born into this relatively independent and inter-mediate class. His lineal and extended family shows all the confu-sions and precarious complexities of just this group. Thus his father's mother was a charity child and his mother had been very poor; his father, by energy as a builder and mason, came to employ as many as fourteen men. The mixed and precarious character of these 'inter-mediate' people can be seen in the number of his relatives who were workingmen and labourers; he is said, characteristically, to have been ashamed of them. At the same time, in the new mobilities of education and the professions, his cousin Tryphena went to training college and became a headmistress at twenty-one, while Hardy him-self became an architect. This is, decisively, a world not of rank but of class, but because it is a world of class, its complexities, its new definitions of relations between destiny, energy and accident, its profound interactions of personal quality and social position, its often crucially determining intermixture of the personality and the sociality of sexual and marriage relationships, created for Hardy a rich, dense, moving world in which, in quite fundamental ways, human lives were always at stake.

The distinguishing quality of Hardy's treatment of class in his fiction follows, as we shall see, from this precise position: at once complex and self-conscious, precarious and mobile. It is because class is at issue, and at a doubtful issue, within the difficult con-sciousness of this intermediate group, that he is both intensely aware of it and that he handles it through a particular fusion of what are elsewhere often seen as 'external' and 'internal' characteristics. . . .

Tess, in *Tess of the d'Urbervilles*, has often been described as a 'peasant'. This is the class language of another class. It is interesting that after it had lost any precise meaning in English rural society, following the rise of capitalist agriculture, it was reintroduced to express a more totalising view: one which suppressed the crucial actual relations and variations. The reintroduction was essentially political, in the reaction which followed the French Revolution. A crucial text is Cobbett, in 1830:

> Pray, my readers, attend to these things, and then (if you be Catholics) *cross yourselves* when you hear Peel and Knatchbull say, that the fires *do not proceed from the 'peasantry'*, a *new* name given to the *country labourers* by the insolent boroughmongering and loanmongering tribes. But if it be not the 'peasantry', who is it?[3]

Cobbett's fine sense of the actualities of rural society is matched, half a century later, by Hardy's. The blocking stereotypes of an urban ruling-class ideology dissolve in his patient application of detail. Tess, quite apart from the d'Urberville-Durbeyfield complication, is the daughter of a haggler or small itinerant trader. The working capital of this extreme marginal occupation is a horse. When it is killed they have nowhere to go but the labour market; they have also lost the life tenure of their cottage on John Durbeyfield's death. Tess takes employment to look after poultry, within a double social irony: that it is on the 'little fancy farm' kept as a hobby by the merchant family (the new d'Urbervilles) who have bought their way into the 'landed gentry'; and that the poultry are kept in an old cottage formerly occupied by 'certain dusty copyholders who now lay east and west in the churchyard' and now 'indifferently turned into a fowl-house by Mrs Stoke d'Urberville as soon as the property fell into hand according to law'. Thus Tess, as a girl, begins at the nadir of this struggling intermediate class, and is forced through the relatively light wage-labour of poultry and dairy work to the heavy work of the fields. But then also, intricately enmeshed in the same process, she is in the special position of a woman labourer, that as a woman as well as a worker she is exposed to the market, with its range of possibilities in seduction, marriage, desertion, kept mistress. The limits and pressures of a declining intermediate group are then an intrinsic part of her history. . . .

What is being charted then, in an exceptional richness and variation of material, is what Hardy saw as crucial: the flattening and in a sense (though this can never be complete) the extinction of the 'intermediate' people who had been not only a 'sector of the economy' but the bearers of a culture. This at once places and limits Hardy in the radical tradition which runs back to Paine and Cobbett but which at the end of the century had to encounter the more systematic rigidities of a fully developed capitalist system. The complexities of this encounter, in the transition from radicalism to socialism, begin to sound in his work, but his centre of gravity is in the earlier rather than the later process. This can be seen clearly in his essay on 'The Dorsetshire Labourer', from which we may complete the quotation given earlier:

> Every one of these banished people imbibes a sworn enmity to the existing order of things, and not a few of them, far from being merely honest Radicals, degenerate into Anarchists, waiters on chance, to whom danger to the State . . . is a welcomed opportunity. . . . But the question of the Dorset cottager here merges in that of all the houseless and landless poor, and the vast topic of the Rights of Man, to consider which is beyond the scope of a purely descriptive article.[4]

It is not only the scope of the article, it is the scope of the experienced social history, now at a point of critical transition, which checks Hardy. The explicit class struggles, like the more integral class formations, of modern industrial capitalist society are beyond and ahead of his world, though he could sense their shadows.

However, at the point of critical transition, and within the perspective of the problems of an intermediate class, he picked up and remarkably embodied one of the characteristic themes of the new social situation: that of mobility through education. This had been present, in minor ways, within an older structure, in the figures of Fancy Day, Grace Melbury and Swithin (in *Two on a Tower*). There it interlocks with the more general problems of the older intermediate mobility. It is again briefly present in *Tess*:

> Mrs Durbeyfield habitually spoke the dialect; her daughter, who had passed the Sixth Standard in the National School under a London-trained mistress, spoke two languages: the dialect at home, more or less; ordinary English abroad and to persons of quality.
>
> (ch. 3)

But it is of course in *Jude the Obscure* that it becomes central.

Mobility through education is often described as if it were a simple functional passage from one class (type of work) to another. In Hardy's social perspective it could never be reduced to this, even if the mobility had been easier than it commonly was. Precisely within the terms of his 'intermediate' perspective, he asked questions about the relations between social position, social experience and social and personal qualities which necessarily supersede merely functional answers. . . .

But at least in the intermediate structure there was an attempt to negotiate the difficult relations between moral purpose, learning and teaching, on the one hand, and social position, financial betterment, on the other. When he came to observe the orthodox educated world, Hardy saw, by contrast, a dull and false congruity, in which learning and privilege were taken to be naturally interchangeable. As he puts it of Angel's brothers in *Tess*:

> . . . he noticed their growing mental limitations. Felix seemed to him all Church; Cuthbert all college . . . Each brother candidly recognised that there were a few unimportant scores of millions of outsiders in civilised society, persons who were neither University men nor Churchmen; but they were to be tolerated rather than reckoned with and respected.
>
> (ch. 25)

Here, at the point of arrival of the most ideal educational mobility, was a deep cancellation of the life of the mind by the specific limitations and perspectives of class.

. . . As we read Hardy's prolonged meditations on the real relations between learning and humanity, between educated and customary ways of feeling and thinking, and between the harsh necessities of material production and the painful complications of every effort towards a higher culture, we find ourselves moved beyond the formulas of the more familiar arguments and returned always to the question which is either left unanswered or at best ironically or precariously answered: 'what is doing well?'. To most of the members of this intermediate group, and to the writer who speaks from within their specific structure of feeling, both the question and the difficulty of the answers are all too well known.

### III

One decisive element must be added to this account: Hardy's deeply original and still exceptional emphasis on work. This is not, except superficially, the consequence of the developing idea of the dignity of labour. Hardy looked at actual work too closely to rest on that abstract formula. In *The Woodlanders*, *Tess* and *Jude* especially, his descriptions of the detailed material processes of labour have an intensity of feeling which in most fiction is reserved for interpersonal relationships or for landscape and scene. It is not, obviously, that Hardy neglects either of these; they are as important in his work as anywhere in fiction. But he provides a further dimension, in which being is expressed in labour, but then is also, in all the variations of social and physical circumstances, exalted or degraded, fulfilled or frustrated, sustained or broken up. This integral connection, as it becomes in the later novels, between the quality and conditions of labour and the quality and conditions of primary and effective being, is very remarkable. Moreover it begins to offer an emphasis which can transform social values. It is very striking that people who do useful work are always, in Hardy, positive characters; the most evident examples are Marty, Giles, Tess and Jude. At the other extreme, people who do no work, like Eustacia or Lucetta or Mrs Charmond, are characteristically negative and disruptive. Nor is this merely an ethic of 'productive values'. The capacity to work and the habit of working are directly connected with the ability to love, to care and to sustain. It is not that the exercise of any of these virtues brings happiness, as in the older formulas. For as unquestioned primary processes, the only true sources of value, they are cut across in two ways: by the sheer hardness and harshness of the material world with which this work is always grappling – a kind of pain which is seen as intrinsic; but also by the arbitrariness, the coldness, the irresponsible power of a social class system which is of course not intrinsic, but which eats into all the processes of life and labour. Both emphases are there: the often intractable world; the historically specific class system. Hardy did not often extricate them, one from the other. What was experienced in a single dimension was responded to in a single dimension. This also, it can be said, is the limit of consciousness of an intermediate class. Yet the emphatic linking of labour and value, with the corresponding detachment of value from property, is a remarkable exploration of a new kind of consciousness, beyond a class system. That he held to this exploration while at the same time recording, ironically or bitterly, its practical difficulties, its repeated frustrations, its terrible actual losses in the people who, consciously or unconsciously, were attempting to live in these new ways, is at once the paradox and the triumph of his work.

From *Thomas Hardy: The Writer and His Background*, ed. Norman Page (London, 1980), pp. 29–40.

## NOTES

[Merryn Williams's early book on Hardy, *Thomas Hardy and Rural England* (1972), was a genuine attempt – little developed or improved upon by others since – to situate his work in a specific social and historical *locus*. A revised and enlarged edition of her later *Preface to Hardy* (1976) was published in 1992. Her father, Raymond Williams, who wrote the present essay based on Merryn's research, was, until his much lamented early death in 1988, one of the most influential intellectual figures in Great Britain since the Second World War. 'Cultural materialism', Williams's particular inflexion of a marxist analysis of 'culture and society', combined sophisticated theoretical underpinning with a close attention to specific cultural practices, be they the development of literacy, the mass media or literary texts. His works, theoretical, critical and fictional, are too numerous (and too well-known) to be listed here, but he wrote about Hardy specifically in *The English Novel from Dickens to Lawrence* (1970, much of which was later reprinted in *The Country and the City*, 1973), although there are further illuminating comments in *Politics and Letters* (1979, pp. 223, 245–7, 264). The present essay, from which several paragraphs referring to novels other than *Tess of the d'Urbervilles* have been cut, is a significant, because relatively rare, analysis of the coordinates of Hardy's own class of origin and of his subtle and knowledgeable deployment of class in his fiction. *Tess* here becomes material evidence of such a consciousness at work. Ed.]

1.  F. M. L. Thompson, *English Landed Society in the 19th Century* (London, 1963), p. 25.

2.  'The Dorsetshire Labourer' in *Thomas Hardy's Personal Writings*, ed. H. Orel (London, 1967), p. 189.

3.  William Cobbett, *The Political Register*, 70: 1 (13 November 1830), 695.

4.  'The Dorsetshire Labourer', ed. Orel, p. 25.

# 2

# 'Tess of the d'Urbervilles': Towards a Materialist Criticism

*GEORGE WOTTON*

## I MOMENTS OF VISION

In *Tess of the d'Urbervilles* the structure of perceptions is deployed in the construction of two major *scenarios*. The first and more general is that of the repression and displacement of the customary and experiential relationships in which the inhabitants of Wessex stand to their world; the second and more specific is that of the contrasting ways in which Tess herself is exploited and subjected by the distracted gaze and the idealising vision.

In chapter two Hardy *places* Tess in her natural environment, that 'engirdled and secluded region', the Vale of Blackmoor. Here we first see her engaged in celebrating the 'local Cerealia . . . a gay survival from Old Style days, when cheerfulness and May-time were synonymous – days before the habit of taking long views had reduced emotions to a monotonous average'. Among the onlookers of this Pagan festival were the Clare brothers, 'the regulation curate', the 'normal undergraduate', and the 'desultory tentative student of something and everything'. Unlike his brothers who think it beneath their dignity to be seen dancing in public with a troop of country hoydens, Angel takes a partner. Significantly he does not dance with Tess because he fails to see her, and he senses afterwards 'that she was hurt by his oversight'. It is a significant oversight because throughout the novel Hardy makes a point of emphasising Tess's profoundly physical presence. He writes of her 'exceptional physical nature',[1] her 'luxuriance of aspect', her 'fulness of growth',[2] and her 'bouncing handsome womanliness'.[3] Indeed, despite the constraints of Victorian censorship, Hardy conveys a powerful sense of Tess's sexuality as well as her sexual attractiveness. But what Angel's idealising vision fails to see is immediately apparent to the distracted gaze of Alec d'Urberville.

From the outset Tess's spontaneous relationship to her world takes a non-Christian form of expression. She reacts with horror to the biblical texts which the itinerant painter daubs on the walls and stile-boards about the village of Marlott. This 'hideous defacement – the last grotesque phase of a creed which had served mankind well in its time', she finds 'horrible . . . crushing! killing!'[4] After her 'fall' she becomes terrified by the 'cloud of moral hobgoblins' which these accusatory texts create in her imagination. But Hardy stresses that it was they that were 'out of harmony with the actual world, not she. . . . She had been made to break an accepted social law, but no law known to the environment in which she fancied herself such an anomaly'. Accredited dogma forces an 'unnatural' perception upon Tess in which she 'looked upon herself as a figure of Guilt intruding into haunts of Innocence'.[5] This stands in stark contrast to the 'natural', spontaneous and harmonious relationship which is evoked when this 'daughter of Nature' comes to the Valley of the Great Dairies 'in which milk and butter grew to rankness'.[6] Here Tess manifests that 'invincible instinct towards self-delight',[7] the 'irresistible, universal, automatic tendency to find sweet pleasure somewhere, which pervades all life'.[8] Angel has a fleeting glimpse of this when he looks at Tess and seems 'to discern in her something that was familiar, something which carried him back into a joyous and unforeseeing past, before the necessity of taking thought had made the heavens gray'.[9] This moment of vision reawakens in him memories which have long been repressed. Tess's spontaneous relation to her world is associated with the pagan, the flesh, with the customary and experiential forms of the native inhabitants of Wessex and 'the old-fashioned revelling in the general situation'.[10] On the other hand, confronting that relationship, stands the Wilhelm Meister intellectual. Here the associations are with the disease of flesh, with the spirit, Christianity, the ache of modernism, the modern vice of unrest, and with consciousness. Like all Hardy's intellectuals Angel floats about uneasily, restlessly, peculiarly unattached, seeking some ideological structure in which to live. It is not, of course, that the intellectuals live 'outside' ideology but that in abandoning that 'creed which had served mankind well in its time', they are deprived of a potent and effective ideological structure in which to inscribe their fundamentally religious 'ideas'. These ideas are manifested in a variety of idealising visions. Thus when thinking about those 'feelings which might almost have been called those of the age – the ache of modernism', Angel reflects that what are called 'advanced ideas are really in great part but the latest fashion in definition . . . of sensations which men and women have vaguely grasped for centuries'.[11] Whatever the apparent form of the individual subject's idealism, we notice that whenever the conflicts in which the intellectuals are involved reach a crisis and they must *act* according to their ideas, those actions are almost invariably determined by the religious ideology upon which, in the end, their ideas depend.

When Tess is drawn into the wild and overgrown garden by the sound of Angel's harp-playing[12] we have a sense of her profoundly physical intimacy with the natural environment. I have already mentioned the way Hardy suggests Tess's sexual presence, a presence which had to be fudged for the sake of the censor, hence the misty ambiguities about the incident in the Chase and the incongruity of the protestations of this country girl who did not know about Alec's intentions because she had not read novels! Nevertheless, as far as Tess (and Hardy) is concerned the only thing wrong with her relationship with Alec is that she does not love him. Tess, Hardy writes, was 'temporarily blinded by his ardent manners, had been stirred to confused surrender awhile: had suddenly despised and disliked him, and had run away. That was all.'[13] Tess's sexual relationship (but not the manner of its commencement) was, in this sense, 'natural'. The harm comes from the ideological equation of sexuality with ownership. The idea of a woman 'belonging' to the man who first 'possesses' her – which is the way Angel sees it – depends upon the ambiguity of the word possession. Tess 'belongs' to Alec because he 'took' her in the Chase and 'made her his' (we can see here how the language of romantic love reproduces the possessive individualism of male sexist ideology); thus Tess is bound to him by powerful ideological fetters as later Sue is to Phillotson. In this sense Tess really has nothing to lose but her chains and her slaughter of Alec could be read as a throwing off of shackles little short of revolutionary. But the repression of Tess exercised by Alec's view of her as a sexual object is different from that exercised over her by Angel.

From the moment of the meeting in the garden the harmonious relations between Tess and her world begin to be repressed and displaced by certain abstractions mediated by Angel's idealising vision. She is transformed in Angel's sight: 'She was no longer the milkmaid, but a visionary essence of woman – a whole sex condensed into one typical form.' He calls her Artemis, Demeter and 'other fanciful names'.[14] Angel's idealisation has a profound effect upon Tess for she is treated according to how she is perceived and she is subjected by Angel's idealising vision in a way which is totally different from the way she is exploited by Alec's distracted gaze. Perceived by Alec as a sexual object she is treated accordingly, but her seduction and subsequent pregnancy is represented as merely a 'passing corporeal blight' from which she emerges intact. In this part of her story (that of the pretty maid seduced by the squire, retold in ballad and popular song and here in the novel which alludes to those popular and superseded forms) we see the ideological reflex of those 'feudal' social relations where individuals enter into relation with one another as individuals imprisoned within a certain definition (landlord and 'peasant', squire and milkmaid) which appears as a personal restriction of one individual by another.[15] The relationship between Tess and Angel is different because whereas Alec appeared quite definitely as a man to Tess, Angel appears as an intelligence.[16] The material, physical relationship is replaced by a spiritual, idealised relationship. Here Tess is no longer subjected by the relations of personal dependence but rather by certain abstractions, that is not by the new conditions of existence themselves, but by the ideological reflex of new material conditions, by the 'reign of ideas' which was the peculiarity of this new age. But these abstractions are nothing more than the ideological expression of 'the material relations which are their lord and master', the belief in the permanence of which is 'consolidated, nourished and inculcated by the ruling classes by all means available'.[17] This transformation is not directly reflected in Hardy's writing, rather it evokes the contradictions of the history of the radical separation through the conflicting ways Tess is perceived and consequently treated, ways which reflect different modes of ideological subjection.

It is at Talbothays that the transition take place. In the dairy farm we have an image of the relations of contradiction between two modes of production. In the working and social relations of the farm we have an image of the productive relations of the patriarchal industries of the yeoman or small producer, and at the same time those of the small capitalist farmer who produces commodities for sale in the large urban centres. Until this point the productive relations of Tess and her family were entirely those of the independent small producer in which the different kinds of their labour were direct social functions, functions of the Durbeyfield family. After Tess leaves Talbothays those relations are transformed. Thereafter the Durbeyfields have the status of propertyless wage labourers with nothing to sell but their labour power. By the time Tess reaches Flintcomb-Ash the radical separation has occurred. It is, however, Talbothays which is the site of that transformation, it is there that the radical break takes place.

Writing of this separation from a certain position, Hardy gives us an image of these superseded relations as 'idyllic'. To stress that this world was as yet unsullied by an alien and false idealism Hardy emphasises the 'physical' nature of these relations in the 'oozing fatness and warm ferments of the Froom Vale'.[18] The associations here are with the communal, the customary, with physical labour, natural instinct, sexuality and with the essential paganism which lay concealed beneath this apparently Christian community where Sunday is a 'Sun's-day, when flesh went forth to coquet with flesh while hypocritically affecting business with spiritual things'.[19] All this is put in jeopardy by the 'spiritual' abstractions of 'the smear of "civilisation"'.[20]

In so far as the aesthetic project of Hardy's writing is to enable the reader to perceive the real, *Tess* is structured upon a series of contradictory perceptions in the conflict between which those abstractions are revealed as inauthentic. The idealising vision here represents the operation of a 'false' idealism which in Hardy's view had to be replaced by a 'true' idealism, true because it is understood not as a subjective projection but as a mode of perception which sees into the heart and inner meaning of things. Hardy believed that it was in the power of imaginative writing to effect that transformation because it allowed the reader to see, perhaps only catch a glimpse of, the possibility of the existence of that inner truth, that deeper reality. The idealist basis of the aesthetic project is revealed in the desired conjunction of perceptions in which the consciousness of the writer and that of the reader are fused into a single idealist point of view, a uniquely revelationary moment of vision. . . .

## II THE PRODUCTION OF MEANING

I have said that Hardy's writing produces a determinate view of the Victorian masculinist alter-ideology of woman as the *sexus sequior*. In this ideological construction woman appears in the image of her innate difference. Her vanity, masochism, capriciousness, her desire to be mastered, her weakness, her wiles, her 'womanliness', are all manifestations of the unfathomable mystery of her essential otherness. But this sexist ideology is not simply reflected in the writing but put into contradiction, not through images or scenes of repression, but by being activated in the structure of perceptions. Trapped and captured by the masculine gaze each of Hardy's women is enmeshed in a conflict of perceptions, a complex of visions of herself. She is constituted as the observed subject whose existence is determined by her reactions to the conflicting acts of sight of the men by whom she is observed. Interpellated as a subject, subjected to the myth of being the weaker sex, internalising and recognising herself in that image, she behaves accordingly. Whatever Hardy's intention, the innumerable acts of sight which constitute the structure of perceptions put the ideological construction of woman into contradiction by showing that the perception of her 'essential nature' is always conditional upon who is doing the seeing.

How is this structure of perceptions (re)produced in the discourse of aesthetic ideology? How do the female characters in Hardy's writing appear in the views of a male dominated critical discourse and how are they ideologically activated? In an attempt to answer these questions I shall look at a (random) selection of views of just two female characters, Tess and Sue Bridehead, produced since the end of the Second World War. The reason for this selection is twofold. The first is simply the necessity to limit the field of choice which is very large. The second is that both Tess and Sue have a very strong presence in contemporary English studies. So far as students are concerned they figure among the best known characters in English writing at this time and are in consequence the source of production of an enormous number of points of view. How they are critically (re)produced and ideologically activated by the discourse of aesthetic ideology is therefore extremely important.

In the following critical views on woman the contradictions Hardy's writing produces are repressed and replaced by an ideal central idea which not only robs the writing of its reality by representing it as the reflection of something outside it, but also ideologically activates it, uses it to reproduce and reinforce a masculinist alter-ideology.

[In a cut passage here, the essay examines critical views of Hardy's women in general over the past one hundred years.]

For H. C. Webster (1947) Tess is the representative embodiment of her creator's essential humanism and the novel to which she gives her name 'a fine contribution to the war against "man's inhumanity to man" which so importantly characterised the last decade of Hardy's career as a novelist'. In the reiteration of Hardy's humanist theme it is hardly surprising that Tess's 'fight seems to have value in itself because of the nobility of her nature . . . she is a tragic character in the truest sense of the word'. It is, however, in this critic's reading of Tess as the subject of two antithetical but equally powerful laws – the law of Nature and the law of society – and her status as the helpless victim of the conflict between these which constitutes the critical work's dominant perception.[21] Douglas Brown's reading of Tess (1954) emphasises the character as the embodiment of meaning by suggesting that 'Tess is not only the pure woman, the ballad heroine, the country girl: she is the agricultural community in its moment of ruin',[22] a view which accords with Holloway's (1960) perception of Tess as 'a protagonist who incarnates the older order, and whose decline is linked . . . with an inner misdirection, an inner weakness'. This weakness is a result of her heredity: 'The race is in decline . . . in Tess there is something self-destroying'.[23] In these and in Roy Morrell's (1965) reading of Tess as the victim of 'a conventional idea of morality, of the condemnation of society'[24] the universal abstract Subject which confronts the subject Tess is History whereas in Tony Tanner's (1968) view it is the Universal Will. He writes that Hardy suggests 'a universe of radical opposition, working to destroy what it works to create, crushing to death what it coaxes into life. From this point of view society only appears as a functioning part of a larger process. . . . Hardy's vision is tragic and penetrated far deeper than specific social anomalies . . . [he] reveals a Sophoclean grasp of the bed-rock ironies of existence' and he concludes that 'Tess is the living demonstration of these tragic ironies'.[25]

Irving Howe (1968) conveys the sense that the process of identification involves the recognition of an essential humanism when he writes that Tess represents something 'deeply rooted in the substance of instinctual life' and that she provides for us 'a standard of what is right and essential for human beings to demand from life'. She is, he writes, 'one of the great images of human possibility' and in responding to her 'radiant wholeness' what we respond to is Tess herself.[26] But whereas in Howe's commentary the identity between subject and subject, between author, character and reader is implicit, in that of B. J. Paris (1969) it is quite explicit. Tess, this critic writes, 'has dignity because she is loved by the author, because he enters wholeheartedly into her experience of the world, because her feelings have for him, and are made to have for the reader, an intense reality. . . . Tess [is] an experience and a passion for us.'[27] And in Kramer's interpretation (1975) we see both the identification process and the confrontation between subject and Subject, Tess and the Immanent Will. He writes: 'Tess, the conscious individual, becomes confronted with the great natural forces which express themselves through her. . . . The awareness of her that the individual reader gains through the interaction of his consciousness with hers . . . permits the reader to participate in tragic vision on his own terms.' Thus we identify with Tess and consequently 'recognise' the tragic human condition which is her and our lot, subjects as we are, of 'the forces of the universe'. Again there is in this critic's interpretation of Tess the discovery of an inevitable humanism for 'despite its ostensible  unconsciousness, Hardy's universe operates in such a way that man does become its centre, its measuring device'.[28] This conflict is also in Southerington (1971) who writes that the basis of Hardy's novel is 'the conflict between sentient man and insentient forces. . . . The basic discrepancy [is] between social laws and natural conduct.' The subject's subjection to the laws of Nature and society is reiterated. 'Tess's eventual fate', he writes, 'is caused solely by ill-adapted social ordinances . . . so long as social codes fail to take account of reality, for so long does man expose himself obtusely to tragic possibilities. Heredity, economic forces, time, chance and consequence shape Tess's career and bring about her downfall. Only social convention *causes* it.'[29] In G. Thurley's reading (1975) of Tess as 'the fable of the Fall, the loss of innocence' Tess appears as the guilty victim of her own sexuality. In this psychological rendering of the relation between subject and Subject 'It is not fear of censure that dogs Tess, but her own sexual knowledge, her own sense of having fallen; and the force of this depends very largely upon her sense of having yielded out of her own sensualism',[30] whereas in Pinion's view (1977) Tess is the victim of her heredity and 'the work of others in the context of chance'.[31]

In the critical structure of perceptions we can see ideology in operation. Functioning through point of view, aesthetic ideology activates writing and when the critical gaze is turned upon Tess then however varied the individual perceptions, Tess is produced in the discourse of criticism as the representative embodiment of an essential humanism. When Ian Gregor writes that Tess 'realises in Hardy a feeling that we can only describe as love'[32] he points to the basic mechanism of identification. Interpellated as subjects and through the process of identification, the seer and the seen, author, character and reader/critic become fused into the single unique subject, the Self. In this figure of the observed spectator – Tess the object of knowledge and the subject that knows – we have a dominant image of humanist thought.

From George Wotton, *Thomas Hardy: Towards a Materialist Criticism* (Goldenbridge, 1985), pp. 89–94, 172–3, 179–81.


## NOTES

[George Wotton is one of the generation of younger marxist critics which was influenced by European theory in the 1970s, especially as mediated in the work of Terry Eagleton at that point. The key term in such criticism (see the next essay by Penny Boumelha in this context, too) was Ideology, which allowed a much fuller and more complex analysis of the relations between literature and history than did earlier reflectionist notions of 'text and context' (or 'background'). Here, literary works could be seen, first, to reveal the ideology which produced them, even when they were held within it, and to challenge and subvert it in the process; and second, to be historically determined not just by their period of production but also by their *re*production as cultural artefacts in later periods (most particularly as they are processed by literary criticism and their inclusion in the education syllabus). Wotton's book, from which the present extracts derive, is an extensive and diverse analysis of Hardy's work and its later cultural reproduction from the above perspectives (see Introduction, p. 9, for a further brief description of it). The first piece, from Chapter 7, entitled 'Moments of Vision' (see Introduction pp. 11 et seq. in relation to this phrase too), examines the ideological implications of the way Tess is perceived both within and by the novel; the second, from Chapter 13, 'The Production of Meaning: "Hardy's Women" and the Eternal Feminine', extends this to critical reproduction by surveying 'aesthetic ideology' at work in modern critics' male-gendered perception of Tess as sexual object – a 'naturalised' ideological stance which feminist criticism (as later essays in this volume indicate) also seeks to demolish. Both excerpts are from longer, general chapters, the first offering similar analysis of *A Pair of Blue Eyes*, *The Woodlanders* and *Jude the*

*Obscure*, the second surveying critical presentation of Hardy's women in general and Tess and Sue Bridehead (in *Jude*) in particular. The edition of *Tess* referred to throughout the essay is the New Wessex edition (London, 1974). Ed.]

1. p. 287.

2. p. 71.

3. p. 43.

4. p. 115.

5. See pp. 120–1.

6. p. 139.

7. p. 136.

8. p. 140.

9. pp. 158–9.

10. *The Return of the Native*, New Wessex edition (London, 1974), p. 191.

11. p. 163.

12. Part 3, ch. 19.

13. p. 117.

14. p. 170.

15. See Karl Marx, *Grundrisse* (Moscow, 1939–41), pp. 164–5.

16. Tess 'seemed to regard Angel Clare as an intelligence rather than as a man', p. 164.

17. Marx, *Grundrisse*, pp. 164–5.

18. p. 189.

19. p. 182.

20. F. E. Hardy, *The Life of Thomas Hardy* (London, 1962), p. 165.

21. H. C. Webster, *On a Darkling Plain* (Chicago, 1947), pp. 176–80.

22. Douglas Brown, *Thomas Hardy* (London, 1954), p. 91.

23. John Holloway, *The Charted Mirror* (London, 1960), p. 98.

24. Roy Morrell, *Thomas Hardy: The Will and the Way* (Singapore, 1965), p. 36.

25. Tony Tanner, 'Colour and Movement in Hardy's '*Tess of the d'Urbervilles*', *Critical Quarterly*, 10 (1968), 219–39. This appears in the Coles Notes on *Tess*.

26. Irving Howe, *Thomas Hardy* (London, 1968), p. 111.

27. B. J. Paris, '"A Confusion of Many Standards": Conflicting Value Systems in *Tess of the d'Urbervilles'*, *Nineteenth Century Fiction*, 24 (1969), 76.

28. Dale Kramer, *Thomas Hardy: The Forms of Tragedy* (London, 1975), p. 134.

29. F. R. Southerington, *Hardy's Vision of Man* (London, 1971), pp. 131–3.

30. G. Thurley, *The Psychology of Hardy's Novels: The Nervous and the Statuesque* (St Lucia, 1975), pp. 153 and 170.

31. F. B. Pinion, *Thomas Hardy: Art and Thought* (London, 1977), p. 135.

32. Ian Gregor, *The Great Web: The Form of Hardy's Major Fiction* (London, 1974), p. 203.

# 3

## 'Tess of the d'Urbervilles': Sexual Ideology and Narrative Form

*PENNY BOUMELHA*

*Tess of the d'Urbervilles* marks a particularly important moment in Hardy's representations of women in sexual and marital relationships. It takes up many of the concerns and narrative modes of his earlier novels: it picks up the ideological tragic polarities of *The Return of the Native*, for example, and that use of the female body to explore contradictory views of nature that I have already discussed in the case of Grace Melbury (in *The Woodlanders*). These concerns are developed in a number of new ways, however. No novel of Hardy's – not even *The Mayor of Casterbridge* – focuses more exclusively on its central character; and that character is, of course, a woman. Tess brings together for the first time the 'types' of woman that have frequently been counterposed in the earlier work – the woman compromised and doomed by her own sexuality, either as victim or as *femme fatale* (Fanny Robin, for instance, or Lucetta Le Sueur), and the young woman poised at the moment of marriageability (Paula Power, or Elizabeth-Jane Newson). Gregor has noted this change, particularly in relation to *The Woodlanders* :

> The novel finds a single person capable of revealing the conflict [between a divided human consciousness and its environment] which, in the earlier novel, had been widely dispersed. The temptations of Su[k]e, the endurance of Marty, the troubled consciousness of Grace, come together and find a fresh definition in Tess.[1]

44

At the same time, the components of Tess's complex class-position (decayed aristocratic lineage, economic membership of the newly-forming rural proletariat, modified by an education that provides her with a degree of access to the culture of the bourgeoisie) enables Hardy at once to evoke and invert his recurring 'Poor Man and the Lady' motif, as Bayley has remarked:

> She was an ideal of the peasant girl, the sort of girl who in his earlier novels would have been regarded sympathetically but without personal sentiment, but who has now become the kind of *princesse lointaine* whom the girl in the grand house once represented. His first conception of Tess stopped there, but the ingenuity of reverie then provided her with an under-image of the distinction – even the hauteur – possessed by his early aristocratic heroines.[2]

*Tess*, then, has no need of shadowy contrasts or parallels to point up or ironise its central character: it is structured entirely by the sexual and marital history of Tess Durbeyfield.

It is also at this period that Hardy's elaborately constructed, resolutely non-controversial public persona begins to break down. Repeatedly during his career, Hardy was careful to distinguish between his private views and those expressed in his novels, and, indeed, to disclaim any personal views at all on their more controversial subjects. Indeed, he never ceased to feel that certain things simply could not be said publicly, such as that 'Fitzpiers goes on all his life in his bad way, and that in returning to him Grace meets her retribution "for not sticking to Giles"'; or that Sue Bridehead wishes throughout their relationship to restrict herself to only 'occasional' intimacies with Jude.[3] He was, furthermore, among those who, in 1910, advocated suppression of a translation of Sudermann's *Das hohe Lied* , on the grounds that 'its unflinching study of a woman's character . . . of a somewhat ignoble type' required more in the way of 'good literary taste' to make it acceptable.[4] Nevertheless, it was during the 1890s that he also began to make more forthright and challenging statements in his own right. The essay 'Candour in English Fiction' records with great bitterness and force the shifts and trimmings to which the 'undescribably unreal and meretricious' narrative conventions of the family serial condemned him (or, rather, to which his insistence on publishing his novels in that form condemned him). Later, he contributed to a symposium on the need for sex education, and expressed his progressive views quite emphatically.[5] These are essays, however, and remain wholly separate from his fiction. His Preface to *The Woodlanders* uses an oblique and distancing irony to imply his real views on the subject of divorce, but it is only with the Explanatory Note to the First Edition of *Tess* that he makes the unusually straightforward and challenging claim to have represented in his novel 'what everybody nowadays thinks and feels' (p. 25). A subsequent Preface will temper this uncompromising account, claiming that 'the novel was intended to be neither didactic nor aggressive' (p. 27), but the tone of the original Note helps to explain why it was with *Tess of the d'Urbervilles* that Hardy came to be thought of as a writer with a philosophical-cum-moral axe to grind. 'Let the truth be told' (p. 133) has almost the air of a manifesto.

It has been claimed that '*Tess* immediately preceded the New Woman fiction',[6] but novels dealing with sex and the New Woman were already no longer a novelty. Some of the attacks on *Tess* – which was greeted with a moral furore and a degree of partisanship that must have made most of the earlier criticisms of his work seem trivial – were surely induced by the fact that Hardy appeared to be lending the weight of his position as a well-established (if slightly controversial) author to the more recent developments of the New Fiction. The early reviews abound in references to French realism (the term being at the time virtually synonymous with 'naturalism'), to Zola, and to Ibsen, and the work is repeatedly characterised as a 'novel with a purpose' or a 'Tendenz-Roman'.[7] What made *Tess* so controversial was not the relatively harmless plot (after all, many another young girl in fiction had 'fallen' to a man more powerful and experienced than herself, and either come to a bad end, like Eliot's Hetty Sorrell, or redeemed herself by a lifetime of self-sacrifice and maternal devotion, like Gaskell's Ruth), but this new element of polemic. A number of factors interacted to ensure that the novel would be read primarily in this light, whatever Hardy's intentions. There was, first, the context of an increasing questioning, both in fiction and in public discussion, of sex roles and of the double standard. There were elements of the plot: the ambivalence of Tess's feeling for her child, and the failure of motherhood in itself to determine the subsequent course of her experience; the fact that sexual and marital relationships are presented in such direct relation to economic pressures and to work; Tess's concealment of her past from Angel; and, of course, that second 'fall' of the more mature and experienced Tess that so scandalised Margaret Oliphant.[8] But above all, there were the sense (reinforced by that aggressive afterthought of a sub-title, 'A Pure Woman') that Hardy was presuming to offer a moral argument in the shape of a structured defence of his central character, and the passionate commitment to Tess herself.

*Tess* presses the problem of what I have earlier called Hardy's urge towards narrative androgyny to the point where a break becomes necessary. John Bayley claims that 'Tess is the most striking embodiment in literature of the woman realised both as object and as consciousness, to herself and to others'.[9] But this even-handed statement of the case smooths out the tension inherent in this androgynous mode of narration, which has as its project to present woman, 'pure woman', as known from within and without, explicated and rendered transparent. In short, she is not merely spoken by the narrator, but also spoken *for*. To realise Tess as consciousness, with all that that entails of representation and display, inevitably renders her all the more the object of gaze and of knowledge for reader and narrator. John Goode has drawn attention to the erotic dimension of this interplay between reader and character:

> Tess is the subject of the novel: that makes her inevitably an object of the reader's consumption (no novel has ever produced so much of what Sontag required in place of hermeneutics, namely, an erotics of art).[10]

And so it is that all the passionate commitment to exhibiting Tess as the subject of her own experience evokes an unusually overt maleness in the narrative voice. The narrator's erotic fantasies of penetration and engulfment enact a pursuit, violation and persecution of Tess in parallel with those she suffers at the hands of her two lovers. Time and again the narrator seeks to enter Tess, through her eyes – 'his [eyes] plumbed the deepness of the ever-varying pupils, with their radiating fibrils of blue, and black, and gray, and violet' (p. 198) – through her mouth – 'he saw the red interior of her mouth as if it had been a snake's' (p. 198) – and through her flesh – 'as the day wears on its feminine smoothness is scarified by the stubble, and bleeds' (p. 117). The phallic imagery of pricking, piercing and penetration which has repeatedly been noted,[11] serves not only to create an image-chain linking Tess's experiences from the death of Prince to her final penetrative act of retaliation, but also to satisfy the narrator's fascination with the interiority of her sexuality, and his desire to take possession of her. Similarly, the repeated evocations of a recumbent or somnolent Tess awakening to violence, and the continual interweaving of red and white, blood and flesh, sex and death, provide structuring images for the violence Tess suffers, but also repeat that violence. It has even been suggested that the novel takes the form it does in part because the narrator's jealous inability to relinquish his sole possession of her causes both the editing out of her seduction by Alec, and the denial to her of consummated marriage or lasting relationship.[12]

But this narrative appropriation is resisted by the very thing that the narrator seeks above all to capture in Tess: her sexuality, which remains unknowable and unrepresentable. There is a sense here in which James' comment that 'The pretence of "sexuality" is only equalled by the absence of it' could be justified.[13] It is as if Tess's sexuality resides quite literally *within* her body, and must be wrested from her by violence. The most telling passage in this respect is Angel Clare's early morning sight of Tess:

> She had not heard him enter and hardly realised his presence there. She was yawning, and he saw the red interior of her mouth as if it had been a snake's. She had stretched one arm so high above her coiled-up cable of hair that he could see its satin delicacy above the sunburn; her face was flushed with sleep, and her eyelids hung heavy over their pupils. The brim-fulness of her nature breathed from her. It was a moment when a woman's soul is more incarnate than at any other time; when the most spiritual beauty bespeaks itself flesh; and sex takes the outside place in the presentation.
>
> (p. 198)

It is most revealing here that, as Mary Jacobus has remarked, the language of incarnation is destabilised by the physicality and interiority of the 'woman's soul', co-extensive with the 'brimfulness of her nature', that it seeks to represent. Jacobus has also significantly noted that 'The incarnate state of Tess's soul appears to be as close to sleep – to unconsciousness – as is compatible with going about her work.'[14] Here, as elsewhere, and particularly at moments of such erotic response, consciousness is all but edited out. Tess is asleep, or in reverie, at almost every crucial turn of the plot: at Prince's death, at the time of her seduction by Alec, when the sleep-walking Angel buries his image of her, at his return to find her at the Herons, and when the police take her at Stonehenge. Important moments of speech are absent, too – her wedding-night account of her past life, for example, or the 'merciless polemical syllogism', learnt from Angel, with which she transforms Alec from evangelical preacher to sexual suitor once more (p. 345). Tess is most herself – and that is, most woman – at points where she is dumb and semi-conscious. The tragedy of Tess Durbeyfield, like that in *The Return of the Native*, turns upon an ideological basis, projecting a polarity of sex and intellect, body and mind, upon an equally fixed polarity of gender. In this schema, sex and nature are assigned to the female, intellect and culture to the male. That this is so would have been even more clearly the case had Hardy retained the Ur-*Tess* version of the relation between Tess and Angel. The relatively crude feminist point made by Angel's flagrant application of a double standard of sexual morality replaces what might have been a rather subtler counterpointing of the varieties of heterodoxy available to (intellectual) man and (sexual) woman: there is some evidence that his original wedding-night 'confession' was to have been primarily of lost faith.[15] Angel Clare's dilemma is compounded primarily of elements given a historical and social location: the difficulties of class transition, the confrontation of liberal education and Christian faith, the establishment of a standard of morality in the absence of transcendentally ratified principles. Tess's situation, unlike that of Eustacia Vye, calls upon similar elements: her entrapment in mutually reinforcing economic and sexual oppression, for example, and the characteristically Victorian morality of the double standard. But still, the source of what is specifically *tragic* in her story remains at the level of nature. Tess is identified with nature – or, more accurately, constructed as an instance of the natural – in a number of ways. She is, for instance, particularly associated with instinct and intuition, those 'natural' modes of knowledge which Clare too will ascribe to her, and which form part of a collision in the novel between formal and heuristic education. So, the 'invincible instinct towards self-delight' (p. 128) sends her to Talbothays in relatively good heart; her 'instincts' tell her that she must not play hard to get with Angel Clare, 'since it must in its very nature carry with it a suspicion of art' (p. 221); and the 'appetite for joy' moves her to accept Clare's proposal of marriage (p. 218). It is noticeable, too, that Tess is often bound doubly to her sex and to intuition or instinct by a generalising commentary: 'the woman's instinct to hide' (p. 224), 'it would have denoted deficiency of womanhood if she had not instinctively known what an argument lies in propinquity' (p. 269), 'the intuitive heart of woman knoweth not only its own bitterness, but its husband's' (p. 269). Then, too, there is her explicitly remarked continuity with the natural world: she (again in common with other members of her sex) is 'part and parcel of outdoor nature . . . a portion of the field' (p. 116); images of animals and birds, hunting and traps, cluster around her; and in the latter part of the novel she becomes increasingly 'like . . . a lesser creature than a woman' (p. 418). Kathleen Rogers has remarked that 'Tess herself is almost less a personality than a beautiful portion of nature violated by human selfishness and over-intellectualising. She is the least flawed of Hardy's protagonists, but also the least human.'[16] But what might otherwise be simply a process of diminution is modified by the new degree of consciousness with which Tess's assimilation to nature is evoked. The ideological elision of woman, sex, and nature remains a structuring element of the tragedy, but at the same time presses 'the vulgarism of the "natural woman"'[17] to a point where it becomes disruptively visible. Angel Clare, who is patently implicated in Hardy's continuing dialogue with both Shelley and Arnold, is also the bearer of the vestiges of certain Romantic and Christian views of nature in his responses to Tess. For him, Tess is 'a mate from unconstrained Nature, and not from the abodes of Art' (p. 202); during their courtship, he creates for himself a pastoral in which the farm life is 'bucolic' and Tess herself 'idyllic' (p. 232); her wedding-night confession transforms her, for him, from '"a child of nature"' (p. 259) to an instance of 'Nature, in her fantastic trickery' (p. 263). It is through Clare, through the obvious contradictions and inadequacies of his response to Tess, that the novel throws into question the ideological bases of its own tragic polarities.

At the same time there is a remarkable shift in the balance of sympathies since *The Return of the Native*. In *Tess*, the tragic claims of an ironised intellect are subordinated to those of sexuality. The intellectual drama of the male is not itself tragic, but functions rather as a component of the sexual tragedy of Tess. *Tess of the d'Urbervilles*, as one contemporary reviewer remarked, is 'peculiarly the Woman's Tragedy'.[18] If Tess can be said to have a tragic 'flaw', it is her sexuality, which is, in this novel, her 'nature' as a woman. Her sexuality is above all provocative: she is a temptress to the convert Alec, an Eve to Angel Clare. Such are her sexual attractions that she is obliged to travesty herself into '"a mommet of a maid"' in order to protect herself from 'aggressive admiration' (p. 304). Her sexuality is constructed above all through the erotic response of the narrator, and it was surely this that gave rise to Mowbray Morris' sneering objections:

> Poor Tess's sensual qualifications for the part of heroine are paraded over and over again with a persistence like that of a horse-dealer

egging on some wavering customer to a deal, or a slave-dealer appraising his wares to some full-blooded pasha.[19]

Morris had evidently not realised how far he is implicating himself, as a male reader, in that image of the 'wavering customer'. It is interesting to note, by the way, that Edmund Gosse drew a clear distinction between the responses of male and female readers to the novel; he contrasted the 'ape-leading and shrivelled spinster' who had reviewed *Tess* for the *Saturday Review* with the 'serious male public' who appreciated its qualities.[20]

Set against this provocative sexual quality is a lack of calculation, essential if Tess is not to become a posing and self-dramatising *femme fatale* in the style of Felice Charmond. She never declares herself as either virginal or sexually available, and yet her experience is bounded by the power that both these images exercise. Hardy tries to preserve a narrow balance between her awareness of this sexual force (for if she remains wholly unaware, she is merely a passive and stupid victim) and her refusal deliberately to exploit it (for that would involve her too actively as a temptress). The problem becomes acute at the point of her break from Angel:

> Tess's feminine hope – shall we confess it – had been so obstinately recuperative as to revive in her surreptitious visions of a domiciliary intimacy continued long enough to break down his coldness even against his judgment. Though unsophisticated in the usual sense, she was not incomplete; and it would have denoted deficiency of womanhood if she had not instinctively known what an argument lies in propinquity. Nothing else would serve her, she knew, if this failed. It was wrong to hope in what was of the nature of strategy, she said to herself: yet that sort of hope she could not extinguish.
>
> (p. 269)

The archness of that parenthetical 'shall we confess it' and the elaborately distancing abstract and Latinate vocabulary testify to the difficulty of negotiating this area of a consciousness that must not become too conscious. The shared pronoun ('shall *we* confess it') hovers awkwardly between implying a suddenly female narrator and pulling the implied male reader into a conspiratorial secret (women and their little ways) that remains concealed from Tess. He is obliged to fall back on the old standby of instinct (and, on the next page, intuition) for an explanation of a knowledge that Tess must have, in order not to be deficient in womanhood, and must not have, in order to avoid falling into anything 'of the nature of strategy'. 'Purity' is, in a sense, enforced upon Tess by the difficulty of representing for her a self-aware mode of sexuality.

For Tess is doomed by her sexuality in a quite different way from Felice Charmond or Eustacia Vye. She does not share their urgency of desire to be desired, nor their restless dissatisfaction with the actual relationships in which that desire is partially satisfied. Both of those women are complicit in the circumscribing of their identity by their sexuality, and of their experience by their relationships with men. Tess, on the other hand, is trapped by a sexuality which seems at times almost irrelevant to her own experience and sense of her own identity. She is doomed by her 'exceptional physical nature' (p. 269) and by the inevitability of an erotic response from men. That response binds her to male images and fantasies: to the pink cheeks and rustic innocence of Angel's patronising pastoralism (p. 264), and to the proud indifference that Alec finds so piquantly challenging. Her sexuality, provocative without intent, seems inherently guilty by virtue of the reactions it arouses in others: 'And there was revived in her the wretched sentiment which had often come to her before, that in inhabiting the fleshly tabernacle with which Nature had endowed her she was somehow doing wrong' (p. 334). 'Liza-Lu, the 'spiritualised image of Tess' (p. 419), is spiritualised by the execution of Tess, expunging the wrong-doing and expiating the guilt of her woman's sexuality. 'Liza-Lu and Angel Clare give an openly fantasy ending to the novel, in a de-eroticised relationship that nevertheless contravenes socially constituted moral law far more clearly than any of Tess's, since a man's marriage with his sister-in-law remained not only illegal but also tainted with the stigma of incest until the passing of the controversial Deceased Wife's Sister Act (after several previous failed attempts), in 1907. The echo of *Paradise Lost* in the last sentence of *Tess* has often been remarked, but it is notable that the novel in fact offers a curiously inverted image of Milton's fallen world. The post-lapsarian world of *Tess* is attenuated ('Liza-Lu is only 'half girl, half woman', and both she and Clare seem to have 'shrunk' facially [p. 419]) by expulsion from sexuality, and not by the loss of a pre-sexual innocence. In Tess are imaged both a Paradise of sexuality (abundant, fecund, succulent) and the guilt of knowledge that inheres within it.

For *Tess of the d'Urbervilles* draws an illusion of cohesion from its single-minded concentration on the figure of Tess herself – an illusion that is rapidly dissipated by attention to the detail of the text. The text is divided not into a series of chapters adding up to a more or less continuous narrative, but into discontinuous Phases which repeatedly edit out the most crucial episodes of the plot. Mowbray Morris, in his rejection of *Tess* for *Macmillan's Magazine*, noted accurately enough that 'All the first part therefore is a sort of prologue to the girl's seduction, which is hardly ever and can hardly ever be out of the reader's mind'.[21] It is all the more noticeable, then, that after this build-up, the seduction itself is given only obliquely and by implication. The physical particularities of the incident, as Allan Brick has remarked, are transposed graphically enough on to the episode in which Alec persuades Tess to take into her mouth a strawberry – forced and out of season – that she only half resists.[22] But at the point when access to Tess's consciousness would do most to 'fix' the text into a particular significance, it is abruptly withdrawn. The same can be said of other crucial narrative moments – Tess's account of her past on her wedding night,[23] her return to Alec, and her murder of him. It has frequently been remarked, and usually deplored, that these moments fall into a hiatus between Phases. Stanzel, for example, has argued that such gaps in the reader's knowledge are a kind of pre-censorship whose effect is to prevent the formation of an independent opinion or interpretation that might act against Hardy's vindication of his heroine.[24] But it seems, rather, that they at once sharply indicate the way in which Tess's sexuality eludes the circumscribing narrative voice, and point up the disturbing discontinuities of tone and point of view which undermine the stability of Tess as a focal character and which, John Bayley has argued, give the novel its form.[25]

These discontinuities, incidentally, have enabled a critical dismembering of Tess. For some, concentrating on such scenes as the Lady-Day move and the threshing-machine, she is the representative of an order of rural society threatened by urbanism, mechanisation, and the destruction of stable working communities. Thus, for Kettle, she typifies the proletarianisation of the peasantry; for the agrarian traditionalist Douglas Brown, she embodies 'the agricultural community in its moment of ruin'; for the Weberian Lucille Herbert, she marks the moment of transition from *Gemeinschaft* to *Gesellschaft*; and John Holloway finds in her evidence of Hardy's increasing awareness of flaws within the traditional rural order that has hitherto functioned to establish a moral norm.[26] For all of these, the significance of Tess's womanhood is negligible, except insofar as it provides an appropriate image of passivity and victimisation. Others, seizing on the way in which Tess is singled out from her community, both by her own outstanding qualities and by her aristocratic descent with its encumbering heritage of omens and legends, have followed Lawrence to find in 'the deeper-passioned Tess' (p. 164) who can assert that '"I am only a peasant by position, not by nature!"' (p. 258) a natural aristocrat, the suitable subject of a tragedy.[27] Alternatively, by taking up the novel's allusions to, or recapitulations of, Biblical and literary plots (Eden and Fall, *Paradise Lost* , *Pilgrim's Progress* , and so on), or by following through the chains of imagery centring upon altars, druids and sacrifices, it is possible to find in Tess the shadow of innumerable cultural archetypes (Patient Griselda, the scapegoat, the highborn lady in disguise).[28] That each of these views finds its point of departure in the detail of the text indicates how complex and contradictory Tess is, viewed in the light of a critical practice that demands a stable and coherent consolidation of character.

And there is more to the discontinuity than this. The narrator shifts brusquely between dispassionate, long-distance observation (Tess as 'a fly on a billiard-table of indefinite length, and of no more consequence to the surroundings than that fly' [p. 133]) and a lingering closeness of view that particularises the grain of her skin, the texture of her hair. The transparency of her consciousness is punctuated by the distancing reflections of a meditative moralist who can generalise ('women whose chief companions are the forms and forces of outdoor Nature retain in their souls far more of the Pagan fantasy of their remote forefathers than of the systematised religion taught their race at later date' [p. 132]), allude ('But, might some say, where was Tess's guardian angel? . . . Perhaps, like that other god of whom the ironical Tishbite spoke, he was talking, or he was pursuing, or he was in a journey, or he was sleeping and not to be awaked' [p. 101]), and abstract ('But for the world's opinion those experiences would have been simply a liberal education' [p. 127]). Equally, the narrator's analytic omniscience is threatened both by his erotic commitment to Tess, and by the elusiveness of her sexuality. The novel's ideological project, the circumscribing of the consciousness and experience of its heroine by a scientifically dispassionate mode of narration, is undermined by the instability of its 'placing' of Tess through genre and point of view. Structured primarily as tragedy, the novel draws also on a number of other genres and modes of writing: on realism, certainly, but also on a melodrama that itself reaches into balladry, and, of course, on polemic.

The polemic itself also exhibits a series of radical discontinuities. As many of the novel's more recent critics have remarked, what van Ghent has dismissively called the 'bits of philosophic adhesive tape'[29] do not in any sense link together into a consistent or logical argument, and it would be a frustrating and futile exercise to seek in the generalisations and interpretations of the narrator any 'position' on extra-marital sex, or on the question of 'natural' versus 'artificial' morality, that could confidently be ascribed to Hardy as an individual or posited as a structuring imperative of the text. The 'confusion of many standards' of which Paris has written,[30] the overlapping of contradictory and conflictual points of view, probably results in part from Hardy's successive modifications of his manuscript in the face of repeated rejections. The serial bowdlerisations, irritating though they may be, are insignificant compared to the changes which Hardy made in order to secure publication. There was, for example, a major shift of emphasis, which involved superimposing upon a tragedy of the ordinary (in which Tess is representative by virtue of being like many other girls in her position) a mythic tragedy of the exceptional (in which she is marked out from these other girls by a superior sensibility that assimilates her to prototypes in legend and literature).[31] Further, although some of the 'philosophical' comments on Tess's experience are present from the earliest stages of composition, others (including the idea that Tess remains innocent according to natural morality) are added in later revision.[32] The 'argument' that seeks, contradictorily, both to exonerate Tess and to secure forgiveness for her is partly an attempt to rescue her for a conventionally-realised purity; as Jacobus has remarked, 'Tess's purity . . . is "stuck on" in retrospect like the sub-title to meet objections which the novel had encountered even before its publication in 1891.'[33] By a series of modifications, both to the original conception of the story and to those parts of the text that had been written first, Tess is rendered innocent in a revealingly double sense: that is, lacking in knowledge and lacking in guilt. A number of revisions, for example, emphasise chastity and reticence at the expense of passion and spontaneity; so, a passage suggesting that Tess would have been willing to live unmarried with Angel Clare is cancelled in manuscript. There is evidence, too, in the earlier versions of the text, that Tess's relationship with Alec was to have been far more that of equals, and certainly it is only when she must be retrieved from sexual guilt that any suggestion that '"A little more than persuading had to do wi' the coming o't"' (p. 118) is added (the phrase being inserted in the 1892 revisions). As Tess is purified, so there is also a far-reaching and wholesale blackening of Alec and Angel that transforms them unequivocally into rake and hypocrite.[34]

The contradictions in the defence of Tess, however, cannot all be ascribed straightforwardly to textual revision. They are also closely related to the diverse and conflicting accounts of nature that inhabit the text. Tess, like Grace Melbury before her, acts as the site for the exploration of a number of ideologies of nature that find their focus in her sexuality. The Darwinist nature of amoral instinct and the 'inherent will to enjoy' (p. 310) runs close to a naturalist version of sexuality, which posits an organicist continuity between the human and the non-human.[35]

The broody hens and farrowing pigs of Talbothays, the 'stir of germination' (p. 127) and the 'hiss of fertilisation' (p. 176), give a context of impersonal biological process to the equally impersonal instinct that torments the women dairy-workers:

> The air of the sleeping-chamber seemed to palpitate with the hopeless passion of the girls. They writhed feverishly under the oppressiveness of an emotion thrust on them by cruel Nature's law – an emotion which they had neither expected nor desired. . . . The differences which distinguished them as individuals were abstracted by this passion, and each was but portion of one organism called sex.
>
> (p. 174)

Yet, even as the 'naturalness' of the sexual instinct is proclaimed, it is simultaneously perceived as 'cruel' and 'oppressive', by virtue of its extinction of difference and its imperviousness to circumstance. Here, almost implicitly, there dwells a hint of the tragic potential of sexuality in this novel: individual consciousness, or consciousness of individuality ('She was not an existence, an experience, a passion, a structure of sensations, to anybody but herself' [p. 119]), in conflict with non-human biological process, instinct.

But, further, Romantic ideologies of nature, themselves divergent, are also invoked through the philosophical commentary. There is a strain of Rousseau-ism, positing nature as moral norm: 'She was ashamed of herself for her gloom of the night, based on nothing more tangible than a sense of condemnation under an arbitrary law of society which had no foundation in Nature' (p. 303). There is also a version of the pathetic fallacy:

At times her whimsical fancy would intensify natural processes around her till they seemed a part of her own story. Rather they became a part of it; for the world is only a psychological phenomenon, and what they seemed they were.

But this encompassment of her own characterisation, based on shreds of convention, peopled by phantoms and voices antipathetic to her, was a sorry and mistaken creation of Tess's fancy – a cloud of moral hobgoblins by which she was terrified without reason. It was they that were out of harmony with the actual world, not she.

(p. 114)

Here there is a quite openly paradoxical argument, confronting two views (the world as a 'psychological phenomenon' and the 'actual world') which clearly cannot be reconciled. There is, again, an intensely ironised evocation of the benevolent Wordsworthian nature, akin to the Christian providence, which works out a '"holy plan"' through individual lives (p. 49). Christian nature, 'fallen' along with Tess, is implicit in the allusions to the *Paradise Lost* motif, and is tellingly drawn upon in the description of Tess in the rank but fertile garden of her sexual response to Angel. Clearly, there can be no synthesis into a philosophically or logically coherent argument of such contradictory and paradoxical fragments of commentary. It has been claimed that these 'recognisably limited perspectives – partial insights', and the multiplicity of 'explanations' offered for Tess's tragedy, form part of the novel's onslaught on moral dogma and absolutism, and that they have as their primary effect to undermine the authority of the whole notion of explanation.[36] And it is true that they deter the reader from repeating Alec d'Urberville's act of appropriation or Angel Clare's moment of repudiation, by highlighting the partiality of such views. For both of these male characters, Tess is representative of her sex. For Alec, she says what all women say, but does what all women do:

'I didn't understand your meaning till it was too late.'
'That's what every woman says.'
'How can you dare to use such words!' she cried . . .
'My God! I could knock you out of the gig! Did it never strike your mind that what every woman says some women feel?'

(p. 106)

For Angel, on the other hand, she represents a spiritualised version of her sex:

She was no longer the milkmaid, but a visionary essence of woman –
a whole sex condensed into one typical form. He called her Artemis,
Demeter, and other fanciful names half teasingly, which she did not
like because she did not understand them.
'Call me Tess,' she would say askance; and he did.

(p. 158)

Tess, it should be noted, resists both of these representative roles.
And, of course, they are not the opposites that they might at first
appear; they are precisely complementary, as is emphasised, not only
by Alec's temporary conversion to evangelicism and Angel's momentary transformation into a rake with Izz, but also by the similarities
between their ways of gaining Tess's acquiescence. It is not only Alec
who is associated with the gigs and traps that, on occasion, literally
run away with Tess;[37] it is during a journey in a wagon driven by
Angel that he finally secures Tess's acceptance of his proposal. Equally,
the two ride to their wedding in a sinister, funereal carriage, and
when Angel makes his proposition to Izz, she is riding in his gig. It is
noticeable, too, that during their wagon-ride, Angel feeds Tess with
berries that he has pulled from the trees with a whip, recalling the
scene at The Slopes when Alec feeds her with strawberries.

Clearly, then, the novel's narrative method in a sense enacts the
relativism of its structuring argument. But there is more to the
discontinuities than this. They also mark Hardy's increasing interrogation of his own modes of narration. The disjunctions in narrative voice, the contradictions of logic, the abrupt shifts of point of
view, form what Bayley has called 'a stylisation . . . of the more
natural hiatus between plot and person, description and emotion';[38]
they disintegrate the stability of character as a cohering force, they
threaten the dominance of the dispassionate and omniscient narrator, and so push to its limit the androgynous narrative mode that
seeks to represent and explain the woman from within and without.
The formal characteristics of *Tess of the d'Urbervilles*, its increasingly overt confrontation of subjectivity and subjection,[39] will enable
the radical break in the relation of female character to narrative voice
that intervenes between the violated subjectivity of Tess Durbeyfield
and the resistant opacity of Sue Bridehead.

From Penny Boumelha, *Thomas Hardy and Women: Sexual Ideology and Narrative Form* (Brighton, 1982), pp. 117–34.

## NOTES

[A socialist-feminist critic, Penny Boumelha sees theories of ideology as helping to establish a basis for the analysis and interpretation of cultural texts, whilst the latter at the same time contribute to an understanding of the workings of ideology in their society. Her earliest major attempt to realise this, and the first full-scale poststructuralist analysis of Hardy, was the book in which the present (uncut) essay is Chapter 6. As I have implied in the note to the preceding essay (see p. 41), the influence of Louis Althusser and his followers, and especially the Terry Eagleton of *Criticism and Ideology* (1976), is strong here. But ideology is, in Boumelha's work, overdetermined by the new feminism of the post-1968 women's movement and reinflected in terms of gender: 'it will also encode other relations of power and dominance, and principally that of male dominance' (p. 5). The chapter on *Tess* reproduced here focuses on perceptions and presentations of sexuality in the novel, and in so doing alludes to a number of the issues which this New Casebook foregrounds: the uncertainty of narrative focus, the 'emptying' of Tess's character, the dislocations of the text (partly, but not exclusively, because of textual revision), the self-interrogation of the novel's own narrative strategies – all pointing to a 'radical break' in which Hardy's narratives confront their own informing ideology. The force of Hardy's representations of women lies, then, in 'their resistance to reduction to a single and uniform ideological position' (p. 7). All references to *Tess of the d'Urbervilles* are to the New Wessex edition (London, 1974). Ed.]

1. Ian Gregor, *The Great Web: The Form of Hardy's Fiction* (London, 1974), p. 178.

2. John Bayley, *An Essay on Hardy* (Cambridge, 1978), pp. 167–8.

3. See, respectively, Carl J. Weber, 'Hardy and *The Woodlanders*', *Review of English Studies*, 15 (1939), 332; and F. E. Hardy, *The Later Years of Thomas Hardy, 1892–1928* (London, 1930), pp. 41–2.

4. Hardy's letter is reprinted in the Publisher's Note of Hermann Sudermann, *The Song of Songs: A New Translation by Beatrice Marshall* (London, 1913), p. x. For an account of the whole affair, see Samuel Hynes, *The Edwardian Turn of Mind* (London, 1968), pp. 273–9.

5. 'Candour in English Fiction', in *Thomas Hardy's Personal Writings*, ed. Harold Orel (London, 1967), p. 130; and 'The Tree of Knowledge', *New Review*, 10 (1894), 675–90.

6. Gail Cunningham, *The New Woman and the Victorian Novel* (London, 1978), p. 103.

7. French realism is mentioned by, among others, 'Sylvanus Urban', 'Table Talk', *Gentleman's Magazine*, NS 49 (1892), 321; [Thomas Nelson

Page], 'Editor's Study, I', *Harper's*, 85 (1892), 152–3; and Richard Le Gallienne, rev. of *Tess*, in *Retrospective Reviews: A Literary Log* (London, 1896), I, 14. Zola is mentioned in 'Mr Hardy's *Tess of the d'Urbevilles* [sic]', *Review of Reviews*, 5 (1892), 19; and by D. F. Hannigan, 'The Latest Development of English Fiction', *Westminster Review*, 138 (1892), 657. Hannigan, p. 659, also mentions Ibsen, as does Charles Morton Payne, rev. of *Tess*, *Dial*, 12 (1892), 424. Harriet Waters Preston, in 'Thomas Hardy', *Century Magazine*, NS 24 (1893), 358, talks of a 'Tendenz-Roman,' while Andrew Lang, in 'At the Sign of the Ship', *Longman's*, 21 (1892), 106, prefers 'tendenz story'. W. P. Trent, in 'The Novels of Thomas Hardy', *Sewanee Review*, 1 (1892), 19, describes *Tess* as a 'novel with a purpose'.

8. [Margaret O. W. Oliphant], 'The Old Saloon', *Blackwood's*, 151 (1892), 474.

9. John Bayley, *An Essay on Hardy* (Cambridge, 1978), p. 189.

10. John Goode, 'Sue Bridehead and the New Woman', in *Women Writing and Writing about Women*, ed. Mary Jacobus (London, 1979), p. 102.

11. E.g. by Tony Tanner, 'Colour and Movement in *Tess of the d'Urbervilles*', *Critical Quarterly*, 10 (1968), 219–39.

12. Bayley, *Essay*, p. 183.

13. 'To Robert Louis Stevenson', 17 February 1893, *Letters of Henry James*, ed. Percy Lubbock (London, 1920), I, 205.

14. Mary Jacobus, 'The Difference of View', in *Women Writing*, ed. Jacobus, p. 13.

15. See Mary Jacobus, 'Tess: The Making of a Pure Woman', in *Tearing the Veil: Essays on Femininity*, ed. Susan Lipshitz (London, 1978), p. 87.

16. Kathleen Rogers, 'Women in Thomas Hardy', *Centennial Review*, 19 (1975), 249–50.

17. Bayley, *Essay*, p. 176.

18. 'Mr. Thomas Hardy's New Novel', *Pall Mall Gazette*, 31 December, 1891, p. 3.

19. Mowbray Morris, 'Culture and Anarchy', *Quarterly Review*, 174 (1892), 325.

20. 'To Thomas Hardy', 19 January 1892, *Life and Letters of Sir Edmund Gosse*, by Hon. Evan Charteris (London, 1931), p. 226. In his reply, Hardy repudiated the distinction: 'I hardly think the writer in the *Saturday* can be a woman – the sex having caught on with enthusiasm'; 'To Edmund Gosse', 20 January 1892, *Collected Letters*, p. 255.

21. 'To Thomas Hardy', 25 November 1889, Dorset County Museum. See Michael Millgate, *Thomas Hardy: His Career as a Novelist* (London, 1971), pp. 284–6.

22. Allan Brick, 'Paradise and Consciousness in Hardy's *Tess*', *Nineteenth-Century Fiction*, 17 (1962), 118.

23. Though two versions of this by Hardy can be found in *'Tess' in the Theatre: Two Dramatizations of 'Tess of the d'Urbervilles' by Thomas Hardy, One by Lorimer Stoddard*, ed. Marguerite Roberts (Toronto, 1950), pp. 49 and 182.

24. Franz Stanzel, 'Thomas Hardy: *Tess of the d'Urbervilles*', in *Der Moderne Englische Roman: Interpretationen*, ed. Horst Oppel (Berlin, 1963), pp. 38–40. Cf. Laurence Lerner, *The Truthtellers* (London, 1967), pp. 113–31. For an interesting but sharply contrasting view of this aspect of the novel, see Joseph Hillis Miller, 'Fiction and Repetition: *Tess of the d'Urbervilles*', in *Forms of Modern British Fiction*, ed. Alan Warren Friedman (London, 1975), pp. 43–71.

25. Bayley, *Essay*, p. 189.

26. See, respectively, Arnold Kettle, Introduction, *Tess*, rpt. in *Twentieth-Century Interpretations of 'Tess of the d'Urbervilles'*, ed. Albert J. LaValley (Englewood Cliffs, New Jersey, 1969), pp. 14–29; Douglas Brown, *Thomas Hardy*, Men and Books (London, 1954), p. 91; Lucille Herbert, 'Hardy's Views in *Tess of the d'Urbervilles*', *ELH*, 37 (1970), 77–94; and John Holloway, 'Hardy's Major Fiction', in *The Charted Mirror: Literary and Critical Essays* (London, 1960), pp. 94–107.

27. D. H. Lawrence, 'Study of Thomas Hardy', in *Phoenix: The Posthumous Papers of D. H. Lawrence*, ed. Edward D. McDonald (London, 1936; rpt. 1961), pp. 482–8.

28. Myth critics include Jean Brooks, *Thomas Hardy: The Poetic Structure* (London, 1971), pp. 233–53; Henry Kozicki, 'Myths of Redemption in Hardy's *Tess of the d'Urbervilles*', *Papers on Language and Literature*, 10 (1974), 150–8; and James Hazen, 'The Tragedy of Tess Durbeyfield', *Texas Studies in Literature and Language*, 11 (1969), 779–94.

29. Dorothy van Ghent, *The English Novel: Form and Function* (1953; rpt. New York, 1960), p. 196.

30. Bernard J. Paris, '"A Confusion of Many Standards": Conflicting Value Systems in *Tess of the d'Urbervilles*', *Nineteenth-Century Fiction*, 24 (1969), 57–79. Cf. David Lodge, 'Tess, Nature, and the Voices of Hardy', in *Language of Fiction: Essays in Criticism and Verbal Analysis of the English Novel* (London, 1966), pp. 164–88.

31. Cf. Jacobus, 'Pure Woman', pp. 81–2.

32. According to the invaluable account of textual revision by J. T. Laird, *The Shaping of 'Tess of the d'Urbervilles'* (Oxford, 1975), pp. 190–2.

33. Jacobus, 'Pure Woman', p. 78.

34. See Jacobus, 'Pure Woman', pp. 83–4.

35. For a detailed discussion of *Tess*'s relation to Darwinist theory, see Peter R. Morton, '*Tess of the d'Urbervilles:* A Neo-Darwinian Reading', *Southern Review* (Adelaide), 7 (1974), 38–50; J. R. Ebbatson, 'The Darwinian View of Tess: A Reply', *Southern Review*, 8 (1975), 247–53; and Morton, 'Tess and August Weismann: Unholy Alliance?', *Southern Review*, 8 (1975), 254–6.

36. Robert C. Schweik, 'Moral Perspective in *Tess of the d'Urbervilles*', *College English*, 24 (1962), 18.

37. See Jacobus, 'Pure Woman', pp. 82–3.

38. Bayley, *Essay*, p. 189.

39. Cf. John Goode, 'Woman and the Literary Text', in *The Rights and Wrongs of Woman*, ed. Juliet Mitchell and Ann Oakley (Harmondsworth, 1976), p. 255.

# 4

# Tess: A Less than Pure Woman Ambivalently Presented

*LAURA CLARIDGE*

> How strange that one may write a book without knowing what one
> puts into it – or rather, the reader reads into it.
>
> Thomas Hardy

Over the years many readers have tried to solve the problem of just
what, finally, is wrong with Hardy's *Tess of the d'Urbervilles*. These
same critics have commonly admitted the novel to the first ranks of
our literary canon, but they nonetheless feel compelled to address the
niggling question of 'the flaw'. Weaknesses singled out with some
regularity include the heavy dependence upon coincidence, the 'ab-
surdity of Alec's conversion and deconversion', and the indubitable
hypocrisy of Angel Clare.[1] But with rare exceptions, criticism has
failed to glean the higher fault: the novel's fundamental conflict of
purposes. Indeed, Hardy's philosophy of life has been heavily in-
dicted for its inconsistency or implausibility, but the deeper problem
of textual incoherence generally has been ignored. In what is perhaps
the most notable exception, Bernard Paris has offered an incisive
analysis of the thematic confusion arising from Hardy's treatment of
nature versus convention.[2] My thesis, however, deviates from Paris's
account of the closeness of author to his protagonist by my use of
this relationship to explore a complete undermining of formal coherence. Hardy's intense identification with his heroine creates an almost compulsive authorial exoneration of Tess's mistakes, mistakes

63

that instead must function as signs of the heroine's moral culpability if the novel's unity is maintained. In spite of Hardy's efforts to present Tess as a modern-day tragic hero with whom we are meant to sympathise deeply, a subtle reading suggests too many cross-currents that undermine his intention.

Such a subtle reading, however, is not (perhaps happily) always the novelist's fate. Because of the novel's undeniable poetic grandeur, it is easy for the first-time reader of *Tess* to be blinded to its textual incoherence. It is, as one early reviewer recognised, the second reading that 'leaves a lower estimate than the first'.[3] Lionel Johnson, one of Hardy's first serious critics, devoted himself to the novel: 'I read *Tess* eight or ten times with perfect enthusiasm – it is great literature – but finally, difficulties at first unfelt began to appear.'[4] Johnson's analysis is credible in part because he does acknowledge the book's beauty; he recognises that the novel yields pleasure, *but on a different plane than that of textual consistency*. He locates as a requisite for a novel informed by didactic purpose (a purpose which Hardy denied) a particular coherence: 'Either the story should bear its own burden of spiritual sorrow, each calamity and woe crushing out of us all hope, by its own resistless weight: or the bitter sentences of comment should be lucid and cogent' (p. 389). In Hardy's indictment of society, Johnson 'can see . . . but a tangle of inconsistencies' (p. 391); Hardy's narration creates in Johnson a yearning for 'definitions of *nature, law, society*, and *justice*', for the story grants these words first one premise than another (pp. 390–1). If it is largely Hardy's philosophical inconsistencies and his reliance upon determinism that worry Johnson, it is also his 'apparent denial of anything like conscience in men, that makes his impressive argument so sterile' (p. 394), conscience in Tess as well as the other characters. Finally, Johnson alludes to Thomas à Kempis to suggest that, like Maggie Tulliver, Tess could make 'true use' of her passage through 'fire and water', but she never does (p. 397).

It is because we are more attuned to the subtext upon subsequent readings, after the novel's obvious splendours dazzle us less, that we begin to sense the inconsistencies which weaken our 'appropriate' author-guided identification with Tess. Bernard Paris borrows from John Stuart Mill the phrase 'a confusion of many standards' to explain the undermining of the text.[5] Virginia Woolf went a step further: 'It is as if Hardy himself were not quite aware of what he did, as if his consciousness held more than he could produce.'[6] These critical insights direct us to the heart of the problem: the ambivalence that readers have too easily justified as a deliberate part of the novelist's art is in fact a serious weakness of authorial control. Hardy creates a heroine who does not, in the end, deserve the full sympathy that the thrust of the dominant narrative demands.

Certainly the surface movement of the plot directs us to understand Tess herself as a passive heroine, acting most often out of a last resort in order to survive. In fact, it is necessary that she function as a tractable, victimised girl in order for the characterisation of Alec as stock villain to cohere. Thus we tend to downplay at best or, in some cases, suppress the startling portrait of Tess as assertive, shrewd young woman that surfaces throughout at the expense of the novel's unity.

From the beginning of what D. H. Lawrence called the most important relationship in the book, Tess is sharp-tongued and sure. As she rides to Trantridge with Alec, she exclaims angrily in response to his race downhill, 'Thank God we're safe in spite of your fooling.'[7] She is too quick to be taken in by Alec's teasing; her cleverness in fact suggests her way out of the dogcart: she allows her hat to blow off in order to force Alec to stop. It is Tess's strong will that must help guide our apportioning of responsibility to both Alec and Tess in the course of their relationship. It becomes somewhat difficult, for instance, to marry the headstrong Tess who, riding off with Alec, 'pants in her triumph' (p. 58) to the Tess who is so tractable that any villain can have his way with her. But Tess's malleability, singled out frequently by critics as her dominant trait, functions to sustain her necessary innocence throughout the story. Her submissiveness allows Hardy to explain – and to come close to exonerating – Tess's two accommodations to Alec. Where the subtext insists upon a great deal of at least subtle complicity on Tess's part, the surface narrative denies it in light of her carefully established tractable nature as her only 'real flaw'.

As Elizabeth Langland remarks in her essay on another problematic heroine, Sue Bridehead, inconsistency within a character becomes a textual problem only if the inconsistency marks a novelist's confusion of parts rather than the identifying mark of the character's psychology.[8] That is, there are people whose identity theme might be said to consist of inconsistency. Hardy, however, errs by shifting authorial perspective on a character whose textual integrity is essential to a furthering of his plot. He creates a heroine whose 'tractability' is so marked that it represents her defining characteristic, and yet at the same time he presents her as shrewd, sure, strong enough eventually to assert herself against any fate. We confront not the tragic flaw in an otherwise noble character, but a characterisation formed by competing major instincts that never coalesce into an ordered, coherent personality. In 1892 *The Spectator* expressed reader displeasure in this way: 'If she be "faithfully presented", she was not at all faithful to her own sense of duty in the course of the story. Again and again Hardy shows her shrinking from the obvious and imperative duty of the moment when she must have felt that the whole sincerity of her life was at stake.'[9] This condemnation no doubt implies as much moral indignation as disinterested criticism, yet it neatly suggests the formal difficulties with the novel as well.


# I

Hardy's disclaimer aside, *Tess* is a didactic novel.[10] As *Longman's* insisted from the start, it is 'a story with a moral',[11] or, as *The Speaker* more long-windedly proposed, Hardy has given us a tale that is 'powerful and valuable as a contribution to the ethical education of the world'.[12] What is exasperating, however, is our confusion as to the exact lesson we are meant to learn.

Certainly the author's most obvious intent was to admonish a society that lived according to restrictive rules rather than by feelings of the heart. When Hardy published the chapter on Sorrow's baptism separately and entitled it 'The Midnight Baptism, a Study in Christianity', we can be sure that no one missed his indictment of hypocritical values. But what remains confused throughout his novel is his definition of sexual hypocrisy. What constitutes licit versus illicit sexuality? This question assumes great significance as Tess's erotic entanglements with both Alec and Angel increasingly come to define her fate. That her innocence is important to Hardy is clear in the novel's subtitle: *A Pure Woman Faithfully Presented*. Yet the author compromises the unity of his text through his implicit emphasis on appropriate sexual conduct as a measure of morality. He strongly indicts Alec as the treacherous thief of Tess's virginity, and he condemns Angel as a hypocrite who dares to care about that theft. But at the same time, by allowing a sense of confusion to pervade the text over the right circumstances in which a sexual encounter may occur, Hardy inevitably, if accidentally, suggests the very convention he would deny: that an unmarried woman be sexually inexperienced remains of utmost importance in judging her value.

There can be little doubt that Hardy wanted to liberate sex as a forbidden type of knowledge. Certainly the respect Hardy and Havelock Ellis entertained for each other is consonant with the novelist's real life concerns. It is in his fictional creation that the author seemed unable to decide what should constitute the norms for ethical sexual conduct. The controversy over the famous seduction scene points to his ambivalence: in spite of the heavy evidence that finally demands that the scene be read as sex by (reluctant) consent, several textual passages support critics such as F. B. Pinion in their insistence upon rape as the crime:[13] 'A little more than persuading had to do wi' the coming o't [the baby] I reckon. There were they that heard a sobbing one night last year in The Chase; and it mid ha' gone hard wi' a certain party if folks had come along' (p. 76). What complicates our judgement is the narrator's suggestion that there is no distinction between the sexual acts of seduction and rape: 'a little more, or a little less, 'twas a thousand pities that it should have happened to she.'

It is as if the possibility that Tess is raped protects her from the position of having engaged in 'liberated' sex, as if the idea of free choice might sully her important purity. Yet such freedom is, in a sense, precisely the concern of this novel. We are to censure Angel for his prudishness and society at large for its callous sensibilities. At the same time, however, if we are to take a more expansive attitude toward sex, then the typical reader's severe condemnation of the licentious Alec is exaggerated.

The point is that it does matter, within the textual constraints Hardy sets for himself, whether or not Tess 'accepted' Alec. If Tess is seduced, if she gives in to Alec's flattering, unremitting advances that allow her the chance to flout the gypsy women upon her escape with Car's former lover, her motivation for even their short-lived initial relationship remains unclear. Perhaps Alec's local power lures her, as she insists 'my eyes were dazed by you for a little and that is all' (p. 65). Indeed, Tess justifies her escape with Alec because with 'a spring of the foot' she can transform her 'fear and indignation' at the gypsies into a 'triumph over them' (p. 58). If we are to read here a case of a particularly modern (sexually liberated) attitude wherein 'pure' physical attraction alone warrants sexual consummation, Tess herself appears to disavow such motivation. But the conventional justification of affection does not suffice either; Tess despises herself precisely because she has *not* loved Alec. If she had, she 'should not . . . hate myself for my weakness as I do now' (p. 65). If neither love nor physical attraction, what moral code informs Tess's actions? The narrator, who never hesitates to jump to Tess's defence, especially if he considers her blind to her own virtue, allows her perspective here to stand; for once he fails to contradict her sense of guilt over her encounter with Alec.

What does this failure of narrative control do to Tess's essential formal function as victim? She stays for two weeks after her 'weakness' with Alec. Of course, there is gross inequality in the relationship: Alec's financial control over her family immediately implicates him in a coercive role. But at the same time, and at the expense of defining Tess as an innocent, the narrative implicates Tess too as bearing some kind of responsibility for a 'wrong' relationship. This confusion over Tess's role surfaces as early as the garden scene in which Alec and Tess become acquainted. Here the context of an Edenic bower – a profusion of fruits and flowers – creates a frame for the story that at times will work against the dominant and necessary motif of Tess's innocence. At first glance, the garden sequence appears orchestrated solely by Alec, but upon scrutiny, it bears much in common with the later seduction/rape scene. Inevitably an 'ideal' reader brings to the garden setting an awareness of the sexual complicity implicated in bowers, with the Ur-text, of course, the Edenic garden of Adam and Eve.

Victorian literature often appropriated the lushness of nature to foreground sexual initiation. In Tennyson's *Maud*, for example, the narrator and his lover meet in a garden of innocence which their liaison transforms into a lair of knowledge, passion, and death: 'the honey of poison-flowers and all the measureless ill' [where Maud has] 'but fed on the roses and lain in the lilies of life'.[14] Nature's ripeness functions even more strongly as a prolepsis of the fallen sexual state in Christina Rossetti's fantastic *Goblin Market*, with its alignment of wilful sexual initiation and the bounty of the countryside. The brilliant fruits and flowers that the goblins use to tempt innocent maids into their snare create the taste for 'more' of the same, similar to Tess's quick acquiescence to the pleasure of eating strawberries. In Rossetti's tale, as in *Tess*, the maiden *chooses* whether to become an initiate or not: Laura's sister, Lizzie, remonstrates that the girls 'should not peep at goblin men' but 'Curious Laura chose to linger' until finally she 'sucked and sucked and sucked the more / Fruits which that unknown orchard bore', becoming addicted so that the fruits are necessary food to sustain her life.[15] Similarly, Alec will become the 'poisoned fruit' that sustains Tess as well.

Striking in Rossetti's narrative is the insistence that sexual initiation is always choice: even when Lizzie, the innocent sister, confronts the goblins for Laura's sake, the narrator is at pains (though she never directly indicts Laura) to emphasise the potential for resistance:

> One may lead a horse to water;
> Twenty cannot make him drink.
> Though the goblins cuffed and caught her,
> Coaxed and fought her. . . .
> Lizzie uttered not a word;
> Would not open lip from lip
> Lest they should cram a mouthful in.

In contrast to Rossetti's Lizzie, Tess accedes to Alec's demand that he feed her the strawberry himself: 'in a slight distress she parted her lips and took it in' (p. 34). It is precisely our sense that Tess chooses her sexual initiation – that she knows what she is about – that makes this scene highly erotic (we are not worried about the heroine, but engaged instead in her own deliberate rite of passage into womanhood) *and* that vitiates our sympathy in her later encounters with Alec. After Tess 'takes in' Alec's offering, she wanders 'desultorily . . . eating in a half-pleased, half-reluctant state whatever d'Urberville offered her' (p. 34). Her willingness to sate her appetite before leaving anticipates her reaction to her 'seduction' later on: thus she will stay with d'Urberville two weeks beyond the initial liaison, her eyes 'dazed' a little, until she feels compelled to address other responsibilities.

When we read the subtexts of both the strawberry scene and the seduction scene, then we understand Tess as the Eve who rather too quickly yields to the temptation of the snake in the grass – or brambles – the villainous Alec. Equally interesting is the subsequent conflation of identity, wherein Tess takes on snakelike characteristics herself, a double identity that serves both to underscore the historically negative implications of 'being Eve' and to emphasise her kinship with Alec at a deeper, more essential level than the mere literal relationship that she originally claims, a confused characterisation that again subverts textual unity. In joltingly ugly imagery that parodies the richly sensual strawberry scene at Trantridge, Angel approaches Tess as she is yawning, at which point he sees 'the red interior of her mouth as if it had been a snake's'. She next stretches her arm above her *coiled-up cable* of hair (p. 143; emphasis mine). When Alec later calls her 'you temptress' and she 'recoils' from him as she falsely exclaims that she could not prevent his seeing her again, we wonder how Hardy means for us to understand his heroine now (p. 265). If Tess acts out her Edenic part as snake as well as that of Eve, it is to both Alec's and Angel's discomfort: as d'Urberville notes, it is Tess's scepticism that drives him back to his old ways, so that 'your husband's teaching has *recoiled* upon him' (p. 274).

As Hardy couches his description of Tess in serpent images, we are again forced to read Alec and Tess's earliest meeting retrospectively in light of Tess's complicity in her fate *even then*, a complicity that points more toward Hardy's own confusion over sexuality than to a formal position Tess is meant to embody. Man falls, but woman seduces, perhaps against her will, compelled by an inner sexuality that in fact defines her as female. Woman becomes, in some sense, the first term of the argument, as even the original tempter is ensnared by her beauty. Particularly since Hardy draws upon Milton, we might recall the treatment of his same problem in *Paradise Lost*, for as Satan approaches Eve, who, like Tess in the Garden, is almost hidden by the beautiful rose thickets, he is momentarily stymied by her brilliant innocence and goodness. For a moment, Satan

> abstracted stood
> From his own evil,
> and for the time remained
> Stupidly good, of enmity disarm'd,
> Of guile, of hate, of envy, of revenge.[16]

As Tess and Alec till a humble village plot – yet another 'fallen' garden – Alec quotes lines subsequent to Satan's mesmerisation:

> A jester might say this is just like Paradise. You are Eve, and I am the old Other One come to tempt you in the disguise of an inferior animal. I used to be quite up in that scene of Milton's when I was theological. Some of it goes –
> 'Empress, the way is ready, and not long,
> Beyond a row of myrtles. . . .
> . . . If thou accept
> My conduct, I can bring thee thither soon.'
> 'Lead then,' said Eve.
>
> (p. 289 [*PL*, bk. 9, ll. 626–31])

If we read this Miltonic allusion alongside the serpent images of Tess, Hardy's concern reveals itself: in tandem with the lush sexuality at the woman's disposal, does she possess an innate 'goodness' that protects her, *if she so chooses*, against the 'fallenness' of sexual knowledge? Tess's purity is maintained throughout the dominant narrative line precisely on these terms: in spite of men's abuse, she is pure. Yet again, this position causes formal discontinuities: if this purity is so potent an ingredient in her makeup, why did she open up her lips and take in the strawberry – and then continue to eat? Why, finally, does Eve not refuse Satan? Hardy shifts perspectives on Tess's real responsibility for her eventual fate as he alternately defines her as an unfallen Eve or an Eve who willingly accepts the serpent. Finally, in the parodic Edenic scene, wherein Tess approaches Angel through a fallen garden, 'damp and rank with juicy grass which sent up mists of pollen at a touch' (p. 104), she becomes a conflation of Eve and the dangerous other of the snake-tempter, a function formally assigned to Alec.

What at first puzzles us in seeing Tess switch roles becomes clearer when we recognise Hardy's own uncertainty about how erotic a woman is his Tess. She is surely in part a fantasy to the author as well as to Clare, who sees her as 'a fresh and virginal daughter of Nature' (p. 102). Hardy himself admits that 'I have not been able to put on paper all she was or is to me'.[17] It is even possible for two sensitive and sophisticated readers to draw opposite conclusions: Geoffrey Thurley, in *The Psychology of Hardy's Novels*, claims that Tess's weakness is in fact her overwhelming sensuality, whereas Henry James, in a letter to Robert Louis Stevenson, writes that her 'pretence of "sexuality" is only equalled by the absence of it'.[18]

It is precisely the problem in *Tess* that the heroine is too often caught in the middle of Hardy's own evolving ideas, so that no one, least of all Tess herself, is quite sure how sexual a creature she is allowed to be.


## II

In order to maintain Tess's sexual and psychological purity, a purity necessary (indicated even in the subtitle) for the novel to cohere, readers must condemn Alec as the worst sort of villain and allow Tess her occasional weakness at most. Alec, in fact, becomes for

most readers the stock villain of melodrama. But in our condemnation of Alec that the narrative demands, we can easily fail to see
Hardy's implicit, even unintentional acknowledgement of Tess's own
moral failure. Hardy means to show Tess's strength through her later
relationship with Alec, to dramatise her heroic attempt to 'get back
her own'. But in so doing, he reveals her understanding to be as
limited in its way as is Angel's. Tess is not the victim here, as the
narrative line suggests, but the victimiser. She dangerously fails Alec
in charity – charity that would in fact have saved her as well as him
from destruction. Such a failure works against the ordering of the
text that requires Alec and Angel alone to function as active, deliberate agents of pain to others.

It is through biblical allusions to charity that Hardy subverts the
very characterisations he means to support, especially his portrait of
Tess. That the novelist comments frequently on his story with quotations from the Bible is, of course, a commonplace of criticism. Yet
the extent to which these quotations *undermine* his text in *Tess* has
gone unexplored. Hardy describes Tess's devotion to Angel in the
terms of Paul's letter to the Corinthians on charity (1 Cor. 13): she
was not 'unseemly; she sought not her own; was not provoked;
thought no evil of his treatment of her'. At this point, the narrator
allows, she might well seem 'Apostolic Charity' itself (p. 202). The
narrator further explains Tess's vulnerability to Angel's arguments
by asserting that '[her] heart was humanitarian to its centre'. This
forefronting of charity serves to define this Pauline virtue as central
to a moral life, as we see even upon the eve of the lovers' joint
confessions, when Angel recites Paul's credo for the righteous man:
'Be thou an example – in word, in conversation, in charity, in spirit,
in faith, in purity' (1 Tim. 4:12). Angel's reflections, of course,
overtly (and consistently) serve the narrative in defining his later
hypocrisy and need for a rebirth. But it is not only Angel who fails
dramatically in the Pauline charity so important a part of this novel.
Earlier Angel's father has reminded him that a wife's knowledge of
farm duties comes 'second to a Pauline view of humanity'. When we
juxtapose this paternal statement with the narrator's insistence on
Tess's 'pure humanitarian' heart, we are clearly meant to read the
father's opinion as an unaware elevation of his son's fiancée, as well
as a foreshadowing of Angel's own lack of vision. Yet events occur
which suggest the Reverend Mr Clare's inadvertent but correct indictment of Tess for a moral failure equal to her husband's: she
knows her farm duties but does not know a 'Pauline view of human-

ity' at all. With the portrait that unfolds in direct opposition to Tess's designation as 'Apostolic Charity', the narrative is subverted once again – this time most seriously yet.

In her first exchange with the 'converted' Alec, in which he embarrassedly tries to justify his new role, Tess reacts by scorning his suggestion of a godly mission: 'Have you saved yourself? Charity begins at home, they say' (p. 255). Alec begs her to pray for him, so that even Tess's omnipresent spokesperson, the narrator, admits that 'the suppressed discontent of his manner was almost pitiable'; but Tess does not pity him (p. 265). She withholds her charity from an Alec too grotesque for her to pity, though she had recently been on the receiving end of just such a harsh judgement:

> 'Forgive me as you are forgiven! I forgive *you*, Angel.'
> 'You – yes, you do.'
> 'But you do not forgive me?'
> 'O Tess, forgiveness does not apply to the case! You were one person; now you are another. My God – how can forgiveness meet such a grotesque – prestidigitation as that.'
>
> (p. 191)

Even earlier in the story Tess has asked that letter of the law morality be overturned by a spiritually expansive charity in order to comfort her. She desperately pleads with her pious minister to agree that Baby Sorrow has been legitimately baptised, and he subsequently yields to her need for pity. Not satisfied with only partial charity, however, Tess condemns him for not allowing her baby to be 'properly buried' (p. 82). Charity, it appears, is a demand Tess makes of others, not of herself, except where she judges it earned, quite in contrast with the Pauline injunction. Yet it is precisely their lack of charity that has informed our reactions to, even definitions of, Angel and Alec: Angel as he fails Tess upon her confession; Alec in his initial focus on his physical pleasures alone. If we attune ourselves to the underlying subversive impulses of the text, we must re-evaluate 'Tess as pure woman' in her lack of the same virtue whose absence condemns her two lovers.

It becomes easier to appreciate the importance that Tess's charity would hold for Alec when we unearth the surprising evidence that he has, in whatever grossly inadequate fashion, loved Tess. Such evidence works against our dominant impression of Alec as a caricatured, melodramatic villain. Yet there are incipient signs of his real affection as early as the seduction scene, where he removes the overcoat protecting him from the September chill and 'tenderly' places it around Tess so that she will feel warmer (p. 61). He wildly chases after her when she returns to Marlott – though, significantly, he fears that she will not go back with him – in order to ease her journey home and to assure her of any support she might need for the future. Her total lack of affection for him bothers Alec; he says, within the space of only a few minutes, 'You didn't come for love of me [to Trantridge]' (p. 65) and 'You'll never love me, I fear' (p. 66). The evidence of Alec's desire to make human connections – to make contact emotionally as well as sexually – helps pave the way for his desperate conversion attempt as well as for the equally fierce revival of feelings that Tess's reappearance in his life provokes.

When Alec and Tess do meet again, Alec's lips start to tremble and his eyes hang 'confusedly in every direction but hers' (p. 254). He later apologises for his disorientation by explaining that 'considering what you had been to me, it was natural enough' (p. 255). He risks humiliation by asking Tess to marry him, and when he draws the marriage licence out of his pocket, it is with 'a slight fumbling of embarrassment' (p. 261). After Alec finds out that Tess is already married, he offers to help both Tess and her husband financially even before he knows that they are separated (p. 263). Alec chafes at his impotence in removing Tess from Groby's abuse and exclaims that he feels mad to think he has no legal right to protect her from the malevolent farmer (p. 268). In her former lover's reflective state of redressing past iniquities lies Tess's chance for safety, but rather than seek refuge there, she (and the demands of the text) insists that he remain a villain. Tess continues to define Alec only as a sexual threat until he resumes, almost in response to her expectations, his role as predator. The sharp words that issue forth from his bedside when Tess confronts him with Angel's return are different from the sardonic laughter we might have expected earlier: he loves her, and he will finally pay 'to the utmost farthing' for his surprising and textually disruptive fantasy that one day the affection might be mutual.

It is in light of such complex undercurrents that the necessary sympathy for Tess and hostility toward Alec become complicated. Indeed, it is even possible to laud Alec's fidelity of sexual desire versus Tess's 'use' of Alec, a real twist to the obvious dominant demands of the narrative. Most damagingly, such confusion of character subverts the novel's climax – Tess's killing of Alec – into a dishonest narrative move: rather than the inevitable act of a manipulated, maltreated hero, instead it appears, while certainly not unmotivated, as *unnecessary* by now. Tess could run away with Angel without killing Alec. Angel's catharsis in the desert has clearly left him a changed man; even as she talks from the staircase, Tess is the one in command, both in station and in physical power, while Angel, beneath her, looks so weak that Tess infers that he is dying (p. 315). Tess's apparent supposition that even this new Angel will not accept her in adultery is hard to credit, since she believes he will accept her in the role of murderer.

Thus what vitiates the strength of the murder scene is our uneasy intuition that *Alec does not deserve to be killed*: deserted, yes, though by now we might still flinch at what could be interpreted as injustice. After all, Angel accepts the d'Urbervilles' putative rebuke of him because 'his had been a love "which alters when it alteration finds"' (p. 305), unlike Alec's affection which, despite its possessor's in-adequacies, had been unwavering. Even the narrative description of Alec's murder creates a subtext of confusion over lover versus predator, over what roles Alec and Tess are meant to fulfil. 'The wound was small, but the point of the blade had touched the heart of the victim, who lay on his back, pale, fixed, dead, as if he had scarcely moved after the infliction of the blow' (p. 317). Yet Tess justifies her killing of Alec in her old justificatory terms of *his* power over her: '. . . you had used your cruel persuasion upon me. . . . you moved me. . . . you taunted me. . . . you have torn my life all to pieces . . . made me be what I prayed you in pity not to make me be again!' (p. 315).

But even earlier, Tess's refusal to act upon her admitted know-ledge of the Sermon on the Mount already had revealed an inner spiritual poverty rather than the moral richness a superficial reading suggests. 'I believe in the *Spirit* of the Sermon on the Mount, and so did my dear husband', she tells Alec, but we know what that sermon says and that Tess acts no more in accordance with it now than Angel did upon his wife's confession:

> Ye have heard that it hath been said, An eye for an eye, and a tooth for a tooth: But I say unto you, That you resist not evil: but whosoever shall smite thee on the right cheek, turn to him the other also.
>
> (Matt. 5:38–9)

Tess's earlier reference to the following passage suggests her familiar-ity with the Sermon's radical message of charity and thus further indicts her selective application of its message:

> Ye have heard that it hath been said, Thou shalt love thy neighbour
> and hate thine enemy. But I say unto you, Love your enemies, bless
> them that curse you, . . . for he maketh his sun to rise on the evil and
> on the good, and sendeth rain on the just and on the unjust.[19]
>
> (Matt. 5:43–5)

Tess betrays fully the spirit of this passage; she scorns Alec's
pitiable, even absurd attempts to give a moral direction to his life and
refuses to forgive him. Certainly she had not hesitated to ask Angel
to 'forgive me as you are forgiven' (p. 191) in tones resonant of the
Lord's Prayer, an evocation that the narrative emphasises, since that
prayer is contained in – and central to – the Sermon on the Mount.
By invoking the biblical words of Paul and Matthew, Hardy reminds
us that without charity we are as nothing, and, as illustration, Angel,
in fact, becomes depleted, a mere skeleton on his South American
journey into the self. It is only through a painfully won vision of
charity that he can come to life again. But if Hardy completes Angel
Clare, he leaves us wondering what constitutes the centre of Tess
herself.

### III

Thomas Hardy is on record as wishing his audience to read *Tess of
the d'Urbervilles* for its 'inner Necessity and Truth' alone. Thus he
justifies our sense that he meant something, that he pointed to 'a
truth'. Precisely such a compelling 'inner Necessity' is lacking, however, and fails to control a close reading of *Tess*. And it is for this
reason that the dissatisfaction with the novel exists for some readers;
this is the reason some of us feel uncomfortable when its devotees
explain away its weakness by the illumination of some specific,
basically minor, flaw. I suggest instead that it is the whole, not the
parts, that ails.

But what do we as readers have the right to expect from the text?
We assume that within the context which the author creates she or he
will fulfil the expectations aroused. We expect a realistic novel to
function according to a particular logic that Franz Kafka, for instance, will necessarily subvert in his fiction. As Dorothy Van Ghent
has pointed out, we desire an ordering of life within the realistic
novel that cannot exist in the chaos of the real world. Thus we
encounter the paradox of reality in the text: to make fiction real, we
make artificial good sense of the environment it inhabits. It is, of

course, true that readers impose coherent shape by reading back-ward, so that we create a unified whole a posteriori from the tele-ology that the closure suggests.[20] Yet in spite of current theoretical tendencies to escape the notion of determinate meaning, we must confess to making literary sense most often through a norm of ordering, even as we share Michel Foucault's dismay at the political manipulation such a system encourages.

Thomas Hardy structured *Tess of the d'Urbervilles* so that it demands to be read in a way that a careful scrutiny of its form disallows. It is true that the novel succeeds on some terms nonethe-less; too many generations of 'ideal readers' have indeed been enam-oured of the text to suggest that it does not deserve its place in the canon. But the particular pleasure of *Tess* comes from the genre it constantly evokes: the realm of poetry, not prose. It is Hardy the master of dark poetic truths who speaks so persuasively throughout this novel, and it is Hardy the novelist who works *against* his own text. Thus it is that there exists some recalcitrant coterie of critics, among whom I sit, who see the novel as giving pleasure only in spite of itself. And that pleasure, I suggest, is severely limited for part of its audience precisely to the degree in which the novel deviates from textual coherence.

From *Texas Studies in Literature and Language*, 28 (1986), 324–38.

## NOTES

[Laura Claridge's essay addresses once more the issue of whether *Tess of the d'Urbervilles* is 'flawed' – it asks the question 'what is wrong' with the novel? – albeit, in this case, not from the conventional perspective of 'im-probability' discussed in the Introduction (p. 5), but by way of a searching structural analysis of its contradictory discourses. Although it does not mention J. T. Laird's work (see Introduction, pp. 6, 10), and has only a passing reference note to Mary Jacobus's influential article 'Tess: The Mak-ing of a Pure Woman' (see Introduction, Note 16), Laura Claridge's essay is a kind of response to such work, which has exposed Hardy's increasing emphasis, in the gestation of the novel, on Tess's purity. It argues, through a close textual reading, that Tess is in many respects *anything but* 'pure', and that this contradictory subtext at the heart of the book produces a formal and thematic incoherence which accounts for its 'unsatisfactoriness'. Despite retaining the view (see its final paragraphs) that *Tess* is operating within a realist paradigm, the essay highlights again the radical indeterminacy of the novel, its competing narrative discourses and ambivalent narratorial stance – especially with regard to women's sexuality. Ed.]

1. For these respective criticisms, see Rosemary Benzing, 'In Defence of Tess', *The Contemporary Review*, 218 (1971), 202; Geoffrey Thurley, *The Psychology of Hardy's Novels* (St Lucia, 1975), p. 179; and Mary Jacobus, 'Tess's Purity', *Essays in Criticism*, 26 (1976), 332.

2. Bernard Paris, '"A Confusion of Many Standards": Conflicting Value Systems in *Tess of the d'Urbervilles*', *Nineteenth-Century Fiction*, 24 (1969), 57–92.

3. Francis Adams, *The Fortnightly Review*, July 1892, quoted in *Thomas Hardy and His Readers*, ed. Laurence Lerner and John Holmstrom (London, 1968), p. 89.

4. Lionel Johnson, *The Art of Thomas Hardy* (London, 1895), pp. 245–56, 262–4, 267, 269, 274–6; rpt. 'The Argument', in Thomas Hardy, *Tess of the d'Urbervilles*, ed. Scott Elledge (New York, 1965), p. 389. All further references to this work will be included parenthetically in the text.

5. Paris, '"A Confusion of Many Standards"', 59.

6. Virginia Woolf, 'The Novels of Thomas Hardy', in *The Second Common Reader* (New York, 1932), pp. 266–80; rpt. 'Hardy's Moments of Vision', in Elledge (ed.), *Tess of the d'Urbervilles*, p. 401.

7. Scott Elledge (ed.), *Tess of the d'Urbervilles* (New York, 1965). All further page references will be cited in the text.

8. Elizabeth Langland, 'A Perspective of One's Own: Thomas Hardy and the Elusive Sue Bridehead', *Studies in the Novel*, 12 (1980), 17–18. Perhaps there actually is a kinship of sorts between Sue Bridehead and Tess Durbeyfield; Michael Millgate in *Thomas Hardy: A Biography* (New York, 1982), p. 295, reminds us that 'Tess herself was for a long time called Sue in Hardy's manuscript, and in July 1889 he was suggesting that the novel [*Tess of the d'Urbervilles*] be called "The Body and Soul of Sue"'.

9. R. H. Hutton, *The Spectator*, Jan. 1892, quoted in Lerner and Holmstrom (ed.), *Thomas Hardy*, p. 69.

10. In the Preface to the fifth edition of *Tess*, Hardy claimed that 'the novel was intended to be neither didactic nor aggressive' (see Elledge [ed.], *Tess*, p. 2).

11. Andrew Lang, *Longman's Magazine*, Nov. 1892, quoted in Elledge (ed.), *Tess*, p. 384.

12. *The Speaker*, Dec. 1891, quoted in Lerner and Holmstrom (ed.), *Thomas Hardy*, p. 61.

13. F. B. Pinion, *Thomas Hardy: Art and Thought* (London, 1977), pp. 122, 134.

14. Alfred Tennyson, *Maud, Selected Poems*, ed. Michael Millgate (Oxford, 1973), ll. 157, 161.

15. Christina Rossetti, *Goblin Market* (Boston, 1981), ll. 49, 69, 134–5. All subsequent references will be cited by line from this edition and will be included in the text.

16. John Milton, *Paradise Lost, Complete Poems and Major Prose*, ed. Merrit Y. Hughes (Indianapolis and New York, 1957), bk. 9, ll. 463–6.

17. Robert Gittings, *The Older Hardy* (London, 1978), p. 68.

18. Thurley, *Psychology*, p. 152, and Henry James, quoted in Lerner and Holmstrom (ed.), *Thomas Hardy*, p. 85.

19. Tess laments to Angel that 'I shouldn't mind learning why – why the sun do shine on the just and the unjust alike' (p. 107).

20. For an illuminating discussion of the artificial nature of formal coherence, see D. A. Miller, *Narrative and Its Discontents: Problems of Closure in the Traditional Novel* (Princeton, 1981), p. xiii.

# 5

# Fallen Woman as Sign, and Narrative Syntax in 'Tess of the d'Urbervilles'

*PATRICIA INGHAM*

## I  FALLEN WOMAN AS SIGN

It was Hardy (and others like George Moore) who helped break the constraints against which novelists had fretted in their critical discussion of what to do in the novel. Already he had extended the treatment of women's physicality by developing a sub-erotic register in some early novels. After *Two on a Tower* (1882), he told a correspondent he determined to get rid of 'the doll of English fiction', an essential change 'if England is to have a school of fiction at all'.[1] The new register to which this refers continued to be used and extended into a more fully erotic range in *Tess*. After 1887 he took always the topics, dropped after *Desperate Remedies*, now made familiar by the sensation novels – adultery, marital breakdown, divorce, bigamy, even hinted-at incest, abandoning the false colouring 'best expressed by the regulation finish that "they married and were happy ever after"'.[2]

I now wish to examine the role of women in *The Woodlanders*, *Tess* and *Jude*, to show the evolution of a new set of feminine signs, recodings that are developments as much as innovations: Grace of the womanly, Tess and Arabella of the fallen woman, Sue of the New Woman. These women are all involved in feelings and actions previously excluded by taboo; yet they are not, like Lucy Audley, freaks and beyond the pale. They all make for themselves by a certain autonomy a new meaning, though as yet no descriptive language exists for it. They are seen deviating from the former womanly ideal without moving into the unwomanly category. Hence the preoccupation of males – both narrators and characters – with establishing a reading for them; and hence the contradictions in those readings. The superficial self-contradiction of Hardy the critic (visible also in letters to male, compared with female, correspondents) gives way to the profounder ambivalence of Hardy the novelist that enacts a contemporary confusion felt most strongly by a liberal-minded and sensitive male.

Central to this change is a focus on the issue of women's sexual feelings – read under the old signification as existing only vicariously. Spontaneous sexuality is now, however, an essential characteristic of all four women. . . .

Tess presents an overt attempt to replace a more marginal figure, the fallen woman as sign – exemplified by Fanny and Eustacia – with a positive image:

> Let the truth be told – women do as a rule live through such humiliations, and regain their spirits, and again look about them with an interested eye. While there's life there's hope is a conviction not so entirely unknown to the 'betrayed' as some amiable theorists would have us believe.[3]

She is an explicitly sexual being, her appearance described with the same directness as Grace's feelings: 'She had . . . a luxuriance of aspect, a fulness of growth, which made her appear more of a woman than she really was' (p. 56). This directness was noticed by the hostile reviewer who wrote of this passage: 'The story gains nothing by the reader being let into the secret of the physical attributes which especially fascinated him in Tess. Most people can fill in blanks for themselves, without its being necessary to put the dots on the i's so very plainly; but Mr Hardy leaves little unsaid.'[4] The new erotic rhetoric is pinpointed here, though the reviewer might have chosen more extreme examples such as Tess's yawn, or the passage in which Clare studies the curves of her lips: '. . . and now, as they again confronted him, clothed with colour and life, they sent an *aura* over his flesh, a breeze through his nerves, which well-nigh produced a qualm' (p. 213). Perhaps the culmination of this passage in a sneeze was one which the critic shrank from mentioning.

Nor is Tess's sexuality evoked only through others: she is aware of her own 'impassioned nature', and has for some time, perhaps always, 'the invincible instinct towards self-delight' (p. 141). Under the shock of Clare's finding her living again with Alec she can assert (according to an insertion made by Hardy in his 1912 copy), with the colloquialism seen to mark these women, what the Clarendon editors call 'the primacy of the sexual instinct'[5] by telling him that 'the step back to him was not so great as it seems. He had been as husband to me: you never had!' (p. 514).

As when confronted with Grace, the males of the novel cannot, with the men's language at their disposal, define and place her. Clare believes he can: '"she is a dear, dear Tess," he thought to himself, as one deciding on the true construction of a difficult passage' (p. 309). From early on he, as well as Alec, imposes the signifying framework of men's language upon her. When Tess resists his wooing it is as though ' . . . he had made up his mind that her negatives were, after all, only coyness and youth, startled by the novelty of the proposal' (p. 261). He reads her as 'a pure woman' of the approved kind, complementary and powerless: 'Do I realise solemnly enough how utterly and irretrievably this little womanly thing is the creature of my good or bad faith and fortune?' (p. 309). When he experiences her sexual attractiveness and response he can interpret it in a generalisation of a literary kind that appropriates her in the old way: 'He called her Artemis, Demeter, and other fanciful names' (p. 186).

Tess, literally not understanding, resists, asserts her claim to her own identity, and begs 'Call me Tess' (p. 186). When he finds she has failed in 'purity' he is astonished: 'She looked absolutely pure. Nature, in her fantastic trickery, had set such a seal of maidenhood upon Tess's countenance that he gazed at her with a stupefied air' (p. 335). The only conclusion that the categories of his language allow him to draw is that if she is not 'pure' then she is a fallen woman: 'You were one person: now you are another' (p. 325).

This erasure of Tess's identity and its replacement by a Magdalen figure is one resisted by that other interested male, the narrator. He deliberately sets aside the generalised reading of the unmarried mother who is innately wretched:

> If she could have been but just created, to discover herself as a spouseless mother, with no experience of life except as the parent of a nameless child, would the position have caused her to despair? No, she

would have taken it calmly, and found pleasures therein. Most of the misery had been generated by her conventional aspect, and not by her innate sensations.

(p. 128)

He wishes to insist on the recognition of individuality as she changes from a simple girl to a complex woman, 'whom the turbulent experiences of the last year or two had quite failed to demoralise'. He goes still further: 'But for the world's opinion those experiences would have been simply a liberal education' (p. 139). But he cannot entirely shake off the language of men even, or perhaps particularly, in his defence. The last minute addition to the novel of the subtitle 'A Pure Woman', though peripheral, deflects attention from meanings that Tess herself conveys, by attempting to rehabilitate her under the old womanly category: she may not look it but she is, he says. This subtitle is a reminder of the unitary generalisations of the early novels. It is again referred to when the narrator says of Clare: 'In considering what Tess was not he overlooked what she was, and forgot that the defective can be more than the entire' (p. 369). The antithesis of 'defective' and 'entire' is of course itself a conventional one, and, like 'pure', assesses Tess in inappropriate terms. In his most emotional defences of her this tainted terminology undermines the narrator's account by measuring her against the old norms. He slips back into the familiar terms of early generalisations with the description of the rape–seduction (or more correctly, seduction–rape) as he muses on: 'why it was that upon this beautiful feminine tissue, sensitive as gossamer, and practically blank as snow as yet, there should have been traced such a coarse pattern as it was doomed to receive . . .' (p. 103).

Thus the narrator's defence of Tess involves his recognition of her sexual nature and, as he sees it, its naturalness; but his reading of that aspect of her is an eccentric one, expressive of bewilderment. Since she is not sexless he construes her as all sex, reaching a description of generic 'woman' which is highly reductive:

> She was yawning, and he saw the red interior of her mouth . . . She had stretched one arm so high . . . that he could see its satin delicacy above the sunburn . . . The brim-fulness of her nature breathed from her. It was a moment when a woman's soul is more incarnate than at any other time; when the most spiritual beauty bespeaks itself flesh; and sex takes the outside place in the presentation.

(pp. 242–3)

Tess's own meaning, then, is only fully spoken to the extent that she acts it out in deeds. The narrator's attempts at interpretation evoke the ambiguities of a language in transition. The shifting signification of the fallen, as of the womanly woman, involves problems of perception for those who encounter her. . . .

## II NARRATIVE SYNTAX

Underlying *The Woodlanders* and *Tess* are the familiar structures that underlie the earlier novels. But the previous tentative interrogation of their conventional assumptions here becomes forthright; and the narrator now subsumes this discourse, hostile to patriarchy, into his commentary. This new distancing from the old misogynistic generalisations is evident for instance, in the recantation of the reductive assertion in *Desperate Remedies* that for a woman 'her dress is part of her body'.[6] The narrator articulates a new credo in relation to Grace Melbury: 'there can be hardly anything less connected with a woman's personality than drapery which she has neither designed, manufactured, cut, sewed, nor even seen, except by a glance of approval . . . The woman herself was a conjectural creature who had little to do with the outlines presented to Sherton eyes . . .' This is pushed further, to a point that questions the generic notion of 'woman'. The individual woman's 'true quality' can only be 'approximated', and that by careful analysis, 'by putting together a movement now and a glance then, in that patient attention which nothing but watchful loving-kindness ever troubles itself to give'.[7]

The displacement of earlier clichés about women helps to inscribe a reader different from the long-standing, blushable 'Young Person' attacked by Hardy and others. . . . Given this greater freedom, the narrators' accounts are complicated only by that incomplete comprehension of the opposite sex shared by all males in the late novels and sketched in the preceding section. The explicit defence of women in the narratorial commentaries is enhanced by Hardy's now distinct transformations of narrative patterns. With the choice of a husband in *The Woodlanders* and the fallen woman who atones in *Tess* he negates the conventional implications of such plots. Even with the newly developed variant of the 1880s in which a woman seeks her fulfilment by rejecting marriage he alters a discontinuity in syntax by eradicating sequences that tended in other New Woman fiction elsewhere to re-emerge from the earlier tainted patterns. . . .

In *Tess* the belated subtitle 'A Pure Woman' is itself already a direction to read the text as an over-writing of the traditional fallen-woman-atones stories. I now wish to examine such a reading and also to show the underlying lack of agency involved. In fact the subtitle accepts in advance some of the conventional assumptions that usually underlie such a narrative. Generic 'woman' is up for moral assessment and it is in respect of sexual morality that it is felt appropriate, even essential, to assess her: is she pure or not pure? To that extent the text colludes with the familiar pattern. What is destabilised, however, is the account of what it means for a woman to be sexually pure or blameless.

Characteristically Havelock Ellis grasped the problem that faced Hardy here and wrote of *Tess*:

> I was repelled at the outset by the sub-title . . . I have always regarded the conception of *purity*, when used in moral discussions, as a conception sadly in need of analysis, and almost the first time I ever saw myself in print was as the author of a discussion . . . of the question: 'What is Purity?' . . . It seems to me doubtful whether anyone is entitled to use the word 'pure' without first defining precisely what he means, and still more doubtful whether an artist is called upon to define it at all, even in several hundred pages. I can quite conceive that the artist should take pleasure in the fact that his own creative revelation of life poured contempt on many old prejudices. But such an effect is neither powerful nor legitimate unless it is engrained in the texture of the narrative; it cannot be stuck on by a label.[8]

What Ellis seems to be saying, and with approval not disapproval, is that the artist *should* question the axiom and deny the formula. He does not realise that his unease with the subtitle suggests that *Tess* does precisely this: it destabilises the notion of 'purity' in a way that undermines that subtitle.

It is important not to assume that Tess is pure merely because she is not the victim of outright rape by Alec. This is made clearer by Hardy's progressive alterations of the text. Though he added in 1891 a description of Alec as 'the spoiler' (p. 102) and one to Tess being overheard sobbing on the night of the scene in the chase (p. 127), other revisions render the scene more ambiguous by suggesting co-operation on her part. For instance, in 1892, he removed the reference to Alec as 'the spoiler' and to his drugging Tess with cordial or (earlier) spirits (p. 100) which had been in the text from the manuscript stage. After her escape from Trantridge Alec says to her in an early version: 'You didn't come for love of me . . .' She replies: ''Tis quite true . . . If I had ever really loved you, if I loved you still, I should not so loathe and hate myself for my weakness as I do now!' In 1892 'really' was changed to 'sincerely' and Tess concluded: 'My eyes were dazed by you for a little, and that was all' (p. 109). Similarly in 1891 to a description of her thoughts when confessing to her mother was added:

> She had dreaded him, winced before him, succumbed to . . . advantages he took of her helplessness; then, temporarily blinded by his flash manners, had been stirred to confused surrender awhile: had suddenly despised and disliked him, and had run away.
>
> (p. 117)

Even this was taken a step further by the replacement in 1912 of 'flash' by 'ardent'. As others have pointed out, the rape–seduction scene is followed by 'some few weeks' in which Tess remains Alec's mistress (p. 107). She describes herself as 'mastered' (p. 111) by him, with implications not only of force.

The breaking down of the line between rape and seduction is only one aspect of this sequence in the narrative. Another is that Tess has been physically drawn to Alec in a way retrospectively described as 'natural'. There develops a subtext about Tess, sexuality and naturalness that urges the exclusion of purely sexual relationships from the sphere of moral judgement. By implication Tess in a less artificial world might have regarded such a relationship as an available option. This is paradoxical: it cannot be logically reconciled with the equally urgent assertion that she is the victim of exploitation. But it seems to be the main ground for regarding her as pure, and alludes to some contemporary accounts of naturalness such as one of several produced by 'George Egerton' that Hardy copied out in January 1894: 'Men manufactured an artificial morality, made sins of things that were as clean in themselves as the pairing of . . . birds on the wing; crushed nature, robbed it of its beauty & meaning, and established a system that means war . . . because it is a struggle between instinctive truths and cultivated lies.'[9] Purity ultimately, as Ellis saw, escapes definition in *Tess*, except through the negation of old prejudices that would equate it with virginity and ignorance.

What is also innovatory in the syntax of *Tess* is that her punitive death is not the direct consequence of her fall: she survives her child's death, Angel's desertion and Alec's reappearance. Between the fall that is not a fall and her death is inserted a new sequence in which, like Elfride Swancourt [in *A Pair of Blue Eyes*], she lives through a period of autonomy before she dies. But whereas Elfride's marriage to Luxellian and innocent death in childbirth are tangential to the narrative, Tess's acts of will represent the culmination of the whole sequence. The events involved figure the monstrousness of the only choice that is left to her, the only meaning she can express after the final shock of Angel's coming to claim her when she has already returned to Alec as his mistress. In stabbing Alec to release herself for Angel she feels free even from guilt. As the latter listens to her confession of murder 'his horror at her impulse was mixed with amazement at the strength of her affection for himself; and at the strangeness of its quality, which had apparently extinguished her moral sense altogether' (p. 524).

But Tess has formulated Alec's death to herself as logical, just as the truly autonomous Ethelberta formulated her marriage to Mountclere in that way: 'I thought as I ran along that you would be sure to forgive me now I have done that. It came to me as a shining light that I should get you back that way . . . I was unable to bear your not loving me. Say you do now, dear dear husband . . . now I have killed him!' (pp. 523–4). Her logic is mad, but for once she dominates him:

> It was very terrible, if true: if a temporary hallucination, sad. But anyhow here was this deserted wife of his, this passionately fond woman, clinging to him without a suspicion that he would be anything to her but a protector. He saw that for him to be otherwise was not, in her mind, within the region of the possible.
>
> (p. 525)

And he submits to her account of the possible.

There is no doubt that in her refusal to escape she still leads Angel, although she is clear as to the consequences of her act. It is she who, ironically, suggests that after her death he should marry her sister, Liza-Lu, realising that this would constitute legal incest: 'People marry sister-laws continually about Marlott' (p. 536). When she stretches out on the oblong slab at Stonehenge she is choosing her place of surrender. The death on the gallows that supervenes reveals the hollowness of her autonomy, a pretence with which Angel has colluded, knowing that they were out of time. Significantly she now says to him, with an understanding that goes beyond madness: 'I have had enough; and now I shall not live for you to despise me' (p. 539). Like all fallen women she dies; all she has really been able to choose is the particular form of her death. Murder and execution as the only available expression of autonomy speak for themselves as to the real limits of agency for a fallen woman. Plot, as so often in Hardy, figures a central statement.

From Patricia Ingham, *Thomas Hardy: A Feminist Reading* (Hemel Hempstead, 1989), pp. 67–8, 71–4, 79–80, 86–9.

## NOTES

[As a specialist in language as well as Hardy's texts, Patricia Ingham devised, in the book from which the present extracts derive, a linguistic model of interpretation that provides an innovative tool for feminist and other critics alike. Following a brief but illuminating critique of recent feminist approaches to Hardy in her Introduction – approaches which, in different ways, remain limited by a reflectionist problematic and an inadequate attention to the 'multiple voices of the texts' (p. 6) – Patricia Ingham writes that her own method explores the 'sense of disjunction', the 'fault-line', in the narrative languages or 'syntax' of Hardy's fiction. In particular, this 'involves the idea that "the subject" of a novel (in this case usually a female subject) is created by the language, which in turn is a product of ideologies' (p. 7). The excerpts included here are from chapters which deal generally with several novels, but they nevertheless clearly indicate, in relation to *Tess*, that a close linguistic and gendered reading of the novel reveals once more the ideological tensions and uncertainties enacted in a late-nineteenth-century male writer's attempts to find a fictional form and language by which to represent female sexuality beyond the limitations of convention and stereotype. Patricia Ingham's essay may also be seen indirectly to challenge Laura Claridge's reading (essay 4) of the 'pure woman' discourse in *Tess*, seeing Hardy's figuring of the issue in language and plot as pressing against the constraints of his own ideological positioning. Some of the ideas contained here are expanded in Patricia Ingham's introduction to the new Everyman edition of *Tess of the d'Urbervilles* (1991); and a second book, on *Dickens, Women and Language* (Hemel Hempstead, 1992), further applies her linguistic model to Dickens. Ed.]

1. *The Collected Letters of Thomas Hardy*, 7 vols, ed. Richard L. Purdy and Michael Millgate (Oxford, 1978–88), vol. 1, p. 250.

2. Harold Orel (ed.), *Thomas Hardy's Personal Writings* (London, 1967), pp. 127–8.

3. Thomas Hardy, *Tess of the d'Urbervilles*, ed. Juliet Grindle and Simon Gatrell (Oxford, 1983), p. 151. All further references are to this edition – the Clarendon edition – and appear as bracketed numbers in the text.

4.  R. G. Cox (ed.), *Thomas Hardy: The Critical Heritage* (London, 1970), p. 189.

5.  Grindle and Gatrell, Introduction to Clarendon edition of *Tess of the d'Urbervilles*, p. 54.

6.  Thomas Hardy, *Desperate Remedies*, ed. C. J. P. Beatty, 'New Wessex' edition (London, 1975), p. 155.

7.  Thomas Hardy, *The Woodlanders*, ed. Dale Kramer, Clarendon edition (Oxford, 1981), p. 40.

8.  In Cox (ed.), *Thomas Hardy*, p. 305.

9.  Lennart A. Björk (ed.), *The Literary Notebooks of Thomas Hardy*, vol. 2 (London, 1985), p. 61.

# 6

# A Tess for Child Molesters

*JANE MARCUS*

We go to baseball games to see a batter hit the ball. We expect Pavarotti to sing the right notes at the opera. A film-maker can take liberties with a novel or a play and sometimes can succeed in winning a new audience for an old tale, as, my teenagers tell me, Zeffirelli wins adolescents to *Romeo and Juliet* because he appeals to their own instincts for feuding and loving. But Roman Polanski takes liberties with Hardy's book the way Alec d'Urberville takes liberties with Tess.

Thomas Hardy's characters may be victims of fate, but they are never willing victims. They shake their fists at the gods, and Tess of the d'Urbervilles is no exception. Polanski's film is a long, slow rape by the scriptwriter of Thomas Hardy's text, a long, slow rape by the camera of Natassia Kinski's lovely face, and a long, slow rationalisation by the rapist imagination that that's how it is with helpless, hopeless victims. They never fight back.

The words 'To Sharon' creep down the right-hand side of the screen during the opening credits to produce the measured shock of 'oohs' from a suburban audience. For everybody knows that the director's wife was brutally murdered, not, however, like a fly, killed by the gods for their sport. If the memory of a woman raped and murdered is the muse who inspired the making of this film, she has not taught the director methods for depicting the truth of experience. Tess belongs to history, like Antigone and Lady Macbeth. Her story is known by heart by thousands of people who probably couldn't tell you what Lady Macbeth's crimes were or why Antigone was a heroine.

The young middle-class audience going to see the film have prob-ably encountered Hardy mainly in a classroom. And birth control and changing sexual mores have made Tess a less heroic figure for them. But Hardy's novel has also been loved by another audience across the years. Older women, Catholics, the poor, and those from cultures where woman's chastity is her most important possession, still identify with Tess' plight. She is the great Unwed Mother. And, when she kills Alec d'Urberville, women weep for joy. For Tess revenges all the women wronged by men, raped, taken advantage of, impregnated, battered, harassed and despised for her lost virtue. Hundreds of women must be going to Polanski's movie for one reason, to see Tess kill Alec d'Urberville.

Hardy's novel was censored, like Lawrence's *Lady Chatterley's Lover* and Joyce's *Ulysses* for sexual frankness on a taboo subject. He was harassed and forced to revise for his magazine audience, so he conveys the murder with the apt figure of blood dripping through the ceiling of the parlour of a seaside boarding house in the shape of the ace of hearts. Polanski is a cheat. He does not have to operate under such censorship. We sit through three hours of suffering only to see a cowed Tess sleeping on a rock at a fake Stonehenge to be meekly led off to death by the police. Not only are we deprived of the sight of Tess taking justice into her own hands, we do not hear her tell Angel Clare that it is his duty to marry her sister and so save one member of the ill-fated Durbeyfield family.

In the novel Tess grows and changes. She has two great moments in which she challenges the men and social forces which have op-pressed her. She usurps the power of the priesthood and baptises her baby when the vicar refuses to bless a child born out of wedlock. It is a powerful and moving scene with a powerful heroine. But Polanski won't show us Tess the powerful; his image is of a poor, pretty creature disturbing the bumbling vicar at his bee-keeping, meekly telling him of her blasphemous baptism. Polanski must have his reasons for failing to show this legendary scene in graphic detail on the screen. And the reason is that there is an unwritten rule against showing a woman justified in usurping male power. Only a priest can baptise. And a priest has a penis.

The second deliberate omission is her justified murder of Alec d'Urberville. Not that the audience could have any idea of how diabolically evil Alec really is in Polanski's sympathetic portrait of a simple rake. How far has women's liberation really come if it is still taboo to show a wronged woman kill the man who has ruined her life? Why can't we see a woman enraged on the screen? We see male violence against women all the time. Is the male film-maker afraid that if we see an angry woman kill her 'lover' with a bread knife that the murder rate will go up?

It is the political implications of this act which are important. For here Tess usurps the male power of judgement. The law will not protect her from rape or redress the wrong she has been done, or punish the rapist, or give her back her child or her lost virtue. She takes the law into her own hands and punishes the offender, as she took Christianity into her own hands to get her dying baby into heaven. But Tess' hands are a woman's hands. They are not supposed to administer sacraments and they are not supposed to administer justice.

They are fine for milking cows, threshing wheat, and hoeing turnips. But even here Polanski cheats. There are no callouses on the hands of his cherubic eleven-year-old stilted fixed figure of Tess. We do not see her hardened and coarsened by work. It is cheating to sentimentalise the circumstances of women's seduction. It is somehow even more of a cheat to sentimentalise human labour. Milkmaids' hands are covered with sores. Hoeing turnips out of the frozen earth in a bleak November is not a pleasant task. Another gasp goes through the suburban audience when Tess takes a swig of gin to keep body and soul together in the turnip fields. But so brief is Polanski's picturesque tableau that it is like seeing Kathe Kollwitz' drawings of women field workers for the first time and then only for long enough for the eye to register the beauty of the brown and sepia tones of the drawings, not the suffering and brutalisation of the workers. The same is true of the filming of the threshing machine, that red monster in Hardy's novel which represents the brutal industrialisation of farm work which breaks the rhythm of people's lives. And it titillates a modern urban audience in the electronic age, because its quaint rhythm and noise seems idyllic. There is none of Hardy's attack on industrialisation, nor his portraits of the brutalised and degraded workers, no sense of people working and feeling the work in their bodies. In the film Tess romantically unbinds a few sheaves of wheat which makes her very hungry and allows Polanski another shot of that pretty mouth, now wolfing down its food. Earlier he had a long obscene sequence in which she purses her lips to whistle to Alec's mother's birds, which reminds one of the equally obscene moments in Bergman's *Magic Flute* where the camera lingers lovingly on the candy-coated lips of the director's little girl at precisely the moments when little girls and big are being taught a moral lesson by the opera and the film about loyalty to daddy. Come to think of it, Polanski presents Joan Durbeyfield as another bad mother, the Queen of the Night, who embodies sex, death and social chaos.

If Polanski had wanted to make a modern Tess, he had a ready-made culture where these scenes are still repeated. Hardy's Tess is a working woman, a field woman, he calls her. Polanski could have given us a Teresa of the lettuce fields of the Southwest among similar migrant workers as deeply attached to the earth as Tess is to her Dorset fields. He could have given us a tragedy instead of a slick melodrama for male eyes. But then his camera can hardly equal the sophisticated irony of Hardy's narrator's view. He will not let Tess speak or act. She is passive throughout, and lying down for much of the film. Hardy's Tess is upright. She walks and talks and works and struggles and grows from child to woman under the loving hands of her creator who subtitles his novel 'A Pure Woman', taking the part of a male sympathiser of heroic womanhood. Polanski is a voyeur of victimisation who infantilises our Tess. Hardy makes it clear that the 'President of the Immortals' who has his sport with Tess is the author's enemy. Polanski is angling for a seat as Vice-President of the Immortals. His demand for sympathy for the victimised Tess turns tragedy into melodrama for voyeurs.

From *Jump Cut* (26 December 1981), 3.

## NOTES

[Jane Marcus is a socialist-feminist critic who has lectured, reviewed and published extensively since the late 1970s on feminist theory, women's writing and women writers. A particular specialism running throughout her career to date is the work of Virginia Woolf, on which she has written and edited several books. The present short essay of 1981 is a review, from the alternative film magazine *Jump Cut*, of Roman Polanski's film *Tess* (for details of this, see the Widdowson essay below [number 7] which also takes issue, in a minor way, with Jane Marcus's piece). I am particularly grateful to Professor Marcus for allowing me to reprint for the first time such an 'ephemeral' early piece of work, which she herself describes in a letter to the editor as 'that pretty rough piece on "Tess" – the work of a jobless Marxist-feminist critic'. In fact, it is a tough, highly and properly political demolition of a commercial movie, which also indirectly raises at once the critical chestnut of how 'faithful' a film should be to the book on which it is based and the ideological significance of the cultural reproduction of canonic literary works. Along the way, it also alludes to a number of debates the present volume emphasises: Hardy's attitudes to class and gender, to female sexuality, to Tess as 'pure woman' heroine. Ed.]

# 7

# A 'Tragedy of Modern Life'? Polanski's Tess

*PETER WIDDOWSON*

Roman Polanski's *Tess*, made some twelve years after Schlesinger's *Far From the Madding Crowd* and almost simultaneously with the BBC TV *Mayor of Casterbridge*, has similarities to both in their different ways; but it is markedly dissimilar in its historical reproduction of Hardy by offering, unlike them, a modern re-interpretation – of the main character especially. Released in France in 1979 and elsewhere in 1981, it was produced by Claude Berri and Timothy Burrill, with screenplay by Gerard Brach, Polanski, and John Brownjohn, and it stars Nastassia Kinski as Tess, Peter Firth as Angel Clare, and Leigh Lawson as Alec d'Urberville. What is immediately apparent, then, is that Polanski not only directs the film but also has a hand in the screenplay, and that the main actress and actors are relatively unknown. In other words, Polanski's interpretative mark is very much on the film, and the faces of the protagonists, unlike those in *Far From the Madding Crowd*, are unfamiliar: invoking neither a 'period' physiognomy nor other roles in which they have starred. Polanski can thus construct his own 'private' representation of Hardy's novel; and, not surprisingly, a recurrent message in interviews with him is that *Tess* is *his* film: 'All my films have been the result of an inner necessity and yet, until *Tess*, I've never had the impression of making a film that *exactly* matched my deepest feeling. *Tess* is that film. *My* film. Certainly the film of my maturity.'[1] (The force of this is emphasised, perhaps, by the dedication 'to Sharon' on an otherwise blank screen at the end of the credits [a point I shall return to] – Polanski again repeatedly claiming in interviews that it was Sharon Tate, his murdered first wife, who had introduced him to the novel, which he became very excited by, offering her the part of Tess, although that film of course was never made.) Polanski was already, by the time of *Tess*, a well-established and highly-regarded director, albeit with a controversial private and public life, who had made such films as *Knife in the Water* (1962), *Repulsion* (1965), *Cul de Sac* (1966), *Dance of the Vampires* (1967) *Rosemary's Baby* (1968), *Macbeth* (1971), *What?* (1972), *Chinatown* (1974), and *The Tenant* (1976), in many of which his fascination with psychological disturbance, violence, and destructive sexuality had appeared as motifs. *Tess* was therefore something of a surprise, being restrained in all those areas which had been most characteristic of Polanski's previous work – although, as we shall see, it still evinces strong elements of his world view. The film was widely, but by no means unproblematically, acclaimed by the critics; was nominated for many awards (although those it won were mainly for its 'craft' – cinematography, costume design, and art direction); and it was hugely successful with the public.

For an independent production, *Tess* was a large-scale and lavish affair (it cost just under £5,000,000 – at the time, the most expensive film ever made in France). It started shooting in July 1978 (the year the copyright on *Tess of the d'Urbervilles* ran out), Polanski having bought the film rights from the estate of David Selznick whose greatest dream – apart from making *Gone With the Wind* – was to film *Tess*. The film was stricken with disaster: the shooting took over eight months, using forty different locations in Brittany and Normandy (many of which had to be returned to at different seasons of the year) and involving the reconstruction of Stonehenge (in France) as it would have been in the nineteenth century. It was filmed by Geoffrey Unsworth (who died while it was being made) and then by Ghislain Cloquet. The result is beautiful to look at and very long: its running time is three hours.

The film was conceived, in Polanski's own phrase, as 'a great love story' and as a faithful, artistic reproduction of Hardy's novel: his 'masterpiece', the Press Release says, 'and the most emotionally powerful of all his novels' [which] 'paints a vast canvas of rural life in nineteenth-century England and contains some brilliantly perceptive comments on human nature – then and now'.[2] The brooding romanticism of *Tess*, both in cinematic and thematic terms, is inescapably confronted in the symptomatic features of Nastassia

Kinski, looking out from the advertising poster and from the innumerable publicity stills which focus on her face. (The trailer – 'a
lyrical series of dissolving shots . . . set to Sarde's haunting music',[3]
or, more cruelly, 'a sticky confection of scenic schmaltz and apparently risible acting'[4] – also promotes this aspect of it.) This is, of
course, the 'general public' presentation of the film, and although it
is highly influential in the reproduction of 'Hardy' in the 1980s –
'required viewing', as one critic symptomatically put it, 'for girls [sic]
with Tess on their "O" Level syllabus'[5] – it is not, as we shall see, an
entirely accurate representation either of Polanski's intentions or of
the effect of the film itself. The trade papers, by no means uncom-
promisingly positive, nevertheless emphasise these aspects of Tess:
'physically handsome in the sumptuous manner of those adaptations
of classic novels to be found in the "Masterpiece Theatre" series on
Public Broadcasting Service'; 'sensitive, intelligent screen treatment
of a literary masterwork', 'lambent colour photography', 'superb
production design'; 'exquisitely beautiful to look at', 'very good in
selected up-market popular cinemas and art houses'.[6] Even so, they
are worried by the length of the film, by Polanski's 'slavish' faithfulness to the novel, Nastassia Kinski's emotional range, and the film's
apparent failure to achieve the 'accumulative emotional power'[7] of
the book.

Much of the reviewing of the film also focuses on similar points.
The 'positive' critics admire Polanski's faithfulness to the novel: 'the
result is pure Hardy' (which means, 'its pure romanticism, its scale,
passion, grandeur, drama'); Tess's cinematic beauty – a 'ravishing
spectacle', 'it glows with brilliant "optical effects"'; and its historical
accuracy – 'it looks, to my eyes, convincingly Wessex', 'the camera
captures much of the spirit of Wessex: the innocent gaiety of the
dancers in their white frocks, the wrinkled pathos of the aged instru-
mentalists, the languorous beauty of the countryside at dusk'.[8] Paradoxically, many of the 'negative' critics focus on the same features
but from the opposite point of view: it is a 'sluggish film of ponder-
ous beauty'; 'little more than a mountingly tedious sequence of pretty
picture postcards'; 'a collation of second-hand picturesque effects
. . . [of which] probably the most offensive . . . is the ubiquitous gold
light that shimmers around and about almost everything on the
screen, as if this were a Biblical movie and we were awaiting the
Incarnation'.[9] Partly because of this, but also because of its reveren-
tial yet simplistic adaptation of the novel, it fails to evoke the reality
of the world of the book: 'what is lacking . . . is the pervasive sense

of poverty and drudgery that the novel abounds with . . . a certain grimness of life. . . . The Durbeyfield family's poverty, and the village's poverty, is obscured in *Tess* by the magnificent photography and landscapes, and Tess's beauty, rather than a contrast to the hardship and poverty the family is mired in, is, instead, an extension of the beauty of the land'; 'the image of Wessex that Polanski has conjured up . . . is the kind traditionally used on television to extol the wholesome, back-to-nature properties of sliced bread or dairy butter'; 'shorn of its extraordinarily complex ramifications, this allegory [of theological dispute] is reduced in the film to piddling proportions, with Angel playing rustic shepherd to Tess' shepherdess in a coy homage to pagan bliss'; 'there is none of Hardy's attack on industrialisation, nor his portraits of the brutalised and degraded workers, no sense of people working and feeling the work in their bodies'.[10] At best, for such hostile critics, the film is 'a lethargic form of realism . . . a realistic presentation of romantic sentiments'; a good attempt which misses 'an all-important beat, a heart-beat'; at worst, it has 'the air of an expensive classy/commercial product, the result more of market research than intimate inspiration'.[11]

Much of this criticism contains some truth, particularly given the way the film was received by the public and its consequent contribution, therefore, to the reproduction of 'Thomas Hardy' in conventional terms. But ironically, much of it also rests on the reviewers' own reading of the novel itself, and hence on preconceived expectations of Polanski's film version. If one reads the novel as social drama and then finds the film failing, or if one perceives the film as a factitious cinematic extravaganza, slavishly faithful to the novel but essentially lacking its passionate romantic force, then one is reading the film as though one were reading the novel. But film and novel are not the same thing: the film remakes the novel as a late twentieth-century cultural product; as, in a sense, an autonomous artefact. Neil Sinyard offers a classic example of what we might call the 'originalist fallacy' when he remarks of the film: 'there is nothing very Hardyesque about it. It is a subdued and sober film, Hardy without the glaring faults, but without the sublimity as well.'[12] To be 'Hardyesque' – at least within the conventional critical paradigm – there have to be 'faults' of course. Would the film have been more 'Hardyesque' if it had retained them? What we must 'read', in fact, as late twentieth-century cultural critics, is the film, and then see how, why, and to what effect, it recasts the novel. In this context, but without falling into intentionalism, and before I offer my own reading of the film (which, in any event, was made quite independently), I want to look at some of Polanski's public statements about the film he was making. In the light of this we can see how beside the point is much of the criticism noted above, and also how accurate it is, at times, in its unwitting perception of the film's ideological trajectory.

In interviews, Polanski is quite emphatic that the film of Tess is a 'modern tragedy' and that it relates to his other earlier works (which, as one critic has put it, 'depict the claustrophobic lives of ordinary individuals caught in an ever-tightening web, a web that seems to be spun from their own emotional entanglements and yet bears the external shape of destiny').[13] In an interview in Screen International, while shooting the film, Polanski said: 'I hope there is something that remains, some sort of line that goes through all the films, that makes it possible to say "That is a picture made by that director."' Unwilling to be drawn on the 'connecting line' to Hardy's novel – which, the interviewer proposes, is 'the darker aspects of Victorian society – poverty, ignorance, its unforgiving religion and rigid class system – that are largely the cause of Tess' suffering' – Polanski merely replies: 'I just do what I feel at a given moment of time.'[14] But in a later interview with Continental Film Review, he says: 'Actually Tess should be a film about intolerance, a very romantic, very topical story. This modern aspect was already in Hardy, all we did was focus on it.'[15] And in October the same year (1979), in American Film, he observes that although he has been 'influenced a great deal by surrealism and the theatre of the absurd . . . the world itself has become absurd and almost surreal', and so now he wants 'to go back to the simplicity and essence of human relationships'. Hardy, he notes, 'links the girl to the rhythm of nature, within a Victorian society at odds with everything spontaneous and natural', and adds emphatically: 'Tess belongs to the present, to the modern age, to you and me. She is the first truly modern heroine.'[16] Whether or not Polanski had read John Fowles's novel The French Lieutenant's Woman (1967; the film version appeared in 1981 – the year Tess was released in the USA and Britain, and with strikingly similar poster advertisements), the coincidence of Fowles's Hardy-influenced presentation of Sarah Woodruff as early existentialist woman, and Polanski's conception of Tess as 'the first truly modern heroine' is striking. For what we undoubtedly have in Polanski's Tess is a late twentieth-century existential heroine: 'Maybe if Tess were less noble in the mind, if she lied, if she accepted certain things that she finds instinctively repulsive, she could have lived a happier life than she did. But then, she wouldn't be Tess of the d'Urbervilles, and we wouldn't be here talking about her.' And Polanski concludes his interview by saying: 'Tess, you must remember, was a pure woman . . . She broke Victorian moral codes, but she responded to natural law, to nature, her nature. That's what the whole book is about. The film is an accusation of the hypocrisy and injustice of that rigid society – and by extension of any rigid and repressive society.' Such a world view – of a society's 'rules and mores . . . based on irrational prejudices and superstitions' and of a 'hypocrisy' opposed to the spontaneous natural self[17] – governs Polanski's film and explains, if not justifies, its particular articulation. Andrew Rissik, in a venomously hostile review, sees the film's central failure as the mismatch between the schmaltzy romanticism of the film's visual style and the 'resolutely anti-romantic' sensibility which directs it as a 'modernist novel' in an 'existential universe'.[18] Rissik may have a point about the general effect (although my feeling is that he enjoyed hating the film so much that he misrepresents it), but he is quite wrong to see Polanski's existential sensibility as 'anti-romantic'; indeed, one could say that an uncompromising focus on the 'natural' individual in a hypocritical world, on personal freedom and 'good-faith', is the late twentieth century's own (pessimistic) form of romanticism. Rissik sees the film as only a 'bloodless and anaemic' sequence of inauthentic pretty pictures; Polanski conversely believed that *Tess* is 'such strong material that we mustn't be worried about beautiful pictures', that 'people don't go to the cinema to see a collection of beautiful photographs. They go to experience something. The *emotion* is the thing. . . . Emotion is the main thing in all art.'[19] It all depends, I suppose, on what one conceives of as 'the emotion': the 'passion' Rissik finds in the novel and misses in the film, or the deep existential despair belied by the visual beauty of Polanski's *Tess*.

But let me turn for a moment – before returning to its 'cultural meaning' – to some consideration of the film itself. Sensitively acted and beautifully set and photographed, its leisurely, even self-indulgent pace allows the film to establish its environments in great depth and solidity, to juxtapose, for instance, the sense of unchanging antiquity in the dirt and poverty of the agricultural labourers' lives with the almost modern environs of Alec d'Urberville's house or the seaside town of Sandbourne. There are also superb individual scenes: for example, the deadly Victorian 'interior' of Angel and Tess's first breakfast together after their wedding-night confessions, or the turnip-grubbing at Flintcomb-Ash. The film thus attains the sense of solid historical realism which is a feature of the BBC *Mayor of Casterbridge*, although it does not fetishise it as the serial did. *Tess* is not interested in the past as a museum-piece (neither, as we shall see later, as a dynamic set of social relations), rather as an appropriate 'period' environment for its story. But in this, therefore, it also avoids the modern pastoral images of *Far From the Madding Crowd*. The characters are convincingly located in this physical setting, although the film's predictable focus on Tess's tragic love-story and her personal relations with Alec and Angel once more detaches them from the 'environment' in a larger sense, so that the film can in no way be seen as a social drama. Indeed, while the blurb on the video tape of *Tess* gets it wrong in almost every way – 'Today, he would be tried for rape. In her day, she was accused of seduction. What she did shattered her world for ever. "Tess" – Roman Polanski's brilliant evocation of a woman's struggle against the hypocrisy of her age'[20] (the film is by no means clear that Alec actually rapes Tess [no more is the novel], nor is she ever 'accused of seduction') – it is most emphatically wrong in that final suggestion (perhaps with the 1981 film of Fowles's *The French Lieutenant's Woman* in mind) that Tess is locked in conflict with the social ethics of her time. Although this may be the major thrust of Hardy's novel (but even there the character herself is not conscious of her 'struggle'), it is only implicit in the film because it is played down in Polanski's fascination with the romantic tragedy, the embryonic existentialism of Tess, and with the very modern sense of her *anomie*. The film of *Tess* effectively dehistoricises the nineteenth-century novel, and rehistoricises it by its interpretative frame, as did the film of *Far From the Madding Crowd* and the serial of *The Major of Casterbridge* in their different ways. If, as critics suggest,[21] one of the problems with film in general, and *Tess* in particular, is its 'literalness', its non-figurative presentation of 'the actual', then it can be seen here as the 'modern' existential heroine detached from the 'real' historical determinations which should account for her. Certainly Tess is superimposed on a realistic 'period' background, but she is not organically related to it. This may reinforce the sense of her 'alienation' from her society, but it is a characteristically ahistorical existential alienation in which the particular and specific historical conjuncture is finally immaterial.

Nevertheless, the film is, in many respects, closely faithful to the book: most of the main scenes are present in the correct order, large amounts of the dialogue are reproduced *verbatim*, and there are only a few added or extended scenes. But it is, of course, in some of the more significant changes that we can see the existentialising 'inter-pretative frame' at work. For example, the early scene is cut in which Tess has to drive the cart to Casterbridge because her father gets drunk after hearing of his noble heredity, and Prince the horse is impaled on the mail-cart's shaft, splashing blood on Tess's dress. In its place is merely a reference to the family 'needing a new horse'. The scene's loss reduces the sense of Tess caught in the toils of economic and historical process: doomed by the potent power of the past (heredity), caught in the social and economic relations of her present class (family), and subject to the potentially destructive forces of modern change (the mail-cart) – all factors which the novel's discourses emphasise. In this respect, Tess is very exactly determined by her environment, which the film, as I have suggested, detaches her from. (A number of reviewers noted how this absence of the 'connec-tions' which Hardy insists on causes an otherwise 'faithful' reproduc-tion to become a *reductio ad absurdum*; how Tess is meaningless as a character unless she is seen as 'a victim of class'; how the film's 'absent' violence [unusual in Polanski's work] is 'the brutality of poverty'; and how, 'for all its superb emphasis on landscape and the rhythms of rural life, Polanski's film fails to establish the ties which root Hardy's Tess so firmly in the earth'.[22]) This lack of social determinants is reinforced by the film's underplaying of the corruptive influence of the *nouveau-riche* Alec on the community of Trantridge around his house, The Slopes (there is no suggestion, either, that Alec's money derives from money-lending in the north); and later, when she and Angel arrive at their honeymoon house, by the surpris-ing (because very filmic) omission of the sinister d'Urberville por-traits on the landing in which Tess's features are discernible. Polanski, after all, makes quite a lot of the heredity issue – although mainly, in effect, to highlight, on the one hand, the superstition which the film (rightly) presents as endemic to Tess's 'old' rural society; and on the other, Angel Clare's half-baked socialism (in the novel he is only a half-baked 'free-thinker'), represented by his repeated hostility to 'old, wormeaten families' and – in one of the film's few obvious anachronisms – by the presence of a copy of Marx's *Capital and Capitalist Production* as Clare's bedside reading. A great deal of the sense of Tess as a victim of history is dispelled by playing down the 'old' d'Urberville connection. For Tess, at least as the novel presents her, and despite her 'ache of modernism', is not a proto-'French Lieutenant's Woman', the existentialist 'free woman' cutting her way out of the stifling thickets of Victorian society; she is very precisely a figure imprisoned by history, beset by the moribund past and the entrepreneurial present and future, whose tragedy is that she is dimly conscious of her plight.

But to be fair to the film, it does attempt to show the social and sexual exploitation of Tess, while not factitiously trying to make her an embryonic feminist. Indeed, one reviewer of Tess, Jane Marcus in *Jump Cut*, under the title 'A Tess for child molesters', furiously belabours Polanski for 'raping' Hardy's text; for failing to see that Tess is 'the great Unwed Mother' who causes women to 'weep for joy' when she kills Alec; for showing Tess as meek and passive rather than enraged and powerful; and for being 'a voyeur of victimisation who infantilises *our Tess*' (my italics). That last phrase is, I think, significant: for Tess in this guise may be a strategically feminist reconstruction, but she is in no sense the quiescent and historically-disabled country girl of the novel. What Jane Marcus wants is what she says Polanski fails to give us: 'a Teresa of the lettuce fields of the Southwest among similar migrant workers as deeply attached to the earth as Tess is to her Dorset fields.'[23] Marcus would be quite justified in criticising the film's persistent voyeuristic delight in Kinski's face (although the novel does it, too, in presenting Tess as an innocent *femme fatale*), but to criticise it for not being faithful to a notion of '*our Tess*' is beside the point. A modern female director might properly do it, but to 'expect' it of Polanski is politically naïve. Nevertheless, it is in its treatment of the heroine and her relations with her two lovers that we find the film's most noteworthy contemporary 'reinterpretation' of Tess.

Tess is played as naturally beautiful and sensuous (the close-ups of Kinski's mouth echo the novel's obsession with it), and hence as artlessly but fatally attractive to men. She is also played, for the most part, as in a passive, dreamy, almost trance-like state. The most obvious examples are the scenes (not in the novel) after her seduction by Alec, when she has become his mistress and he rows her on the river and entertains her in the garden marquee; the romantic idyll, immediately before the wedding (and again not in the novel), when she and Angel run through the countryside and she adorns his room with wild flowers; and the scene when Angel rediscovers her in the boarding house at Sandbourne, where she is Alec's kept woman, dolled up in whorish style, who acts and speaks like a zombie. The effect of this is to reinforce the sense of her estrangement from her society and her 'Age'. The novel implies it; the film brings it into bold relief. Nastassia Kinski's own comments on her role are illuminating here: she found herself 'taking on [Tess's] patience and strength and courage'; and adds: 'I've always dreamed of being a person like her. She's not spoiled by the society she moves through. She stays untouched. She goes through everything for love.'[24] Polanski's Tess is someone trying to be her own woman, adrift in a world whose values she cannot relate to, who wants to love and be loved as an existential human subject in a society of exploitation and sham. She is doomed, not so much by history, but by her difference. She is, in late twentieth-century terms, *l'étranger*: the authentic individual whom the world must destroy. Polanski's comments in the interviews cited earlier underwrite this interpretation, as does his statement in the Press Release:

> I had always wanted to film a great love story, but what also fascinated me about this novel was its preoccupation with the vicissitudes of fate. The heroine has every attribute that should make for happiness – personal beauty, an engaging personality and a spirited approach to life – yet the social climate in which she lives and the inexorable pressure it exerts upon her gradually entrap her in a chain of circumstances that culminates in tragedy.[25]

(Is this where the dedication to Sharon Tate, pregnant and ritualistically murdered by the 'Manson family' in 1969, finds its relevance?) It is an inflexion of late twentieth-century liberal tragedy, in which individual good faith is held to be the only true political action: 'a pure woman faithfully presented by Roman Polanski' – for Tess's existential being is what the film really portrays.

It is implied, paradoxically, even in the famous scene in The Chase, when Tess is seduced by Alec. There is no hint of rape; the novel is by no means explicit, but the film is deeply ambiguous as to what happens here. Tess, mesmerised, relieved, grateful, first of all lets Alec kiss her; it is unclear whether Kinski's face at this point registers passivity or pleasure. As Alec becomes more ardent, the film slides into fuzzy soft-focus which makes it difficult to see the sexual act unambiguously: is Kinski/Tess struggling with Alec, or writhing with pleasure; does she fight, or does she succumb to the release of sex, of being 'loved' at that overwrought moment? The film, of course, does not say. (Polanski in an interview, however, implies a rather more dubious ambiguity: asked the usual question about rape/seduction, coercion/consent, he replies: 'it's both, actually, or neither . . . It's half-and-half. It happens by insistence, and by using physical strength in certain ways. But physical strength was almost inevitable in those days; it was part of Victorian courtship. Even on her wedding night a woman might be expected to resist.'[26] It is here that a feminist critic might properly challenge Polanski's implication: for it is strongly redolent of the 'woman-enjoys-it-really' explanation of rape.) If anything, this sense of Tess as emotionally adrift is reinforced by the fact that, immediately following her seduction, Polanski inserts the sequence of scenes in which the trance-like Tess has become Alec's mistress (later, confessing to Angel, she admits that she 'became Alec's mistress' – a loaded phrase absent from the novel, as indeed is her whole 'confession'). Only then does she realise that this is *mauvais foi* and she abruptly leaves, wishing she 'had never been born'. It is at this point that the film brings into high relief Tess's flash of spirit when she answers Alec's 'That's what every woman says' with: 'How can you dare to use such words! . . . Did it never strike your mind that what every woman says some women may feel?'[27] It is a moment which the film makes unforgettable in its presentation of Tess, just as later, when the vicar refuses to give 'Sorrow' Christian burial and she does it herself, the film emphasises her defiant selfhood in opposition to the hypocrisies of social convention. Equally, in all her relations with Angel Clare it is her passionate commitment to him (hence the interpolated scene of her decorating his room with flowers), her trust, and her anxiety about her own 'bad faith', which are emphasised. And combined with all this, is the prominence given to Tess's obsession with death, her wish for the 'courage to die', and her final act of *l'étranger*'s expiation: the killing of Alec. The overtly sexual scene with Angel in their hideaway afterwards, which the novel, of course, cannot provide, intensifies this sense of existential being – as does our knowledge that she herself must 'pay' by dying. Significantly, the film ends with Tess's arrest at Stonehenge (the legend on the final screen stating that she was hanged at Wintoncester – 'aforetime capital of Wessex') and not with the novel's stranger coda in which Angel and 'Liza-Lu (Tess's sister who has become her surrogate) watch her hanging from a hill above the town and then walk away hand in hand. Clearly, it would be difficult for the film to carry this off, but its absence also effectively leaves the focus on Tess's 'nobility' and individual tragedy, as Polanski's own comment again implies: 'Even in Hardy the hanging is almost an epilogue. I don't think it's essential. The story is clear enough and sad enough without it. You know Tess is doomed.'[28]

Polanski's film of *Tess*, then, is remarkably faithful to the novel, but in its emphasis and focus, in its selections and inclusions, in its casting and filming, in its interpretative frame, it reproduces a reading that the novel will sustain, but which is essentially late-twentieth-century in its ideological orientation. By freeing Tess from her historical determinants and by locating her in the film principally in her own emotional space, Polanski reproduces her as the existential heroine of her own time and tragic vision, as someone trying to live an authentic life in an inauthentic society. That this world view in fact represents despair at the claims of social being and political action, and can merely affirm the 'free' but doomed individual, may well account both for the film's popularity in the 1980s and for its whimsical anachronism of making Karl Marx the bedtime reading of 'inauthentic' Angel Clare.

From Peter Widdowson, *Hardy in History: A Study in Literary Sociology* (London, 1989), pp. 115–25.

## NOTES

[Like many others of his generation of critics, Peter Widdowson was stimulated and redirected by the impact of European critical theory in the mid-1970s, albeit as inflected by 'native' intellectuals such as Raymond Williams and Terry Eagleton. Never himself much of a theorist, Widdowson sought to realise the practical applications of the new perspectives theory opened up, especially for criticism and for the higher-education literary and cultural studies syllabus. Hence for some years he helped edit the journal *Literature and History*, and in 1982 was responsible for the polemical collection of essays, *Re-Reading English*. The book on Hardy from which the present essay comes is an attempt to put into empirical practice a number of implications theoretical innovations had thrown up – most particularly the way writers are constructed by the (mainly literary-critical) attention paid to them, and the social and cultural meanings ascribed to their work as they are reproduced at different historical moments. The study of this process Peter Widdowson has termed 'critiography', which very much reinforces the work of George Wotton as described in the Introduction (p. 9) and in the note to essay 2 (p. 41). The excerpt included here, part of a longer chapter about Hardy on radio, TV and film, attempts to extend critiographical treatment beyond the discourses of criticism and education. Prior to the section on Polanski's *Tess* are analyses of John Schlesinger's 1967 film of *Far From the Madding Crowd* and Dennis Potter's adaptation of *The Mayor of Casterbridge* for BBC TV (1978). Ed.]

1. Interview in *Continental Film Review*, 26: 5 (1979), 14–15.

2. Columbia Press Release (in BFI Archive), 5.

3.  Harlan Kennedy, 'Tess: Polanski in Hardy Country', *American Film*, 5: 1 (1979), 65.

4.  Andrew Rissik, 'Laurels for Hardy, but less for "Tess"', *Films Illustrated*, 10: 117 (1981), 352.

5.  Mike Sarne, 'Tess', *Films*, 1: 6 (1981), 35.

6.  *Motion Picture Product Digest* (18 February 1981), 72; *Variety* (7 November 1979), 18; Marjorie Bilbow, *Screen International* (25 April 1981), 59.

7.  *Variety* (7 November 1979), 18.

8.  Ann Totterdell, 'Tess: A Second View', *Films*, 1: 7 (1981), 39; John Coleman, 'Country Matters', *New Statesman* (10 April 1981); William V. Costanzo, 'Polanski in Wessex . . . filming *Tess of the d'Urbervilles*', *Literature/Film Quarterly*, 9: 2 (1981), 78; Richard Roud, 'Taking the Sex out of Wessex', *Guardian* (17 November 1979); Costanzo, 'Polanski in Wessex', 73.

9.  Melanie Wallace, 'Tess', *Cineaste*, 11: 1 (1980/1), 36; Tom Milne, *Monthly Film Bulletin* (May 1981), 98; Rissik, 'Laurels for Hardy', 353.

10. Wallace, 'Tess', 37; Rissik, 'Laurels for Hardy', 353; Milne, 'Monthly Film', 97; Jane Marcus, 'A Tess for Child Molesters', *Jump Cut*, 26 (1981), 3 [reprinted in this volume – see pp. 90–4. Ed].

11. Costanzo, 'Polanski in Wessex', 77–9 *passim*; Coleman, 'Country Matters'; Roud, 'Taking the Sex out of Wessex'.

12. Neil Sinyard, *Filming Literature: The Art of Screen Adaptation* (Beckenham, 1986), p. 49.

13. Costanzo, 'Polanski in Wessex', 72.

14. Colin Vaines, 'Hardy Task for Roman in Love', *Screen International* (24 February 1979), 14–15.

15. Interview in *Continental Film Review*.

16. Kennedy, 'Tess', 62.

17. Kennedy, 'Tess', 62, 66–7.

18. Rissik, 'Laurels for Hardy', 355.

19. Kennedy, 'Tess', 67.

20. Blurb on video case, Thorn/EMI video, 1982.

21. Cf. Rissik, 'Laurels for Hardy', and Costanzo, 'Polanski in Wessex'.

22. Milne, 'Monthly Film'; Wallace, 'Tess'; Costanzo, 'Polanski in Wessex'.

23. Marcus, 'A Tess for Child Molesters'.

24. Profile of Nastassia Kinski, in Kennedy, '*Tess*', 64.

25. Quoted in Columbia Press Release, 5.

26. Kennedy, '*Tess*', 67.

27. Thomas Hardy, *Tess of the d'Urbervilles*, Penguin edition (Harmondsworth, 1978), 125.

28. Kennedy, '*Tess*', 66.

# 8

# Language and the Shape of Reality in 'Tess of the d'Urbervilles'

*CHARLOTTE THOMPSON*

The prime of the literary artist occasionally spawns the tour de force in which the maker's art, having reached its apogee, begins to sport with and celebrate its own powers. As the offspring of Hardy's artistic prime, *Tess of the d'Urbervilles* might claim kinship with these works of virtuosity, yet few readers, I suspect, will be prompted to include *Tess* alongside such better known candidates as *Don Juan* or *The Tempest*, not because *Tess* is wanting in observable brilliance, but because the novel's sombre character gives no indication of celebrating anything, certainly not the novelistic art. Considered in terms of its context, *Tess* must probably remain weighted with its received label of 'pessimism'. At the same time, beneath its sober level of discourse, at the substratum of formal arrangement and verbal and visual imagery, *Tess* contains an exhilarating feat of imagination in which the power of the word, if not exactly celebrated, is at least fully exploited and even parodied with a fine irony and a narrative sleight of hand that are pure bravura.

Access to this enterprise may be had by thoughtfully examining the novel's use of the spoken word, especially the imaginative word, as a shaping force empowered to determine the nature of reality. Among the many forces that Hardy invites us to hold responsible for Tess's tragedy, her society's language constitutes one of its most potent, yet most elusive instruments. An old language, by fixing minds in old, preformed mental structures, can vie with old genes in the ability to perpetuate the past by impelling the mind toward predetermined ends. Conversely, language innovatively used in fresh, creative imagining has the power to reorganise those mental structures and to reform the realities they induce. At least Hardy thought so. Even as he was writing *Tess* he was evolving the ontological vision that would emerge allegorically in *The Dynasts*, and among his speculations was a clear belief in the mind's power to influence, even alter, the material world.[1] It is this power of the imaginative mind working in *Tess* that, although not unnoticed,[2] has been vastly underestimated and that I intend to show represents the ruling principle of *Tess*'s universe. The novel divides its mental influences into those of the past and those of the present. By exploiting the properties of an old, allusive vocabulary, Hardy makes out of past beliefs and imaginings a cultural *logos*, a communal *word*, composed of religious precedents, myths, legends, and names, which, in the manner of the biblical *Logos*, seeks to realise itself in living form and succeeds in the person and tragedy of Tess. But even as Tess is being brought to bay an unceasing process, reminiscent of Heraclitan flux, continues. The communal imagination of the novel's present is relentlessly transmuting its universe and already formulating a new *logos*, a Romantic *word*, which, by the novel's end, has begun to crystallise around the persons of Angel and 'Liza-Lu.

[In a long cut passage here, the essay explores the novel's dense textual presentation of the 'alchemy of rhetoric' in figuring the human mind's tendency towards the abstract and the ideal.]

Close scrutiny of the novel's figurative language shows two linguistic forces at work – one innovative, the other reactionary – each defining reality out of its properties, each endowed with its own figurative vocabulary. A limited set of clear, straightforward rhetorical figures – similes, metaphors, personifications – proceeds from fresh acts of imagination performed by the narrator or his characters and originating within the circumference of the novel's action. When examined, these verbal images, together with visual images, prove to constitute a recreative force whose permutations work gradually to reorganise the existing order. Established order, in contrast, expresses itself in an imaginative language from the past: a vast corpus of figurative and quasi-figurative words, of images, ephithets, and allusions drawn from a traditional vocabulary that owes its being to the entrenched ideas of Western culture. Born of early theologies, this language derives from acts of imagination or interpretation performed centuries earlier, yet which continue to exert their influence upon the novel's personae and upon the reader as well. Phenomena are imprisoned in associations imposed by the language used to describe them: 'Valley of Humiliation' (p. 106); 'River of Life' (p. 87); 'witch of Babylon' (p. 268); 'the old Other One' (p. 289); 'Plutonic master' (p. 270). By applying this language to their experience, the novel's personae perform acts of interpretation more mechanical and ritualistic than spontaneous, interpretations not ultimately of their own making but handed down from generations past. Accompanying this allusive vocabulary is a substantial body of words whose usage is neither wholly literal nor wholly figurative. Words such as *fall, reaper, pure, harvest, web, trap, halo,* and *light,* although often used literally, assume figurative meanings nonetheless, telling a story of their own by virtue of their longstanding associations in the cultural mind. Alec's 'trap' offers a case in point. A language originally formulated to describe the physical world, having for centuries been pressed into the service of defining social, moral, psychological, and theological realms of experience, has become so saturated with connotative values that it can no longer be detached from them, no longer used in its pristine form to describe accurately the reality of the moment. When language, used literally, rises up irrepressibly into secondary and tertiary meanings, the boundaries between literal and figurative have been obliterated. This language is a worn-down text, like the *Compleat Fortune-Teller,* 'so worn by pocketing that the margins had reached the edge of the type' (p. 18).

A text that has lost its margins suggests, additionally, a text whose letters persist but the key to whose interpretation has disappeared. In the biblical tradition, and in the King James Bible, the margins contain the explanatory gloss, so that to lose the margins is to be left with only the letter and not the spirit of the text. Similarly, this well-worn language, by habitual usage, loses something of its original meaning, while the letter perseveres with an oppressive power to impose the past upon the present. Just as Angel leaves his words with Tess (who 'adhered with literal exactness to orders which he had given and forgotten' [p. 282]) and goes off, still retaining his control over her, so the originators of the language have vanished but continue to exert a sometimes tyrannical influence over their descendants. Hardy offers parallel instances in which words from absent speakers reshape a character's attitude. Parson Clare's words, which he likens to seeds planted (p. 141), not only reform but transfigure

Alec d'Urberville (p. 253) well after the Parson and Alec have parted company. Next, Angel's dicta, repeated to Alec through Tess, reconvert 'the late Evangelist' back to his original worldliness (pp. 269, 272). Words uttered by a vanished stranger also revolutionise Angel's perspective: 'The cursory remarks of the large-minded stranger, of whom he knew absolutely nothing beyond a commonplace name, were sublimed by his death, and influenced Clare more than all the reasoned ethics of the philosophers' (p. 283). Elsewhere, Hardy calls attention to the power of the departed to manipulate from the grave, but in this case through the power of music:

> She thought, without exactly wording the thought, how strange and godlike was a composer's power, who from the grave could lead through sequences of emotion, which he alone had felt at first, a girl like her who had never heard his name, and never would have a clue to his personality.
>
> (p. 71)

Old ideas reproducing themselves through old words enjoy an equal potential for extending the minds of unknown speakers. Unlike music, however, old language tends to become blurred, its meanings moribund, or misconstrued and misapplied. Tringham also leaves his words with Durbeyfield and disappears. But he fails to provide a gloss on his text, and it is the misapplication as much as the content of his message that wreaks destruction in the life of Tess. A language transmitted and running down through time conforms to a general motif of deterioration from a past original, exemplified in the d'Urberville lineage, declined and corrupted linguistically to Durbeyfield, and misappropriated by Stoke-d'Urberville.

The power this old language holds over the minds of the characters is directly proportional to its degeneracy. It has a biblical word for every occasion, but especially the occasion of guilt, which it can label efficiently, if not accurately. It brands Tess, who 'looked upon herself as a figure of Guilt intruding into the haunts of Innocence' (p. 72), with a ready biblical image: 'He little thought that the Magdalen might be at his side' (p. 110). With no greater accuracy, biblical language serves man's need to magnify himself with such images as inflate Tess's misadventure with Alec into having 'eaten of the tree of knowledge' (p. 88), and her subsequent pain into a crucifixion by the 'thorny crown' she figuratively wears (p. 125). Biblical texts supply comfortable replacements for objective thought as handy words from Lemuel define the good woman for the Clares but somehow fail to pinpoint the special purity still unsullied in Tess. Alec, too, self-described as 'the old Other One' (p. 289), or 'the Old Adam' (p. 255), can cite Scripture for his purposes with equally ready words from Hosea on the woman who vainly sought her lover and returned to her first husband (pp. 274–5). But Tess's lover does return. Hosea proves a rather untrustworthy index of truth. A biblical vocabulary provides convenient models with which to explain or to misunderstand experience. Tess's sufferings compare to Job's (p. 106), her worship of Angel's wisdom to the Queen of Sheba's wonderment at Solomon's (p. 106); Clare is likened to Samson, reviewing the damage after his tragic wedding night (p. 210); Parson Clare compares to Abraham and his 'misnamed Angel' to a 'doomed Isaac' (p. 281); Alec suggests that his encounter with Tess in the garden plot resembles the meeting of Eve and the Tempter in paradise (p. 289). Should anyone consider Tess as promiscuous as Mary Magdalen or as wicked as Delilah, and Angel Christlike or a sacrificial lamb led to the slaughter, or the garden allotment a paradise, he would find nothing inapt in these borrowed robes from the Scriptures. A thoughtful reappraisal should find them a bit grotesque in their misfit.[3] In the minds of these compulsive interpreters, reality becomes contorted to fix ancient stereotypes. And a change of mind consists of not a liberation from biblical language but a change in text, as when an enlightened Angel reconciles himself to his wife's past, saying, 'Was not the gleaning of the grapes of Ephraim better than the vintage of Abi-ezer?' (p. 284):

> he had seen the virtual Faustina in the literal Cornelia, a spiritual Lucretia in a corporeal Phryne; he had thought of the woman taken and set in the midst as one deserving to be stoned, and of the wife of Uriah being made a queen; and he had asked himself why he had not judged Tess constructively rather than biographically, by the will rather than by the deed?
>
> (p. 306)

How, rather, can he judge accurately anything that has been so thoroughly exchanged for a catalogue of ready-made types?

This language seems to corrupt the narrative voice, which begins free of it, an innocent on a blighted star, and ends by succumbing to its vernacular. Aloof from theology, the narrator nonetheless presents the River Froom as 'clear and pure as the River of Life shown to the Evangelist' (p. 87) and sees a 'Last Day luridness' in the fires of the wedding night (p. 190). A mythophile, but by no means

a believer in the 'old-time heliolatries' (p. 73), he has, by the sixth
Phase, lapsed into something like a parody of the language in which
his characters think:

> He who had wrought her undoing was now on the side of the Spirit,
> while she remained unregenerate. And, as in the legend, it had resulted
> that her Cyprian image had suddenly appeared upon his altar, whereby
> the fire of the priest has been wellnigh extinguished.
>
> (p. 254)

Much of this language represents an extension of Tess's thoughts. All
the same, the 'Cyprian image' cannot possibly spring from the mind
of a girl who elsewhere does not even know the name 'Artemis'
(p. 111). Instead, the narrative voice shines through, caught up in the
language of mythology, the same affinity that prompts the 'Aeschylean
Phrase' on the President of the Immortals. '<u>Mythology</u>,' wrote Hardy,
'according to the comparative mythologers, is, forsooth, only a <u>dis-
ease in language</u> – literal understanding of primitive metaphors.'[4]
This 'disease in language' has the power virtually to obliterate reality
by systematically replacing a living event with a construct of the past,
just as Angel replaces a living Tess with his mythological and biblical
women. As 'fire' replaces desire, and 'priest' replaces Alec, 'Cyprian
image' replaces Tess, until the characters have lost their identities,
and the true nature of the event has been swallowed up into a
prefabricated drama to be construed accordingly in a preconceived
way. From the past a scenario of guilt and sacrifice in blood imprints
itself upon the cultural mind, reproduces itself in words, and works
its way inexorably toward realisation. If this process begins with
ideas introduced into the imagination as germs into the bloodstream,
then the first of these verbal 'germs' is biblical, Tringham's 'How are
the mighty fallen', and the effect is a kind of linguistic disease: an
accelerating use of biblical and mythological language that proves
contagious to the sybaritic Alec, the philosophical Angel, and the
rationalistic narrator and proves, moreover, deadly to Alec and Tess.

Hardy objectifies this growing blight upon the mental landscape
in the episode of the sign painter, who similarly blights the countryside as he proliferates his texts wherever space will permit. His
words, burning in red and oddly propped up by commas, give visible
form to the insistent, inflexible character of this language. His uncompromising 'tex' provokes Tess to complain of his words: '"I
think they are horrible . . . Crushing! Killing!" "That's what they are
meant to be!" he replied' (pp. 67–8). Indeed, the letter killeth,

especially when separated from the spirit. The inappropriateness to the actual state of things, together with the speaker's lament for a moribund theology (p. 67), reminds us that this old message exists somehow out of context, unsuited to define the reality into which it intrudes. In the same way, biblical and mythological constructs, formulated two thousand years earlier, impose themselves relentlessly upon a present that they are ill-equipped to define with precision. By their persistence, these constructs determine men's thoughts and inevitably their lives. The accompanying language, perpetuated by the desire to amplify experience, continually detaches itself from reality and rises toward the ideal or toward allegory, forcing thought into those aesthetic categories that Kierkegaard saw as separating man from his ability to see the unvarnished truth.[5] Far from impeding imagination, this old language impels imagination, but impels it toward predetermined ends.

A subtle compulsion to replace empirical with symbolic thinking reaches its consummate expression in Tess's final actions. Tess habitually perceives her life in biblical analogies. Many have noted her moralised view of reality and her susceptibility to the beliefs of her society.[6] Although she possesses natural wisdom and attains considerable understanding, she nonetheless exemplifies that astute but unsophisticated mind that is prone to overlook the complexities of men such as Alec and Angel and to conceive of them in oversimplified, moralised terms. Tess may insist that she does not see Alec as diabolical (p. 289), yet she is unable to transcend a certain mental fixation in which Angel appears godlike.[7] The moralisation of Angel's adversary is thus inevitable. Her final actions indicate that, in the end, Angel and Alec have been distilled in her mind to the simple contraries of 'good' and 'evil'. Alec's destruction has been comparably moralised and simplified: a destruction of evil, an act of cleansing and reparation, which produces little guilt and more a feeling of liberation;[8] concomitantly, a martyrdom to the godlike Angel seems equally justified by the same errors of thinking. By responding more to a symbolic than an empirical reality, Tess fulfills a scenario less of her own than of the culture that produced such symbolic thought.

A cultural consciousness, striving to reproduce itself, offers another, more viable way of understanding the universal mechanism working to realise ideas in substance. The tendency of ideas to materialise comes to its most pertinent focus in the pressures of a cultural scenario working toward fulfilment in Tess. Ideas resident in

the cultural mind – the Fall of Man, the Crucifixion, pagan vegeta-
tion myths or sacrifices to the sun god, folk legends surrounding the
d'Urbervilles or the terrain – planted in the minds of the novel's
personae, express themselves in a conventional vocabulary, crystallise around events, urge a disregard of the idiosyncratic, and impel
conformity to ancient models, effecting what Miller aptly calls the
'irresistible coercion of history'.[9] By forcing the plastic substances of
the present into the rigid moulds of the past, this process might
compare to the alchemical procedure known as fixation. In any
event, language as much as plot urges the impression of an old
culture drama being repeated, so that reference to Aeschylus, for
instance, suggests to Miller that 'Tess reincarnates a pattern of tragic
experience already present in the earliest masterpieces of Western
literature'.[10] The hybrid character of this tragic pattern, with its
mixture of pagan, classical, biblical, and folk elements, attests to the
amalgam of cultural ideas that go into its formation and are reflected
in the figurative hodge-podge spoken by the narrator and by Angel.

Although Tess is the ostensible victim of these cultural pressures,
it is in the reader's mind that the attendant language achieves its
ultimate impact, and his mind, therefore, there is also being skilfully
manipulated. By a subtle coercion of the reader's associations, these
same cultural forces help to create the tight cyclical structure into
which Tess is bound and from which she escapes, incidentally, only
after language has been broken down to the monosyllable 'O-O-O'!
(pp. 314–15).

[In a cut passage here, the essay deals with instances of metaphorical patterning in the novel which, ironically, promote notions of
abstraction and sublimity.]

Visual and verbal images, spontaneously born in response to the
moment, introduce a fresh, recreative force into what we must call
the novel's empirical reality. Each of these images represents an act
of imagination by the narrator or his characters and not by their
forebears. Inserted as they are into the largely factual exposition,
these moments of fancy seem no more than attractive digressions,
lending a poetic delicacy or imaginative 'atmosphere' to an otherwise
realistic account of rural England. Still, by the novel's end, such
imaginings have realised themselves. They have done so by a subtle
process of repeated incursions into the empirical order of things,
each time intruding a second dimension of reality, that of idea, which
builds by slow accretions and by transferring vitalities from one
realm to another, from the phenomenal to the ideal, and between

subdivisions of the phenomenal. While the examples cited [of the 'imaginary'] hint at the transfiguring powers of the visual and rhetorical figure, the same examples illustrate the limitations of the imaginative: the impossibility of creating a truly original second reality that does not dissipate and lead off toward abstraction. The transformation of the country dance in particular demonstrates the limitation imposed upon the would-be renovator and his rhetoric. The narrator can create only a mirror image of the world he knows and only out of the language of his world, in this case the language of mythology, the product of a culture he cannot escape. Even little Abraham, when he changes trees into tigers or giants' heads (p. 24), can only substitute in the second realm objects from the known universe. Rolliver's patrons can glorify only the fixtures of this world and only in the terms of this world. Visual and verbal images, dependent upon known phenomena, cannot create a wholly unique second reality; they can only rearrange already existing elements.

Reorganisation, then, constitutes the primary activity of the novel's imaginative force. If the imagination is confined to a reshuffling of old matter, the verbal creator enjoys special prerogatives not tendered to manipulators of the material universe, chiefly the power to transgress with ease the boundaries dividing the three traditional kingdoms of nature – animal, vegetable, and mineral – and in particular the barrier separating the organic from the inorganic. Hardy's notes find him contemplating the impassability of this barricade:

> The organic & the inorganic worlds. The passage from the mineral world to the plant or animal world is hermetically sealed on the mineral side. This inorganic world is staked off from the living world by barriers which have never yet been crossed from within. No change of substance, no modification of environment, no chemistry, no electricity, nor any form of energy, nor any evolution, can endow any single atom of the mineral world with the attribute of life. Only by the bending down into this dead world of some living form can these dead atoms be gifted with the properties of vitality, without this preliminary contact with life they remain fixed in the inorganic sphere for ever . . . . If there is one thing in Nature more worth pondering for its strangeness it is the spectacle of this vast helpless world of the dead cut off from the living by the law of Biogenesis, & denied forever the possibility of resurrection within itself.[11]

In a literary universe, the pathetic fallacy can readily enliven this 'dead world'. In *Tess*, Hardy employs sophisticated variations of the pathetic fallacy, as his images, working below the level of discourse, effect gradual permutations in nature that lead in due course to the dissolution of Tess and the inversions noted in the novel's culmination.

Tess is the living form selected to be bent down to the earth for its vitalisation as Hardy literally rearranges the elements – plant, animal, and mineral – by a series of comparisons that gradually reduce Tess and diffuse her vitality into the other realms of nature. The process begins imperceptibly, with innocent comparisons of her to insects and animals – a fly, a bird, or a cat – and to plants – to a 'sapling' (p. 109), a plant flinching under the burning sun of Angel's ardour (p. 144), or a 'belated seedling' of the d'Urbervilles (p. 195). Reduction proceeds toward the inorganic, diminishing this plant and her sun to the 'ashes of their former fires' and toward the nebulosity of gases by comparison to a 'soul at large', achieving at length a full dissociation of Tess from her body, which she allows to 'drift like a corpse upon the current', and climaxing in her complete disappearance and replacement by the black flag. As Tess dwindles to nothing, her vitality returns to the soil, a process heralded by the narrator's meditation upon the field hands: 'a field-woman is a portion of the field; she has somehow lost her own margin, imbibed the essence of her surrounding, and assimilated herself with it' (p. 74). This loss of distinguishing identity and assimilation into the landscape then recurs with awesome literalness in the harsh season at the turnip farm. There Tess diminishes to a nonentity while the narrator simultaneously reinvests her animus in the inorganic world. At her approach, Tess is psychologically 'obliterating her identity' (p. 230); next, she is literally effaced as she snips off her brows (p. 233), then figuratively 'effaced', cut off from two families, 'virtually nonexistent' (p. 245); and meanwhile blended into the landscape, 'a thing scarcely percipient, almost inorganic' (p. 234). Inorganic nature, in turn, mirrors back Tess's effacement, having acquired in the process something of a visage of its own:

> the whole field was in colour a desolate drab; it was a complexion without features, as if a face from chin to brow, should be only an expanse of skin. The sky wore, in another colour, the same likeness; a white vacuity of countenance with the lineaments gone.
>
> (p. 237)

At the same time, the 'air afflicted to pallor' (p. 241) also gains a little physiognomy. Meanwhile, vegetable begins to shift into animal:

'the few lonely trees and thorns of the hedgerows appeared as if they had put off a vegetable for an animal integument' (p. 239). In the decidedly inorganic world of Flintcomb-Ash, with its flints, its 'hardened' daylight (p. 242), coppery sunlight (p. 276), and 'glass splinters' of rain (p. 238), living things are hardened to deadness. Angel's words harden to 'crystallised phrases', which, dropping into the 'sea' of Alec's enthusiasm, 'served to chill its effervescence to stagnation' (p. 269), while dead things come to life, as the inorganic storm attains a human deliberation (p. 239), and invisible things materialise: 'Cobwebs revealed their presence on shed and walls where none had ever been observed till brought out into visibility by the crystallising atmosphere' (pp. 239–40). Much earlier, man and vegetable had been intermixed in that 'vegeto-human pollen' out of which the narrator had inverted matter and emotion in an important paradigm of this reorganisation. The next major interchange occurs on Tess's wedding night, when an almost palpable anguish begins to infuse animal energies into insentient objects, the latter, by their very indifference, displaying an irritating vitality of a distinctly human kind: "The fire in the grate looked impish. . . . The fender grinned idly, as if it did not care' (p. 190). As tragedy drains life from Tess, a living spirit begins to flicker in a hitherto lifeless environment.

The novel's creative energies, concentrated in its figures of speech, serve a process of breaking down the divisions between the major realms of nature and shifting vitalities from one realm to another. The linguistic equivalent of this process consists of breaking down the distinctions between the phenomenal and intelligible realms of reality by comparable transgressions in the use of rhetorical figures. The narrator, exchanging man and vegetable or matter and emotion, or exchanging Tess and the field with his brilliant play on 'desolate drab', also changes the phenomenal for the intelligible by the use of metaphor. Metaphor, used infrequently in *Tess*, represents a strong impulsive force for change, and its significance is perhaps best appreciated in the context of Hardy's use of the simile.

Hardy works predominantly with similes, which he clusters around moments of fantasising or intense emotion. While similes appear to describe the process taking place, they may also be recognised as generated by the participants – by the drinkers, for example, aggrandising their surroundings, or the labourers, imagining themselves intermingled with nature:

> the erratic motions seemed an inherent part of the irradiation, and the fumes of their breathing a component of the night's mist; and the spirit of the scene, and of the moonlight, and of Nature, seemed harmoniously to mingle with the spirit of wine.
>
> (p. 58)

Passion spawns a complex of similes, as Tess in the garden listens to Angel's music:

> she undulated upon the thin notes of the second-hand harp, and their harmonies passed like breezes through her, bringing tears to her eyes. The floating pollen seemed to be his notes made visible, the dampness of the garden the weeping of the garden's sensibilities . . . the waves of colour mixed with the waves of sound.
>
> (p. 104)

Both passages show transformations of reality taking place within the imagination, but confined to the imagination, the repeated 'seemed' insisting upon the purely mental and illusory nature of such transformations. Within these confines, however, the permutations of nature slowly advance, intermingling the gaseous spirits of this world with those of the other world, or the sensuality of the vegetable kingdom with the sensibilities of the human heart. In these passages, moreover, Hardy works with the most finely attenuated substances of the phenomenal world, linking them to equally ephemeral referents in the ideational, playing, as it were, at the very border of the material world. Across this border a series of transactions takes place from the phenomenal to the intelligible through the simile, as the interpreting minds repeatedly refer phenomena to their counterparts in the ideal. 'Harmonies' transfer to 'breezes', 'pollen' to 'music notes', 'dampness' to 'weeping' or 'fumes' of breathing to the 'night's mist'. By a continuing process of such references, a second dimension of reality gradually amasses, or fills, if you will, made of the stuff of emotion and imagination: irradiation, spirit of the scene, musical notes, weeping. If in time ideas will realise themselves, then these are the ingredients of the next world to come, and they are all as airy and insubstantial as possible.

Elsewhere, the simile allows a wholesale investment of personality to transfer unnoticed across the border between the realms of matter and mind: 'The evening sun was now ugly to her, like a great inflamed wound in the sky' (p. 114); 'The pollard willows, tortured out of their natural shape by incessant choppings, [became] spiny-haired monsters' (p. 150). Abraham, 'still mentally in the other world' (p. 24), injects giants and tigers, while Tess, in reverie, half witnesses, half participates in the infusion of persona into that other world:

> The mute procession past her shoulders of trees and hedges became attached to fantastic scenes outside reality, and the occasional heave of the wind became the sigh of some immense sad soul, conterminous with the universe in space, and with history in time.
>
> (p. 26)

The intoxicated farmhands breathe a substantial amount of spirit – the spirit of the scene, the spirit of nature – into their surroundings, while a more potent elixir, love, inspires its own animation of the landscape: 'It was a typical summer evening in June, the atmosphere being so transmissive that inanimate objects seemed endowed with two or three senses, if not five' (p. 103).

Were these episodes to be spatialised, one would find the participants on a borderline, at Hardy's 'interspace', a locus halfway between fantasy and reality, which they attain through drink, drowsiness, or the stimulus of emotion. Or one would find the narrator also on a border, neither wholly inside nor outside a character's mind, but somewhere between, mediating between a character's impressions and a factual, external world. Man's mind, located at the intersection of the phenomenal and the intelligible, serves as the arbiter and bridge between the two, but the mind is also the barrier that distinguishes fact from fancy and maintains their separation. More than once the novel insists upon the preservation of this barrier, as when the narrator points out Tess committing the pathetic fallacy (p. 72), and later, when Tess corrects her own rhetoric, saying, 'The trees have inquisitive eyes, haven't they? – that is, seem as if they had' (p. 105). This strict division cannot be maintained in the ubiquitous traditional vocabulary, where component words are so heavily freighted with imaginative values that the margins between the factual and the imaginary have been eroded. Accordingly, they exert a compulsive force. In contrast, the novel's fresh, creative enterprise has been concentrated primarily in similes, whose structure upholds the distinction, even in the most extravagant fantasising, and so sustains the impression that the factual is always winnowed from the illusory. Still, the reader has it on good authority that in this world seeming is tantamount to being: 'for the world is only a psychological phenomenon and what they seemed they were' (p. 72). Despite the reader's illusion that he is at all times in touch with a factual, objective reality, he receives it from a narrator whose recital is continually tempered and mutated by the psychic operations of his characters, to which he periodically adds impressions distinctively his own, foremost among them the Arcadian imagery transfiguring the country dance, imagery that the novel makes plain lies beyond Tess's knowledge. If what things seem they are, then that supposedly factual reality comes to the reader through transmitters to whom it repeatedly seems something other than it is. And, by the novel's end, many things that at first only seemed to be have, in a sense, come to be. Something, therefore, must happen to change seeming into being, and that something must happen rhetorically to violate the integrity of the simile, whose nature it is to differentiate between the realms of things as they are and things as they seem.

In a verbal universe, the structure of reality is intimately bound up with the structure of the simile. The simile, embracing but separating empirical reality on the one hand and idea on the other, is the mental analogue of the bifold universe, a rhetorical microcosm and a paradigm of universal stability. This stability is fragile, however. Between empirical fact and the ideas of the mind are only those minimal words of connection, 'seems like', 'as if', words that are, at the same time, separations. Even when 'the wind became the sigh', the word 'became' represents that last tenuous moment of separation before the implicit being of metaphor replaces the factual with the imaginary and inverts the order of things. This construct appears to be endemic to Hardy's mind, so that, whether intentionally or unconsciously, he pictorialises both his biform universe and the simile itself when he invests the earth and sky with faces:

> So these two upper and neither visages confronted each other all day long, the white face looking down on the brown face, and the brown face looking up at the white face, without anything standing between them but the two girls crawling over the surface like flies.
>
> (pp. 237–8)

Thus visualised, the universe appears in two equal and opposite halves, each holding a mirror to the other, with man and his mind alone positioned between them. The shape of the simile can also be discerned here, with the phenomenal and the ideational divided, yet engaged in a reciprocal reflection of one another, with only those miniscule words of connection and separation standing between them 'like flies'. Remove those inconsequential 'flies', blend those frail beings back into the landscape, and the order of the two realms begins to shift.

[In a cut passage here, the essay considers 'personification' and 'metaphor' in the same way that it has just dealt with 'simile'.]

Taken together, Hardy's rhetorical figures function as little mirrors into which one may peer to observe more closely the novel's imaginative thrust. One traces, first, a consistent diminution or dissolution of the palpable. The sun grows more abstract when compared to a 'wound'; the air, already intangible, grows still more so when it suggests 'an achromatic chaos of things' (p. 241). Most of these figures contribute to the progressive disintegration of Tess, while Angel all but dissolves into a 'ghost' and the revellers sublime into gases. The simile itself presses toward abstraction. With few exceptions, similes in the first six Phases offer up a definite entity, however flimsy, for comparison to a counterpart in the ideal. By the novel's end, however, abstractions are compared to even greater abstractions: 'The gloomy intervening time seemed to sink into chaos, over which the present and prior times closed as if it had never been' (p. 323); 'the night grew dark as a cave' (p. 325). To peer into these little mirrors for a glimpse of the other world is to look into a black hole. A complementary activity, also performed in rhetorical figures, enlarges the commonplace and vitalises the inanimate. An injection of alcohol aggrandises the rustic dancers, sanctifies the labourers, beautifies the tawdry furnishings of reality. Anguish animates the impish fire and grinning fender, the furtive dawn and voracious night. An infusion of mist and narrative enthusiasm invests the sun with an active, masculine identity. Love breathes romantic life into an old, uninteresting dairy house. While the narrative alchemy reduces and dehumanises Tess, divesting her of her features, it simultaneously endows the landscape with a face and invigorates the inanimate kingdom of nature. By recurring impressions and ventures of the imagination, *Tess*'s governing mind reduces, sublimes, and ultimately transubstantiates its world.

Reduction of Tess reaches its penultimate in the compression of her language to the monosyllable of nothing: 'O-O-O!' (pp. 314–15), at which point the novel seems to achieve a kind of liberation. As Tess releases herself from d'Urberville and breaks through social and moral barriers, she attains a liberation from her tragic life already prefigured in the dissociation of her psyche from her body. The novel parallels this release as it breaks out of its customary habit of fixing its characters rigidly in time and space with each new chapter. The action moves relatively unhampered across the chapters of Phase the Seventh as Angel and Tess wander through vast, open spaces in a less carefully defined time for a period of free floating before the forces of established order re-exert their pressures and claims. In this Phase, the narrative as a whole has attained a kind of interspace between an old order, which has by now been largely overturned, and a new, which promises to reform around Angel and 'Liza-Lu. If this history will repeat itself, there is evidence that it will do so without the strictures of a theological scenario and its coercive vocabulary, if only because Tess has so thoroughly satisfied the old words by fulfilling them, a fulfilment helped along, of course, by the comparison of the mourners to Giotto's *Two Apostles* (p. 329), and by the implications of Stonehenge.

As to the nature of the new order, we have observed it in the making. By repeated excursions into the imaginary, an alter-reality has been forming out of the stuff of emotion and sentiment, of self-aggrandisement, by exaltation of the commonplace – the beatified labourers and tender milkmaids – and by repeated commission of the pathetic fallacy. This other world grows gradually more numinous as the novel progresses, filling with the 'spirit of Nature', the soul sighing in the wind, a visaged earth and sky, grinning fenders, a beaming sun, and a ruminating night, until the same novel that once fastidiously pointed out the pathetic fallacy has, by its end, invested the very void with a persona: 'All around was open loneliness and black solitude' (p. 325). A student of *The Prelude*, listening intently to this language, should hear the echo of a familiar voice or glimpse the shadow of a parody, begun at least in the country dance, the glorification of the rustics, and the sublimation that occurs on the walk homeward. In short, the new order is distinctly Wordsworthian.[12] Nor does it seem by chance that the man for the New Age, Angel, shows an uncanny likeness to Wordsworth. As with Wordsworth, Angel eschews a Cambridge education in favour of the rural life whose charms he sentimentalises but also patronises.[13] Like Wordsworth, Angel finds that early 'association with country solitudes had bred in him an unconquerable, and almost unreasonable, aversion to modern town life' (p. 99),[14] finds orthodox religion uncongenial and, preferring 'sermons in stones to sermons in churches' (p. 120), adopts instead his own mixture of Christianity, idealism, and neo-pantheism.[15] Angel, along with Wordsworth, finds it easier to love from afar an idealised humanity in the abstract than a flawed human being, close at hand, in the flesh.[16] And, with a delightful aptness, Angel at Talbothays parodies Wordsworth's self-conscious sublimity by living above it all, in the attic above the *loft*, producing his harmonies and idealising milkmaids.[17] Hardy, who noted impartially both Wordsworth's pompousness and his virtues, asserted that if a new 'golden age' of more honest values, of true democracy, and of greater refinement in the humble and wealthy alike should 'dawn upon the nations, then Wordsworth will be recognised as the prophet & apostle of the world's rejuvenescence'.[18] Whether *Tess*'s world will be so fully reformed is a matter of some doubt. Still, it has undergone a rejuvenation and a form of refinement. The novel's alchemy has produced what alchemy should: gold – the hint of a new golden age about to begin with the refined natures of Angel and 'Liza-Lu, this gold having been brought forth from the lead-encased d'Urberville ancestry in the Durbeyfield girls and purified by Tess's sacrificial death. Meanwhile, no small irony rewards the demystified narrator, whose philosophical posture has rejected Romanticism as flatly as it has theology. Quite unknowingly he has laboriously overturned the universe with his rhetoric, element by element, almost molecule by molecule, dismantling a theologically dominated world only to turn up a Romantic one on the other side.

Hardy, of course, offers many angles from which to assess the novel's overall statement, and it would be a mistake to overstress the importance of this submerged rhetorical process. When considering the novel's covert shaping of reality, we are best served, in my opinion, by regarding it in the broader light of Hardy's philosophical vision, which emerges more definitively in *The Dynasts*. There, J. O. Bailey sees the influence of von Hartmann's philosophy, which posited in the universe a permeating and manipulating mind, yet one lacking the consciousness of a human mind or an anthropomorphic deity. History and evolution consist of this Unconscious striving to realise itself by coming to full consciousness.[19] In *Tess*, the cultural consciousness, transcending time and space and working to bring its ideas to fruition, performs a comparable function. History in *Tess* consists of bringing a theological epoch to its fulfilment and moving on toward its chronological successor, the Romantic Age. *Tess*'s imaginative process also shows traces of Hardy's evolutionary meliorism, his theory that man, consciously suffering, compassionating, exhibiting noble or humane behaviour, modifies the Unconscious by teaching it what it means to be conscious, so that in time the universal mind acquires the requisite sympathy to reform its indifferent, mechanical ways.[28] In *Tess*, a coalition of minds invests human consciousness, and especially human suffering, into an initially lifeless nature, and succeeds in activating it with an increasingly discernible persona. A noticeably more conscious universe, emergent at the novel's end, suggests a slightly more sympathetic one, an improved but far from perfected model, one whose prophet might well be styled after Wordsworth.

Tess is the novel's chosen sacrifice, offered up to vitalise the rundown mechanism of the universe. She also proves well suited to instruct a still manifestly pitiless world on the nature of injustice, tenderness, and selfless devotion. When her death is assessed in the light of the novel's subtler ontology, its tragic character may be somewhat alleviated by a hopeful observation. If the novel bends its efforts to erase Tess from its own realm of matter, it also concludes by subliming her into an abstraction, an idea displaced by the black flag, and, in that sublimation, shifting her into the alternate dimension of mind. The locus of this dimension rests ultimately in the cultural consciousness where legends show a remarkable durability. There – or rather, here, with us – Tess attains a kind of immortality, the only kind Hardy thought allowable on a blighted star.

From *English Literary History*, 50 (1983), 729–62.

## NOTES

[Charlotte Thompson's main field of work is in medieval and early renaissance literature. Indeed, by self-avowal, she is not a Hardy specialist at all, and the present essay represents a 'marked digression . . . and exhilarating holiday' from the mainstream of her work. Nevertheless, her interest in *Tess* was first activated both by its conspicuous medieval elements and, conversely, by its disturbingly modern orientation: most particularly 'the seemingly opposed tendencies of the present time – the much discussed impulse to "reinvent" our society and the reactionary thrust to reassert old cultural paradigms, [which] two forces, in a less intense, less-self-conscious form, are the same ones shaping reality in *Tess*' (letter to the editor). Charlotte Thompson's suggestion here of the 'post-modern' consciousness of the novel is, of course, one which this New Casebook as a whole promotes, and her essay – extensively cut, but with the content of such passages indicated in the text – reveals this ambivalence in its extraordinarily detailed and acute analysis of the novel's languages. Whilst warning against overstressing 'the importance of this submerged rhetorical process' (p. 125), the essay at once demonstrates the efficacy of a deconstruction-alerted analysis of the text's language and rhetorical figures and demonstrates how Hardy transgresses the old order in *Tess* precisely in the dynamic renewal proffered by the 'language of the imagination'. Here, it is the very language of the text which itself enacts the novel's victory in defeating the burden of the past. The edition of *Tess* used throughout the essay is the Wessex edition of 1912 (New York, 1965); all references to the novel are included in the text. Ed.]

1. J. O. Bailey, *Thomas Hardy and the Cosmic Mind: A New Reading of 'The Dynasts'* (Chapel Hill, 1956), p. 7.

2. See, for example, Andrew Enstice, *Thomas Hardy: Landscapes of the Mind* (London, 1979), p. 130, on the forces bringing Tess down, which include 'ideas implanted in Tess' and 'the texts of old Clare's followers'.

3. J. Hillis Miller discusses the inadequacy of prescribed legendary models to fit the realities of *Tess*, in 'Fiction and Repetition: *Tess of the d'Urbervilles*', *Forms of Modern Fiction*, ed. Alan Warren Friedman (Austin, 1975), pp. 62–4.

4. Lennart A. Björk (ed.), *The Literary Notes of Thomas Hardy*, Gothenberg Studies in English 29 (Göteborg, 1974), 1: 61.

5. Søren Kierkegaard, 'The Point of View For My Work as an Author', in *The Point of View*, trans. Walter Lowrie (1939: rpt. London, 1950), pp. 40–3.

6. Dorothy Van Ghent, *The English Novel: Form and Function* (New York, 1953), pp. 208–9; Enstice, *Thomas Hardy: Landscapes of the Mind*, pp. 146–7.

7. Enstice, *Thomas Hardy: Landscapes of the Mind*, p. 127.

8. The expectation that murdering Alec will earn her Angel's benediction (p. 318) along with the calm expectation of her approaching death is rational in the mentality of the martyr.

9. J. Hillis Miller, *Thomas Hardy: Distance and Desire* (Cambridge, 1970), p. 103. See also Miller's discussion of the past imposing itself upon the present, pp. 98–102.

10. Miller, *Thomas Hardy: Distance and Desire*, p. 105.

11. Björk (ed.), *The Literary Notes*, 1: 159. Entry refers to 'Drummond's "Natural Law of the Spiritual World"'.

12. For the recurring language of 'loneliness' and 'solitude' see William Wordsworth, *The Prelude*, ed. Ernest de Selincourt, 2nd edn, rev. Helen Darbishire (Oxford, 1959), 1: 329–37, 469–71; 6: 191–6; 8: 353. On solitude as a theme of Wordsworth's life, see John Jones, *The Egotistical Sublime* (London, 1964), p. 31. On the country dance and Wordsworth's exalted homeward walk, *The Prelude* 4: 308–99. David Lodge also

recognises the novel's trend towards Romanticism in its views of nature and its apparently ambiguous position on the pathetic fallacy ('Tess, Nature, and the Voices of Hardy', in *Language of Fiction* [London, 1966]; rpt. in *Hardy: The Tragic Novels*, ed. R. P. Draper [London, 1975], 165–80, see esp. 176–9).

13. *Tess*, p. 98; see *The Prelude*, 7: 52–7 on Cambridge dropouts. On Wordsworth's idealisation of the pastoral, see Book 8 passim.

14. See *The Prelude* 7: 722–33 on Wordsworth's response to London.

15. See *The Prelude* 2: 376, 405–30 on receiving religious instruction from nature and things natural.

16. Among the commentaries on Angel's defects, Bruce Hugman's anatomy nicely illuminates those humourless, priggish features so well known to Wordsworth's critics (*Hardy: 'Tess of the d'Urbervilles'* [London, 1970], pp. 29–34, esp. 29–31). On Wordsworth, see Jones, *The Egotistical Sublime*, passim.

17. I refer to Wordsworth's famous posture of elevation with its attendant language of heights, exaltation, and particularly 'loftiness', his favourite. See *The Prelude* 1: 143; 2: 463; 7: 496; 5: 223–41.

18. Björk (ed.) *The Literary Notes*, 1: 130.

19. Bailey, *Thomas Hardy and the Cosmic Mind*, pp. 14–15.

20. Bailey, *Thomas Hardy and the Cosmic Mind*, pp. 155–60.

# 9

# History, Figuration and Female Subjectivity in 'Tess of the d'Urbervilles'

*KAJA SILVERMAN*

The first two chapters of Thomas Hardy's *Tess of the d'Urbervilles* form a curiously assorted pair of frontispieces to that novel. Chapter 1 focuses an untroubled eye upon John Durbeyfield, whose physical appearance yields immediate access to his years ('middle-aged'), health ('rickety'), social and economic status ('quite worn away') and moral inclinations ('somewhat to the left of a straight line').[1] Chapter 2 offers no such readable or even consistent a portrait. It introduces the reader to Marlott via a complicated approach, beginning with a distant and unpeopled view of the environs, and concluding with a baffled (and baffling) scrutiny of Tess. During this approach the vantage point shifts constantly, moving from a series of panoramic images to a close-up of an individual human form, and locating the reader variously within the discourses of late nineteenth century ethnology, landscape painting and tourism.[2]

Vision is further problematised by the insistent anchoring of these shifting scenes to a viewer, who assumes in turn the guise of a tourist, a landscape painter, and a random passer-by. This viewer is present initially only through his absence, an absence which is made the implicit precondition for preserving Marlott as a 'virgin territory'. (Chapter 2 opens with the observation that 'The village of Marlott lay amid the north-eastern undulations of the beautiful Vale of Blakemore or Blackmoor aforesaid, an engirdled and secluded region, for the most part untrodden as yet by tourist or landscape-painter, though within a four hours' journey from London' [p. 48]). However, the description which follows insistently routes all access to Marlott through the eyes of that very tourist/artist who has been seemingly banished:

> The traveller from the coast, who, after plodding northward for a score of miles over calcerous downs and corn-lands, suddenly reaches the verge of one of these escarpments, is surprised and delighted to behold, extended like a map beneath him, a country differing absolutely from that which he has passed through. Behind him the hills are open. . . . Here, in the valley, the world seems to be constructed upon a smaller and more delicate scale. . . . The atmosphere beneath is langorous, and is so tinged with azure that what the artists call the middle distance partakes also of that hue . . .
>
> (p. 48)

A viewer is also implied by the ensuing account of a May-Day celebration, which is characterised as an 'exhibition' of women in white dresses, carrying willow wands and white flowers. It is here that the anonymous gaze first comes into open confrontation with its object, generating what might be called a 'crisis of representation' in the younger members of the procession, who experience a 'difficulty of arranging their lips in this crude exposure to scrutiny, an inability to balance their heads, and to dissociate self-consciousness from their features' (p. 50). The youthful celebrants are as yet situated outside coherent figuration, although they are shown to have registered and internalised its demands. Significantly, the inability to present a coherent self-image is adduced as evidence that these celebrants are 'genuine country girls', much as Marlott's neglect by tourists and landscape painters is cited as proof of its 'seclusion' and 'engirdlement'. Specularity is thus twice opposed to what the narrator will later designate, in relation to Tess, an 'intact state'.

Although the landscape has now been peopled, no human shape has yet come into clear focus. Indeed, the blurred image of unspecified girls attempting to arrange their lips and balance their heads draws attention to the diffuseness of the human scene. The members of the procession have been evoked only generally, as a band, and fragmentarily, as clusters of individual features (for instance, we are told that 'their heads of luxuriant hair [reflect] in the sunshine every tone of gold, and black, and brown', and that 'Some [have] beautiful eyes, others a beautiful nose, others a beautiful mouth' [p. 50]). Tess is the first to be identified as an individual. With the entry of her father, the sound of her name, and the answering turn of her head, she is isolated from the crowd, and articulated as *figure*:

> 'The Lord-a-Lord! Why, Tess Durbeyfield, if there isn't thy father riding hwome in a carriage!'
> A young member of the band turned her head at the exclamation. She was a fine and handsome girl – not handsomer than the others, possibly – but her mobile peony mouth and large innocent eyes added eloquence to colour and shape. She wore a red ribbon in her hair, and was the only one of the white company who could boast of such a pronounced ornament.
>
> (p. 51)

With the articulation of Tess, the landscape and the other women in the band recede into a background position. This figure/ground relationship is particularly stressed through the red ribbon which separates Tess from the wash of white – an ornament which the narrator characterises as 'pronounced' (i.e. prominent, jutting forth) – and through the attribution of 'eloquence' to her eyes and mouth, which associates her with expressivity.

Tess's mouth, which is consistently the most privileged feature of her physical appearance throughout the novel, is described in much greater detail a few paragraphs later, where her emergence as figure is explicitly attributed to the gaze – not just any gaze, but that of the tourist/artist whose vision has already proven so indispensable to the delineation of the Vale of Blakemore. It is only within the illumination cast by this unaccustomed look, the narrator makes a point of telling us, that Tess's form springs forth from the crowd that otherwise absorbs her – that she 'figures':

> A small minority, mostly strangers, would look at her in casually passing by, and grow momentarily fascinated by her freshness, and wonder if they would ever see her again: but to almost everybody she was a fine and picturesque country girl, and no more.
>
> (p. 52)

With the departure of this imaginary spectator, Tess drops from view, assimilated once more into the band of women celebrating May-Day. She doesn't reappear until some time after the entry of Angel Clare, when he finally looks in her direction. With his knapsack and refined manners, Angel is the obvious diegetic incarnation of the artistic traveller upon whom the novel has already relied so heavily. He is in the middle of a walking tour when he stops, like his imaginary predecessor, to observe the spring festivities. He, too, is momentarily distracted by the throng of dancers, his gaze unable to discriminate one from another. As before, no figure comes into focus until Angel catches sight of Tess, with whom he has neglected to dance. As he runs after his brothers, he casts one final look in the direction of the celebration, and under the pressure of that look Tess once again assumes a distinct and expressive shape, while the other women become an undifferentiated background mass:

> He had not yet overtaken his brothers, but he paused to get breath, and looked back. He could see the white figures of the girls in the green enclosure whirling about as they had whirled when he was among them. They seemed to have forgotten him already.
>
> All of them, except, perhaps, one. This white shape stood by the hedge alone. From her position he knew it to be the pretty maiden with whom he had not danced.
>
> (p. 54)

Much later the narrator will wonder why Tess was 'doomed to be seen and coveted' by the wrong man, instead of by 'some other man, the right and desired one in all respects' (p. 82), suggesting that Tess comes to an unhappy end not so much because she is subjected to a colonising male gaze, but because she is constructed according to the image of Alec's rather than Angel's desire. He will suggest, in other words, that if Angel's glance had only found its mark during the May-Day dance, all subsequent disasters would have been averted. Tess echoes this fond fantasy when she asks Angel: 'Why didn't you stay and love me, When I – was sixteen?; living with my little sisters and brothers, and you danced on the green?' (p. 261) However, to subscribe critically to this binarism would be to overlook the complexities of vision in *Tess of the d'Urbervilles*. Within that novel the gaze never innocently alights on its object. Rather, it *constructs* its object through a process of colonisation, delimitation, configuration and inscription. To use the novel's own metaphor, it extends representation into virgin territory.

Angel's gaze may be more benign in intent than Alec's, but there can be no doubt that it is informed by a similar mandate. As he leaves Marlott, he looks back at a 'green enclosure' which, unlike the 'engirdled and secluded region' described at the chapter's opening, has been definitively trodden by a sightseer (pp. 54–5). As a result of Angel's passing, this enclosure is no longer quite what it was before.

One figure now stands apart from the group, outside the harmony of the dance. Moreover, that figure has moved to the outer edge of the enclosure, a gesture anticipating further ruptures and invasions of that virgin territory which refers metaphorically and metonymically not just to Marlott, but to Tess.

. . .

More often, however, Tess functions as the surface upon which a pattern is imposed, and it is at these times that the artistic metaphor introduced in Chapter 2 resurfaces most insistently, anchoring her figure firmly to a mastering gaze. For instance, she is likened early in the novel to a canvas upon which her mother paints an image of voluptuous womanhood with which to ensnare Alec (after fluffing Tess up into a veritable concoction of femininity, Mrs Durbeyfield steps back 'like a painter from his easel, and [surveys] her work as a whole [pp. 89–90]). Tess is subsequently compared to a marble bust or 'term' upon which Alec 'imprints' a kiss, which she attempts to erase by wiping her cheek. On the evening of her wedding the winter sun recalls that kiss, as well as other, more violent inscriptions etched upon Tess's body by Alec, through the 'spot like a paint-mark' it casts upon her skirt (p. 284).

The most violent and ineradicable of those inscriptions occurs in The Chase, by means of that action which has been varyingly designated a 'rape' and a 'seduction'.[3] The passage recounting the night in the forest makes unusually explicit that what is at stake in the representation of Tess as a surface upon which certain things are figured is precisely *her accessibility as image* – that whereas John Durbeyfield is posited as having a stable and knowable appearance, co-extensive with his social, economic and physical circumstances, his daughter has *no* integral visual consistency, but must be painted, imprinted and patterned in order to be seen.

As Tess moves with Alec deeper and deeper in The Chase, she is increasingly blanketed in darkness and fog. When Alec deposits her beneath a tree and goes to find directions, and the light of the moon lessens, she actually becomes 'invisible'. On his return, Alec can see 'absolutely nothing but a pale nebulousness at his feet, which [represents] the white muslin figure he . . . left upon the dead leaves' (pp. 118–19). As I indicated above, Tess drops from sight in a similar way during the May-Day celebration, and she will do so again on a number of future occasions, although never quite as dramatically as here. In each case she is absorbed back into the landscape out of which the gaze of the imaginary traveller first carves her.

Alec counters Tess's disappearance with the most obviously coercive and extreme of all the novel's representational events – an event so extreme and coercive that it can only be recorded through protest:

> Why was it that upon this beautiful feminine tissue, sensitive as gossamer, and practically blank as snow as yet, there should have been traced such a coarse pattern as it was doomed to receive; why so often the coarse appropriates the finer thus, the wrong man the woman, the wrong woman the man, many thousand of years of analytical philosophy have failed to explain to our sense of order.
>
> (p. 113)

Not only is Tess's 'white muslin figure' quite specifically re-evoked through the words 'tissue', 'gossamer' and 'blank as snow', but that figure is made the ground for a second articulation. Her violation is thus a double figuration.

I would like to suggest that the action taken by Alec in the druidical darkness of The Chase has assumed the status of a seduction in some analyses of the novel not so much because Tess's 'own' sexuality seems at any point engaged, as because the narrator entertains a complexly ambivalent relation to that action. Others have already remarked upon the narrator's erotic investment in Tess's character,[4] as well as his apparent complicity in her violation.[5] However, it would also seem necessary to examine the narrator's relation to representation – his attraction to Tess *as figure*.

Desire is classically organised and sustained through representation,[6] and the libidinal economy of *Tess of the d'Urbervilles* is no exception. The narrator may parade under the fictional guises of tourist, landscape painter and ethnographer, but he betrays his true erotic colours as soon as he isolates Tess from the other May-Day celebrants on the basis of her 'mobile peony mouth' and 'large innocent eyes'. He returns compulsively to the first of those attributes throughout the rest of the novel, drawn to it as though it were a source of honey. Indeed, he has already found his way back there a few paragraphs later, where he lapses, in mid-linguistic insight, into a rapt scrutiny of its contours:

> The dialect was on her tongue to some extent, despite the village school: the characteristic intonation of that dialect for this district being approximately rendered by the syllable UR, probably as rich an utterance as any to be found in human speech. The pouted-up deep red mouth to which this syllable was native had hardly as yet settled into

its definitive shape, and her lower lip had a way of thrusting the
middle of her top one upward, when they closed together after a word.

(pp. 51–2)

This series of observations clearly exceeds the uninformed gaze of the
imaginary traveller, who is invoked again a moment later, and must
consequently be attributed to the narrator alone.

A subsequent passage, which provides one of the most erotically
charged descriptions of Tess in the entire novel, dwells upon the
same curve of the lip, associating it first with a familiar rhetorical
figure, and then with an image that has been internalised as fantasy:

> To a young man with the least fire in him that little upward lift in the
> middle of her red top lip was distracting, infatuating, maddening. He
> had never seen a woman's lips and teeth which forced upon his mind
> with such insistent iteration the old Elizabethan simile of roses filled
> with snow . . .
> Clare had studied the curves of those lips so many times that he
> could reproduce them mentally with ease: and now, as they again
> confronted him, clothed with colour and life, they sent an *aura* over
> his flesh, a breeze through his nerves which might well nigh have
> produced a qualm . . .
>
> (pp. 208–9)

It is ostensibly Angel's gaze which is here turned upon Tess, but the
reference to 'a young man with the least fire in him' functions more
as an ironic admonition to a character whose passion is 'ethereal to
a fault' than as an 'inside' account of his reactions. This abrupt shift
in point of view, much like the excessive information conveyed about
Tess in the passage devoted to her speech patterns, reveals the
narrator to be the speaking subject, the one whose desires structure
our view of Tess. That desire expresses itself here, as in the scene in
The Chase, through the emergence of shape, form and pattern –
through figuration.

This is not the only narratological desire to come into play either
during the meditation on Tess's lips or the scene in the forest. At both
points attraction toward the figure coexists with revulsion against it,
and a powerful wish for its dissolution. Although the desire to see the
image of Tess's mouth far outweighs the desire for the disintegration
of that image, nevertheless the pleasurable spectacle threatens to
induce a 'qualm' in the viewer – a term implying 'sickness', 'uneasi-
ness', 'doubt' and 'misgiving'. During the scene in The Chase, on the

other hand, the desire for the figure's dissolution is momentarily satisfied as Tess in fact disappears, while anxiety and distress far outweigh any manifest gratification to be derived from her reappearance. The narrator attempts to establish his own moral distance from what happens to Tess by inveighing against providence:

> But, some might say, where was Tess's guardian angel? where was the providence of her simple faith? Perhaps, like that other god of whom the ironical Tishbite spoke, he was talking, or he was pursuing, or he was in a journey, and not to be awakened.
>
> (p. 119)

However, since the narrator himself is the only transcendental agency on the horizon when Alec violates Tess, this outcry constitutes a classic disavowal, implicating him in the very action he abominates.

What largely determines our reading of the scene in The Chase is thus the relative emphasis we give to each of these contradictory desires, both of which are textually operative. To the degree that the narrator's desire for figural disintegration predominates, Alec's 'mastery' of Tess will be perceived as a rape. However, insofar as priority is given to the narrator's erotic gratification at the re-emergence of Tess as image, Alec's action will assume the status of a seduction. In the first instance narratological revulsion is projected onto Tess as non-compliance, whereas in the second narratological desire is projected onto her as acquiescence.

The painter of religious signs Tess encounters on her way home from The Slopes to Marlott takes the discursive operation begun by Mrs Durbeyfield one step further. As Tess watches him cover every available stile with biblical graffiti, she feels herself caught up and implicated by his crimson texts, made a part of their story; she remarks to herself that 'it was as if this man had known her recent history; yet he was a total stranger' (p. 128). Although he does not paint directly onto the surfaces of her body, the sign-painter, who represents yet another diegetic incarnation of the travelling-artist imagined by the narrator at the beginning of Chapter 2, constructs her just as inexorably as do Alec and her mother. The chief difference between those two constructions is that whereas one is chiefly erotic, the other is moral and teleological. However, as if to stress their ultimate symmetry, the narrator describes the religious inscriptions in much the same way he earlier describes the violation of Tess – again a coarse pattern scars a delicate background ('Against the peaceful landscape, the pale, decaying tints of the copses, the blue air of the horizon, and the lichened stile-board, these staring vermilion words shone forth' [p. 128]). The night in The Chase and the encounter with the graffiti-artist mark the transition from Tess as 'an engirdled and secluded region, for the most part untrodden as yet by tourist or landscape-painter' to Tess as a portrait on an easel, a patterned tissue, and a figure sharply-etched in the red letters of damnation.

*   *   *

There remains, nonetheless, a curious instability about Tess's image. Early on, before she has been subjected to the productive efforts of her mother, Alec and the sign-painter, she presents a kaleidoscopic view to the interested gaze ('Phases of her childhood lurked in her aspect still. As she walked along to-day, for all her bouncing handsome womanliness, you could sometimes see her twelfth year in her cheeks, or her ninth sparkling from her eyes; and even her fifth would flit over the curves of her mouth now and then' [p. 52]). Even after those various attempts to organise her visually, Tess slips constantly out of focus, often oscillating between two or more representations. Immediately prior to her sojourn at Talbothays, for instance, we are told that 'Her face had latterly changed with changing states of mind',

> continually fluctuating between beauty and ordinariness, according as the thoughts were gay or grave. One day she was pink and flawless; another pale and tragical.
>
> (p. 157)

Later, in the Talbothays dawns, she changes shape and consistency with the light, shifting back and forth from milkmaid to 'visionary essence of woman' (p. 187). This instability reaches crisis proportions on her wedding night, when the heirloom jewels transform her from a peasant girl into a woman of fashion, and when she is twice identified with the portraits of her d'Urberville ancestors:

> The unpleasantness of the matter was that, in addition to their effect upon Tess, her fine features were unquestionably traceable in these exaggerated forms.
>
> (pp. 283–4)

> The Caroline bodice of the portrait was low – precisely as Tess's had been when he tucked it in to show the necklace; and again he experienced the distressing sensation of a resemblance between them.
>
> (p. 305)

The alignment of Tess with her forebears recalls the visual trans-actions earlier effected by her mother, Alec and the sign-painter; once again her image is conformed to a model or pattern. However, whereas on prior occasions she is shaped according to an erotic or moral fore-conceit, here she is fashioned in the likeness of two women who lived before her. Furthermore, each element in the equation has an historical as well as a metaphorical status, implying the other without being reducible to it. When those two elements are brought together, the effect is analogous to what in cinema would be called a 'lap dissolve' – one is superimposed upon the other without either yielding to or completely fusing with it.

These are very much the terms used by Eric Auerbach to describe a figural view of history, a view within which one person or event is seen as anticipating another while at the same time maintaining its own existential independence:

> Figural interpretation establishes a connection between two events or persons, the first of which signifies not only itself but also the second, while the second encompasses or fulfils the first. The two poles of the figure are separate in time, but both, being real events or figures, are within time, within the stream of historical life.[7]

Within this account, figuration is an historical activity; indeed, it is through the complementary activities of pre-figuration and figural fulfilment that history is seen as moving toward its ultimate goal. *Tess of the d'Urbervilles* is heavily indebted to this representational model. In fact, I would go so far as to say that it is trapped within a figural view of history, albeit one within which the redemptive possibilities are radically curtailed.

[In the course of a long cut passage here, the essay explores this negative 'figural history' – especially in terms of scenes in the novel which emphasise 'disembodiment' (of Tess in particular).]

\* \* \*

We have seen that Tess's body serves as the surface for history as well as artistic and erotic inscription – that she is not just discursively determined, but discursively *overdetermined*. However, the very density of this representational activity attests to difficulties of con-tainment – to a certain slippage of Tess out of the paradigms that structure her. That slippage is also revealed through the hesitation over names (Durbeyfield/d'Urberville, Blakemore/Blackmoor), as well as in numerous passages devoted to a delineation of Tess's appearance. Again and again the dominant scopic regime of the novel is shown to induce anxiety and unpleasure in Tess, and to precipitate her retreat from specularity and the body. Indeed, the more she comes into figural and figurative focus, the more her subjectivity splits into irreconcilable parts.

. . .

As several Hardy critics have remarked, Tess is curiously 'absent' from most of the key events in the novel; from the death of Prince, to the strawberry scene, the night in The Chase, Angel's return and her capture at Stonehenge, she is asleep or in a trance.[8] She also abstracts herself on a number of seemingly less consequential occasions, such as when Alec kisses her goodbye. The abstraction functions as a kind of resistance or defence against the demands of representation, dissociating Tess from her body as the discursive pressure on it intensifies. One such dislocation occurs at the precise moment when Alec first looks erotically at her. As his look assumes possession of her image, the narrator quickly situates Tess 'herself' elsewhere by severing all connections between 'her' and that image:

> She had an attribute which amounted to a disadvantage just now; and it was this that caused Alec d'Urberville's eyes to rivet themselves upon her. It was a luxuriance of aspect, a fulness of growth, that made her appear *more of a woman than she really was.* She had inherited the feature from her mother *without the quality it denoted.* It had troubled her mind occasionally, till her companions had said that it was a fault which time would cure.
>
> (p. 82, emphases added)

Tess's estrangement from her own exteriority becomes much more acute after the scene in the forest, inspiring her recurrent fantasy about travelling 'hundreds and hundreds o' miles away from your body, which you don't seem to want at all' (p. 175). By the time Angel returns from Brazil, that estrangement has reached the proportions of a complete divide; as he stands at the door of her Sandbourne apartment looking at her, he has 'a vague consciousness of one thing, though it [will not be] clear to him till later' –

> that his original Tess [has] spiritually ceased to recognise the body before him as hers – allowing it to drift, like a corpse upon the current, in a direction dissociated from its living will.
>
> (p. 467)

The extremity of Tess's disaffiliation from her 'own' corporeality is suggested not only by the simile of the corpse, which will soon be literalised, but by the odd circumlocution, 'the body before him', which denies all possession.

All of this begs some very large questions as to what 'in' Tess withholds itself from the gaze, and attempts to resist figural history – what constitutes, in other words, the 'real' Tess. The category that comes most immediately to mind – her interiority – does not provide a satisfactory answer, since what the narrator characterises as her 'soul' or 'consciousness' is often so fully exteriorised as to bear little resemblance to any classical definition of those terms. The most striking example of this exteriorisation must surely be the account given of Angel's encounter with Tess after his return from the vicarage, where the categories 'inner' and 'outer', and 'spirit' and 'body' collapse into each other, losing all specificity:

> She was yawning, and he saw the red interior of her mouth as if it had been a snake's. She had stretched one arm so high above her coiled-up cable of hair that he could see its satin delicacy above the sunburn; her face was flushed with sleep, and her eyelids hung heavy over their pupils. The brim-fulness of her nature breathed from her. It was a moment when a woman's soul is more incarnate than at any other time; when the most spiritual beauty bespeaks itself flesh; and sex takes the outside place in the presentation.
>
> (p. 231)

Other passages create an analogous confusion of the demarcations between the spiritual and the material by conflating Tess's interiority with her physical surroundings. In the garden scene, for instance, her spiritual exaltation is identified with the 'floating pollen' and the 'rank-smelling flowers'. Similarly, during the evening walks she takes during her pregnancy, the 'natural processes' around her become 'a part of her own story' (p. 134), blending outer with inner.

Since Tess's 'whimsical fancy' succeeds in marrying mind to matter only after her 'flexuous and stealthy figure [has become] an integral part of the scene', the second of these passages suggests that she can only merge spiritually with the landscape if she first fuses with it visually. Corporeal assimilation would seem to be the precondition for psychological assimilation because Tess's subjectivity begins with the construction of her body, and that construction exercises a determining influence upon what, for lack of a better word, I will call her interiority. As long as her form remains sharply articulated against a generalised background, she is dominated by the awareness of a structuring gaze.

This is obviously the case on a number of occasions, such as the strawberry scene, or the second threshing scene, where Alec is the actual or implied viewer. At these times the gaze instils in her an unhappy consciousness, based upon the 'wretched sentiment . . . that in inhabiting the fleshy tabernacle with which nature had endowed her she was somehow doing wrong' (p. 388). However, it is also the case when the articulation is apparently benign or even benevolent, as is indicated by the breakfast scene at Talbothays where Angel first isolates Tess from the other dairy-maids. She responds to the figurative pressure of his gaze with a sympathetic gesture of her hand, thereby testifying eloquently to the pressure exerted upon female interiority by female specularity:

> Clare continued to observe her. She soon finished her eating, and having a consciousness that Clare was regarding her, began to trace imaginary patterns on the tablecloth with her forefinger with the constraint of a domestic animal that perceives itself to be watched.
>
> (p. 176)

In a closely related passage somewhat later in the novel, Tess's discursive abilities are once again attributed to the same source as her visual coherence ('her admiration for [Angel] . . . led her to pick up his vocabulary, his accent, and fragments of his knowledge, to a surprising extent' [p. 238]). This mirror relay between male gaze, female exteriority, and female interiority renders the distinction between Tess's body and her soul largely irrelevant.

I do not mean to imply that Tess always acquiesces to male vision, but rather to suggest that she is split less between the corporeal and the spiritual than between two compositional poles and their corresponding temporalities – between the figural and the non-figural. Because this opposition always implies a male viewer who does not himself pose any complications for vision, what it really entails are two contradictory notions of 'the feminine' and the conflicting narratological desires behind those notions: woman as image or text, with fixed visual boundaries and formal coherence, and woman as undifferentiated, 'intact' terrain.

The narrator refers to Tess in her non-figural mode, which is increasingly proposed as her 'true' identity, as a 'field-woman pure and simple'. The phrase designates not only the agricultural work she frequently performs, but her semiotic status on those occasions. When Tess binds corn or unearths turnip roots, she recedes into the background, and melts into her environment. This disappearing act is first explicitly described during the Marlott threshing scene, where it is also clearly specified as a female phenomenon ('A field-man is a personality afield; a field-woman is a portion of the field; she has somehow lost her own margin, imbued the essence of her surrounding, and assimilated herself with it' [pp. 137–8]).

The same passage articulates the alternative view of Tess as well. Indeed, through an extraordinary re-enactment of the visual itinerary earlier charted in Chapter 2, the threshing scene brings the two 'femininities' into sharp conflict. The ubiquitous viewer is installed once again in front of the imaginary canvas, this time not merely as landscape painter or tourist, but as the very source of illumination, and everything that follows is mediated through his gaze.[9] As on the occasion of the May-Day dance, that gaze shifts from an initial panoramic survey of Marlott to an ever more microscopic and individualising scrutiny that ultimately reinvests Tess as spectacle. In fact, immediately after extolling the assimilation of woman to landscape, the viewer embarks upon a rigorous differentiation of the former from the latter, isolating one female labourer after another on the basis of her clothing ('There was one wearing a pink jacket, another in a cream-coloured tight-sleeved gown, another in a petticoat as red as the arms of the reaping-machine' [p. 138]). Tess is singled out as 'the most flexuous and *finely-drawn figure* of them all' (emphasis mine), and subjected to an exhaustive visual interrogation and a quick historical overview. At the conclusion of this delineation, harmony no longer reigns between Tess and her surroundings; instead, the stubble of the corn 'scarifies' her 'feminine smoothness', suggesting non-equivalence and incompatibility between woman and landscape. . . .

\* \* \*

At first glance, the two contradictory paradigms of feminity proposed by the novel would seem to conform to the argument, variously formulated by Kristeva and Montrelay, that woman is always divided between language and the drives, the symbolic and the semiotic, representation and the real.[10] Tess certainly literalises the notion of a dark continent whenever she is folded into the landscape, and these moments of integration always pose a quite explicit threat to figuration. Indeed, on those occasions when Tess melts into the landscape she could be said to ruin representation.[11] However, as we have seen, the split in her subjectivity does not at all follow the same body/psyche divide as those writers chart. Indeed, far from resisting the symbolic order, the female body is here shown to be the point of greatest figural coercion, a coercion that extends 'inward' in the guise of an unhappy consciousness of being watched. Tess escapes from cultural structuration by retreating *out of*, rather than *into* corporeality.

Unfortunately for Tess and the female reader constituted through identification with her, the assimilation of figure into background means the abolition not just of hierarchy, but of difference, and hence of identity. Environmental absorption marks her demise as emphatically as the black flag does at the end of the novel. Indeed, both 'femininities' point in the direction of Wintoncester, and could be said to over-determine Tess's death. There is consequently nothing emancipatory about either alternative.

As I suggested earlier, Tess is figured or dissolved according to the vicissitudes of authorial subjectivity and its ambivalent relation to representation. The oscillation between the two compositional poles is thus ultimately the effect of a contradiction at the level of narrative desire. The assimilation of her form into her surroundings attests to her viewer's or marker's nostalgia for an 'intact state' of things – for a moment prior to differentiation. Her construction as image, on the other hand, speaks to her viewer's or maker's desire for visual control.

Each of these notions of 'the feminine' represents a classic, culturally fostered mechanism for disavowing the male subject's symbolic castration – a device for covering over the self-alienation induced in him by the entry into language. Woman-as-intact-state makes good male lack through the fantasmatic restoration of phenomenal plenitude. Woman-as-figure provides a very different solution, reconciling the male subject to symbolic castration by situating him in a position of apparent discursive potency. To the degree that Tess conforms to male desire and vision, the male subject is able to locate himself on the side of the enunciation rather than the enounced – to align himself with the agency rather than the object of articulation. In so doing he seems to master his own lack, to move from a passive to an active relation to representation.

However, the supremacy of the male gaze must be constantly reasserted in *Tess of the d'Urbervilles*, and always in the face of powerful opposition. We need not look very far for the source of that opposition. Symbolic castration entails not only the *aphanisis* or fading of the phenomenal real under the pressure of meaning, but the subject's insertion into a pre-existing discursive network which confers upon him or her a strictly relational identity, and so challenges any assumption either of self-presence or self-determination. . . . With its insistence upon relational identity and the coercive power of the signifier, figural history in *Tess of the d'Urbervilles* would finally seem to be nothing other than a nightmarish view of the symbolic order – a traumatic apprehension of the central role played in the constitution of the subject by the language and desire of the Other.

This glimpse of the symbolic order is perhaps less traumatic for the female reader, since it doesn't teach her anything she doesn't already know about her own castration. There may even be an implicit promise for her in the suggestion that far from remaining outside meaning, immersed in the phenomenal real, her body provides the surface not only for *erotic*, but for *historical* inscription. If Tess's body is produced within one symbolic order, other symbolic orders may very well produce different female bodies, and consequently different subjective possibilities.

From *Novel*, 18 (1984), 5–28.

## NOTES

[Kaja Silverman has written extensively on sexual difference and representation, especially in prose fiction and film. The essay included here, informed by the concepts and terminology of neo-Freudian theories about gender and language (especially those of Jacques Lacan and Julia Kristeva), again offers a close textual analysis of the narratalogical language of *Tess*, showing how 'the complexities of vision', the 'gaze' of the novel, '*construct* its object through a process of colonisation, delimitation, configuration and inscription' (p. 132). In this respect, it extends the earlier perceptions of John Goode, noted in the Introduction (pp. 7–8), and reinforces the discussion of the paradoxical '*de*-characterisation' of Tess as 'pure woman' which the novel seems to effect (Introduction, pp. 16–19, passim). In particular, Kaja Silverman shows how *Tess of the d'Urbervilles* figures two contradictory paradigms of male representation of female sexuality, and relates this (in a long, cut passage of the essay) to a 'figural view of history' (p. 138) which usually implies 'fulfilment' (the title, ironically, of the last section of *Tess*) and therefore contains redemptive possibilities, but which here is effectively negated. Finally the essay suggests that the novel is a 'nightmarish' enactment of Hardy's subconscious apprehension of his own (male) symbolic castration effected by the entry into language – paradoxically the source of the very discourse of representation Hardy the novelist must deploy in order to envision Tess at all. Ed.]

1. Thomas Hardy, *Tess of the d'Urbervilles*, Penguin edn, ed. David Skilton (London, 1978), p. 43. All future citations will refer to this edition.

2. Thus we are informed about local legends and rituals, told where the middle distance is tinged with the deepest azure, and advised (much as we might be by the *Blue Guide*) that Blakemore is a vale 'whose acquaintance is best made by viewing it from the summits of the hills that surround it' (pp. 48–9).

3. For an interesting recent discussion of the rape/seduction scene, see Ellen Rooney, 'Criticism and the Subject of Sexual Violence', *Modern Language Notes*, 98 (1983), 1269–78.

4. See, for instance, John Bayley, *An Essay on Hardy* (Cambridge, 1978), p. 183.

5. In *Thomas Hardy and Women: Sexual Ideology and Narrative Form* (Brighton, 1982), Penny Boumelha observes that 'The narrator's erotic fantasies of penetration and engulfment enact a pursuit, violation and persecution of Tess in parallel with those she suffers at the hands of her two lovers' (p. 120 – land in the present volume, p. 47). Tony Tanner makes a similar point in 'Colour and Movement in *Tess of the d'Urbervilles*', *Critical Quarterly*, 10 (1968), 219–39.

6. This is suggested both by Freud's theory of dreams, and his theory of fantasy. See *The Standard Edition of the Complete Psychological Works of Sigmund Freud*, trans. James Strachey (London, 1958), vol. 5, pp. 565–89, and vol. 17, pp. 179–204.

7. 'Figura' in *Scenes from the Drama of European Literature: Six Essays* (Gloucester, 1973), p. 53.

8. The narrator's ambivalent relation to figuration surfaces here through a tendency to naturalise Tess's image ('She had an attribute'), and to hold her responsible for an action that clearly originates elsewhere ('it was this that caused Alec d'Urberville's eyes to rivet themselves upon her'). An analogous confusion of constructing subject with constructed object leads Ian Gregor to claim in *The Great Web: The Form of Hardy's Major Fiction* (London, 1974), that Alec brings 'to consciousness (Tess's) own sexuality' (p. 182), and Bert Hornback to assert in *The Metaphor of Chance: Vision and Technique in the Works of Thomas Hardy* (Athens, 1971) that 'Tess's tragic flaw is her seduction by Alec d'Urberville' (p. 111).

9. The narrator devotes a whole paragraph of praise to this viewer (here represented by the sun), stressing both his male identity and his superiority to the spectacle: 'The sun, on account of the mist, had a curious sentient, personal look demanding the personal pronoun for its adequate expression. His present aspect, coupled with the lack of all human beings in the scene, explained the old-time heliolotries in a

moment. One could feel that a saner religion had never prevailed under the sky. The luminary was a golden-haired, beaming, mild-eyed God-like creature, gazing down in the vigour and intentness of youth upon an earth that was brimming with interest for him' (p. 136).

10. See Julia Kristeva, 'Motherhood According to Bellini', in *Desire in Language: A Semiotic Approach to Literature and Art,* trans. Thomas Gora, Alice Jardine and Leon S. Roudiez (New York, 1980), pp. 237–43, and Michele Montrelay, 'Inquiry Into Femininity', trans. Parveen Adams, *m/f,* no. 1(1978) 83–101.

11. Montrelay writes that 'feminine eroticism is more censored, less repressed than that of the man. It lends itself less easily to a "losing itself" as the stake of unconscious representation. The drives whose force was demonstrated by the English school, circumscribe a place or "continent" which can be called "dark" to the extent that it is outside the circumference of the symbolic economy' (p. 90). She adds that representation is threatened by this foreclosure (p. 93). For a fuller discussion of this formulation, as well as a general investigation of the female body, see Silverman, '*Histoire d'O*: The Story of a Disciplined and Punished Body', *Enclitic,* 7 (1983), 63–81.

# 10

# The Violence of Style in 'Tess of the d'Urbervilles'

*JEAN JACQUES LECERCLE*

There is a sense in which we must begin our reading of *Tess of the d'Urbervilles* with the last paragraph. But not the obvious sense. For it is too trivially clear that the closing paragraphs of the novel provide material for a retrospective reading and give both meaning and direction (*sens* in French) to the story, so that the whole novel is pervaded with emotional tension towards its catastrophic ending. What strikes one in the last paragraph, however, is not so much the climactic event on which it is the commentary as the violence of Hardy's style. The physical violence of Tess's death (which is not described) is displaced not only to the symbolic black flag (and indeed the word 'hang' which is the meaningful centre of the description is only present in the last chapter concealed within the apparently innocuous clause 'till the horizon was lost in the radiance of the sun hanging above it'[1]) but to the violence of the language. In spite of Hardy's notorious disclaimer in the *Life*,[2] there is stylistic violence in the famous sentence 'the President of the Immortals . . . had ended his sport with Tess'. The allusion is to a Promethean song of revolt against tyranny and torture;[3] the definite description for Zeus, taken out of its original context, takes on sardonic overtones, and the metaphor of the hunt is one of inherent violence. What we have is an explosion of anger, irony giving way to sarcasm and rage, an instance of verbal violence, as if the pent-up energy of a narrator who so far had kept his distance has suddenly been liberated.

Neither the suddenness of this violence nor the narrator's previous distance should be overstressed, although the last paragraph does contrast with the subdued and symbolic rendering of the execution itself. But the retrospective reading of the novel which this ending, like all endings, provokes, will show the importance not only of violence in *Tess* – for although violence is not absent from most of Hardy's novels, the amount we find here is rather overwhelming: a rape, a murder, an execution, etc. – but also of the connection between violence and language, both as a theme (I shall try to show that to a certain extent this is a novel about language) and as a practice – I shall try to show that the violence of style is Hardy's main object in *Tess*.

[In a cut pasage here, the essay reflects on whether the novel is 'tragic', and decides that because of the pervasive violence of its language, it is not.]

As the rest of this chapter will be an attempt to substantiate this thesis, that is, to account for the violence/woman/language nexus, a provisional definition of the phrase 'the violence of language' is in order. The first meaning it can be given is literal: certain implicit speech acts in the novel are violent (slogans, like 'THY, DAMNA-TION, SLUMBERETH, NOT'; the words of various quarrels, but also the insidious words of seduction). The second is social: the language of the heroine is subject to repression by the dominant idiom – this repression often takes pedagogic form. Tess, in Althusserian terms, is submitted to a process of interpellation which transforms her into a subject at the expense of her native language and culture. The process is rife with symbolic, if not physical violence. The theme of possession by language indicates the un-avoidable character of this violence (ideology interpellates all individuals, without exception, into subjects).

My thesis is that the main object of the novel is this 'becoming violent' of language, to use a Deleuzian phrase. From this point of view, 'Tess' is the name for a 'collective arrangement of utterance',[4] i.e. a style as expression of a culture and a collective mode of discourse: a style of life (which is fast disappearing, because a victim of the violence of historical change), a style of speech (*'la femme, c'est le style'*: the essence of Tess is in her language, and what happens to it) and of course also, *en abyme*, a style of writing (the famous question of Hardy's style). The rest of the essay will deal with violence in relation to these two notions: woman and style.

\*   \*   \*

[In a long, cut passage here, the essay explores the relationship between women and violence within cultural history.]

Violence in *Tess* is primarily linguistic. Let us turn to the pedagogic violence of Angel's teaching (that there is such a thing needs to be proved). Tess is peeling lords and ladies, an old custom in her culture, and ironically expresses the truth about the situation: 'I meant there are always more ladies than lords when you come to peel them.'[5] Angel replies: 'Never mind about the lords and ladies. Would you like to take up any course of study – history for instance?' In this scene, a pre-linguistic semiotic activity, a game which does not need elaborate language, is repressed by the articulate language of the dominant culture. Exactly as the unspoken past, which flows in Tess's veins, must be replaced by the spoken past, history as 'a course of study'. Angel's question, in spite of appearances, does not allow Tess any choice: it is preceded by an imperative, and takes on the force of an order (if she wants to reach Angel's elevated position, to be worthy of him, she *must* abandon her culture and her language, she must study). We are entering the world of Deleuze and Guattari's 'signifying semiotics', as opposed to the 'pre-signifying semiotics' of dance and gestures, where the origin of the sentence is the slogan (the imperative mood, or the performative verb implicit in the deep structure of all sentences), where there is no direct speech, only the repetition, as indirect speech, of collective slogans. 'THY, DAMNA-TION, SLUMBERETH, NOT. 2. PET.ii.3.'[6] What is striking about this sentence is the commas that separate the words, thus turning them into the repetition, or quotation, of authoritative speech, in short into a slogan (and the authority which transforms the sentence into an injunction is duly mentioned). The conception of language which we find in Deleuze and Guattari's *Mille Plateaux* (especially in *plateau* no. 4, 'The four postulates of linguistics') provides an account of violence in language. One of the aspects of post-Saussurian linguistics which they criticise is the postulate of a standard language. This theoretical linguistics disregards dialectal variations, whether social or geographical, for it needs to study a stable object. What Deleuze and Guattari point out is that there is no stability in language, that it is a violent and unstable mixture of dialects. I shall add one more source of violence. Another of the postulates of theoretical linguistics, which they do not attack directly, is that of synchrony: for its object to remain stable, linguistics must disregard diachronic variations (or at least carefully separate the two fields of study). But a synchronic state of the language is an abstract construct. In reality, what we find – and this is particularly obvious in *Tess* – is an unstable mixture of various historical layers of language, all combining into a corrupt whole.

The postulate of a standard language has to be abandoned when we realise that a natural language is a battlefield for the struggles between a *major* and various *minor* dialects.[7] Thus, Kafka writes in German, the major dialect of the Austrian empire, but from the linguistic position of a Czech Jew; Yiddish and Czech struggle against the dominant German to produce Kafka's own dialect, his style. In the same way, Tess has to express herself in a no-woman's speech, situated between the dialect of her forefathers and the English of her men. Hers is a situation of minority, by which we must also understand her personal and social minority, her position of irresponsibility as a child or a woman – but also the fact that she and the likes of her are historically 'in a minority', expelled from their traditional territories by the invasion of the urban 'majority'. And this also has consequences for the language of the majority: it threatens and destabilises it. English, far from being reducible to a 'standard language' is the totality of major and minor dialects. If the minor dialect of Wessex is repressed or destroyed by the Queen's English, the process can also be reversed, and both Alec and Angel lose some of their linguistic sense of superiority in their contact with Tess. There is a clash, a source of uncertainty to all concerned, a source of violence also. Angel's adoption of the Wessex phrase, 'a drop of pretty tipple' (p. 155) shocks his brothers, who have been to Cambridge. Tess's description of her family origins, 'we have an old seal, marked with a ramping lion on a shield . . . and we have a very old silver spoon' is corrected by Alec: 'A castle argent is certainly my crest . . . And my arms a lion rampant' (p. 34). The technical terms of heraldry come from the French, whereas Tess's 'mistakes' have a distinctly English sound. The violence of language – nothing as picturesque as rape or murder, of course – appears here in the following nexus: blood (the origin) – language (French vs English) – sex (one of the meanings of 'rampant', so my edition informs me, is 'lustful').

The postulate of a synchronic *langue* must also be abandoned if we realise that language is subject to historical forces, that it is always uttered by a collective arrangement of utterance, in a historical conjuncture: the slogan which provides the deep structure for a sentence is historically determined. Instead of a stable synchronic structure, we have an unstable diachronic process of 'becoming' (*devenir*), subject to the violence of corruption.

This is apparent in *names*. One may recall here Derrida's theory of the violence inherent in proper names.[8] This instability is obvious in the very title of *Tess* – it is not only the subtitle which reminds us of an oxymoron. If Tess Durbeyfield is a corruption of Teresa d'Urberville, we must note that the title combines the nickname (an instance of corruption) and the archaic name. And we can try and follow this process of linguistic corruption: the unchanged element is the syllable *urb*, which contains the 'ur' characteristic of Tess's dialect: 'the characteristic intonation of that dialect for this district being the voicing approximately rendered by the syllable UR, probably as rich an utterance as any to be found in human speech' (p. 9). Here, the situation is reversed: far from being a corruption of pure English, the dialect appears as the rich *Ur-sprache* in which meaning is preserved ('as rich an utterance'), exactly as the country girl is the true descendant of the archaic nobility, much more so than the *nouveau riche* impostor who has appropriated her name, or the petty-bourgeois who dominate her world. So there is violence in proper names. Tess's name is the locus of a struggle for appropriation (of her name by Alec, of her person by the ancient d'Urbervilles, whose name governs her destiny) in a process which Deleuze and Guattari might describe as one of deterritorialisation/ reterritorialisation: being chased from Marlott, obliged to seek work elsewhere, to move from the almost ancestral cottage, as the third life comes to an end, finding one's ancestors by camping in the family vault at Kingsbere.

The phrase 'the corruption of language' is ambiguous between an objective and a subjective genitive: language corrupts, it is corrupt or corrupted. There is violence in both cases. Language corrupts Tess: the contrast between the opening scene, where she keeps silent, and the explanation scene, when she tells Angel at last, is striking. Words do not favour Tess: they create misunderstanding, and in spite of appearances explanations are the opposite of a clarification. They only induce in Angel an unnatural – because culturally determined – hardness of heart. It is when he is 'taken in' by Tess's appearance, by her behaviour, by her gestures, that Angel is *intuitively* right. The explanation scene clears that 'mistake' only by replacing it with a deeper mistake. Far from expressing the truth of the matter, language is the bearer of hypocrisy and illusion. The consequences are duly violent.

But language corrupts because it is corrupt. Tess is not an actor in a synchronic system of communication, a linguistic cosmos, exchanging messages and performing felicitous speech acts. She has to come to terms with the chaos of linguistic corruption. It is not only her name which undergoes the process: customs disappear, words change meaning (the 'lords and ladies' passage is a good example of this – and of Hardy's ironic skill – for 'the terms LORD and LADY, which nowadays refer to high positions of the social order, must originally be seen in the context of an agricultural society: OE *hlāford* and *hlǣfdige* were compounds with *hlāf* 'bread' as their first element'[9]). Perhaps the exact term is 'corrupted' rather than 'corrupt'. For it is ironic that the dialect, which is being superseded by the national tongue for obvious historical reasons, should be less corrupt, less subject to change (because the time of folklore is *aiôn* and not *chronos*), closer to the English of Chaucer and Shakespeare than modern speech. Tess's name is 'corrupt', her blood is tainted because the energy of her line is spent (this is Angel's vision of 'old families'), but her speech is closer to the origins and to nature than Alec's or Angel's. This is her contradiction – the core of the linguistic violence to which she is subjected; on the one hand, she is caught in historical change, the corrupt descendant of a long line of ancestors; on the other hand, she has remained close to nature, and is corrupted – as her dialect is corrupted – by culture and history.

At this point it appears that linguistic corruption is (a) the tenor of a metaphor, the vehicle of which is decay and rottenness, and (b) the vehicle of a metaphor, the tenor of which is moral corruption. The tenor: linguistic corruption is embodied in images of decay (the tombs, the recurrent mention of the old d'Urbervilles) which offer a concrete version of the abstract corruption of language and society. The vehicle: linguistic corruption is the outward sign of the moral corruption which cankers the main characters. Alec, with his sensuousness and his lapses, is corruption incarnate: the serpent does not bother to disguise himself. Angel, a serpent in angel's garb, embodies the sly corruption of pride, narrow-mindedness and conventionality: his temptation is all the more devastating as it is offered with the best of intentions. Confronted with this double serpent, what can Tess, a daughter of nature, do, except be a daughter of Eve, and follow her mother's advice (and Mrs Durbeyfield is always ready with ill advice). The very first letter of her name, in the shape of a cross, the cross of St Anthony, a saint celebrated for his temptation, but also in the shape of a gallows, indicates her fate – it is not only inscribed in her speech, but in the writing of her name.

In the light of Deleuze and Guattari's analyses, I can now propose a better definition of the phrase 'the violence of language'. It has literal meaning (the illocutionary force of the slogan which is to be found beneath every utterance), symbolic meaning (language is an unstable rhizome-like proliferation, rather than a hierarchically ordered tree-like structure; it is subject to the corruption of diachrony). And it is itself contradictory and unstable, for the violence of language has two sources: the paranoid violence of triangulation, which interpellates the individual into a subject; and the schizophrenic violence of the subject's attempt at liberation, when he or she crosses the frontiers, follows his or her lines of flight. This is why Tess is not only the object, but also the subject of violence.

So the violence of language is central in *Tess*. But it does not only concern the heroine: an obvious *abyme* makes it also the violence of the author's style. For Tess's linguistic and social minority, which determines her subject position, is close to Hardy's. Her difficult relation to language is paralleled in the contradiction of Hardy's style. What Tess embodies is perhaps not so much the position of women in late Victorian times: the social minority of the heroine becomes a metaphor for the minority of the author's writing, for the struggle of his style against the major, i.e. established, literary English. Seen in this light, the plot of the novel is a reflection of Hardy's linguistic strategy.

There is indeed a striking parallel between Tess's relation to language and Hardy's. She is torn between two languages and two lives, he is torn between three lives and several languages, as a well-known passage in his autobiography notes: 'his inner life . . . might almost have been called academic – a triple existence unusual for a young man – what he used to call, in looking back, a life twisted of three strands – the professional life, the scholar's life and the rustic life.'[10] As in *Tess*, the languages which correspond to the three lives, tend to clash. Tess, as we have seen, they destroy – with Hardy, according to the critics, they threaten his style. A common type of criticism of Hardy is that sometimes he writes well, and sometimes atrociously. He himself was conscious of this 'stylelessness': he wanted to improve his style, and for that purpose read Addison and *The Times*, much to the scandal of the academic critic.

And it is certainly true that Hardy speaks several languages, that, to use his own metaphor, his text is woven of several strands of discourse. There are at least two Hardys: the speaker of dialect – often with rich comic or dramatic effect – and the reader of penny cyclopaedias, desirous to share his knowledge. The usual criticism accuses him of being a pedant, as a compensation for being an autodidact. Raymond Williams has exploded this myth.[11] The truth is that in his writing, as in the story of Tess, the themes of language and school are inextricably mixed. It is at school that one learns the correct language, at university that one is taught to write in the approved style.

For an author who finds himself in Hardy's position, a position of linguistic plurality and contradiction, of potential stylistic violence, there are two solutions: suture or polyphony. Suture, a psychoanalytic concept,[12] means the weaving together at all costs of the various threads of the text into a unified whole – an obsessional activity, a case of paranoid repression. A 'polished' style, as approved by Dr Johnson and his disciples, is the result of suture: all contradictions, all dialectical variations are erased in the perfection of a unified text. The major has eaten up the minor – a situation which is obviously rife with the violence of repression. The other choice, a more difficult one, is to let violence erupt on the surface of the text, to follow the lines of flight it indicates, to let the minor voices engage in their babble/Babel, in other words not to erase the contradictions from the text. To describe this choice, we can borrow Bakhtin's term, 'polyphony'. And this is indeed Hardy's choice: he accepts the violence of an unstable language as an integral part of his style, he lets the different languages within him speak out and contradict one another. This is why the narrator speaks like Tess, but also like Alec and Angel; why he indulges in flights of lyrical fancy, and also speaks the pedantic words of improving knowledge. Hence this impression of instability, of eruptive violence. This is a style which is not as controlled as the academic critic – I am thinking of David Cecil[13] – would wish it. And it is the stylistic equivalent of Tess's position in the novel.

Against the academic critic, we shall maintain that this style, with all its 'defects' (which are only the symptoms of linguistic violence) is particularly apt, that it is faithful to the violent reality of language. If the novel is based on a contradiction (if it is a myth retelling the age-old opposition between Nature and Culture, folklore and history, *aiôn* and *chronos*), and if this narrative contradiction is a metaphor for the instability and violence of language, Hardy's own stylistic contradiction is the best possible reflection of this. Hardy's stylistic gift is that he dares unleash the violence of language, that he does not attempt a mythical solution to the contradiction, but lets it stand and be perceived.

To sum up. Starting from the theme of physical violence in *Tess*, i.e. violence in the strictest sense, I have tried to show that another type of violence is at the centre of the novel: symbolic violence, the preferred locus of which is language. The novel is about the passage from the one to the other – and, *en abyme*, the novel is also about the violence of style: in *Tess* Hardy comes to terms with his own linguistic contradictions. The position of women in *Tess* I have interpreted as the crucial point where physical violence becomes symbolic: Tess is subjected to physical violence, she is subjected *by*, i.e. made a subject by, a process of symbolic violence, in which her relation to language plays the essential part. Behind my reading of the novel, there is a rather contentious theory of violence, distinctly continental in flavour.[14] I make no apology for this: it allows me to move from a purely metaphorical conception of the violence of Hardy's language, interpreted in psychological terms as the expression of his 'rage', to a more literal description of the violence of language as constitutive of his style.

From *Alternative Hardy*, ed. Lance St John Butler (London, 1989), pp. 1–2, 6–7, 17–25.

[Inspired by the work of the linguist and semiotician, Gilles Deleuze (to whom he devoted most of his first book), Jean Jacques Lecercle's main fields of research are philosophy of language, critical theory and nineteenth-century English literature (especially nonsense literature), and his stated aim as a critic is 'to reside on the frontier between literature and philosophy (of the continental kind)'. The present essay, also beholden in part to Deleuze, is a sophisticated exploration of violence as the determining characteristic of the language of *Tess*. In its deconstructive analysis of the latter, it relates well to the two previous essays in this collection and to Patricia Ingham's, while its discussion on women and violence (some of which, for reasons of space, is cut from the present excerpt) reiterates the issue of female sexuality which is also a recurrent theme of this New Casebook. In particular, the essay alludes to previous academic critics' hostility to Hardy's 'flawed' style, and counters with an emphatic affirmation of Hardy's achievement as lying, precisely, in his 'polyphonic' text – where different languages contradict each other giving the 'impression of instability, of eruptive violence' (p. 154) – and in his refusal to resolve contradiction, but to 'let it stand and be perceived' (p. 154). In all of this the essay tends to confirm the notion of *Tess* as a post-modern text before its time. Ed.]

1. *Tess of the d'Urbervilles*, p. 387. All the references are to the Everyman edition (London, 1984).

2. F. E. Hardy, *The Life of Thomas Hardy* (London, 1962), pp. 243–4.

3. It comes from Aeschylus, *Prometheus Bound*, I, 169.

4. G. Deleuze and F. Guattari, *Mille Plateaux* (Paris, 1980). For the English terms, see the glossary to F. Guattari, *Molecular Revolution* (Harmondsworth, 1984).

5. *Tess*, p. 122.

6. *Tess*, p. 76.

7. See Deleuze and Guattari, *Kafka* (Paris, 1975), especially pp. 33–45.

8. J. Derrida, *De la grammatologie* (Paris, 1967), p. 162. English translation by Gayatri Chakravorty Spivak, *Of Grammatology* (Baltimore, 1976).

9. A. Bammesberger, *English Etymology* (Heidelberg, 1986), p. 99.

10. F. E. Hardy, *Life*, pp. 32–3.

11. See R. Williams, *The Country and the City* (London, 1973), ch. 18; see also T. Eagleton, *Walter Benjamin* (London, 1981), p. 129.

12. See J. A. Miller, 'La suture – éléments da la logique du signifiant', *Cahiers pour l'analyse*, 1 (Paris, 1966). English translation in *Screen*, 18: 4 (1977/8). For the use of the concept in the field of political science, see E. Laclau and C. Mouffe, *Hegemony and Socialist Strategy* (London, 1985).

13. D. Cecil, *Hardy the Novelist* (London, 1943). Apart from the notorious strictures on Hardy's style and the rather snobbish assessment of his lack of formal education, the book contains many remarkable insights.

14. See the use of the concept 'violence' in the Marxist tradition, for instance in Althusser's distinction between repressive and ideological apparatuses; see his 'Ideology and Ideological State Apparatuses', in *Lenin and Philosophy*, translated by B. Brewster (London, 1977).

# 11

# Geographies of Hardy's Wessex in 'Tess of the d'Urbervilles'

*JOHN BARRELL*

I have never been to Dorset – though I believe I may have passed through it on the train to somewhere else. But I make that confession, not to disqualify myself from writing this essay, but to indicate at the outset the sort of essay it will not be. It will not be concerned with the identification of places in the Wessex novels with their possible originals in Dorset and the neighbouring counties. That task has already been performed more than a few times, most convincingly by Denys Kay-Robinson, and by Andrew Enstice whose work is especially useful where it points out how Hardy manipulated the geography of Dorset to create the imaginary space called Wessex.[1] Nor am I offering – I would be equally incompetent to offer – the sort of study that H. C. Darby has made of the regional geography of Hardy's Wessex – a study whose implications have still to be taken up by literary critics and humanist geographers, in that it would seem possible to base upon it an understanding of how the plots and the narrative structures of Hardy's novels might have been to a degree determined by their various settings.[2]

This essay sets out instead to examine how localities and spaces in Hardy's novels are constructed, are mapped, by the characters in the novels, and therefore also by Hardy in his narrative and by us as we read. I am concerned, then, with different, subjective geographies, and with geographies as modes of cognition. This is a topic we can approach, traditionally enough, through a consideration of the development of theme and character in the novels, but it has implications, too, for the study of Hardy's narrative method, particularly the problem of who speaks what in the narrative – a problem more salient, perhaps, in Hardy than in any other nineteenth-century novelist, and one well-described by David Lodge in some remarks on *Tess of the d'Urbervilles*.[3] It is to *Tess* (1891) and to *The Return of the Native* (1878) that this study will address itself.

The context for my discussion (particularly of *Tess*) will be Hardy's concern with the mobility, with the migration of agricultural labourers in Dorset in the second half of the nineteenth century by the system of annual hirings, at statute fairs, described in *Far From the Madding Crowd* and referred to in *Tess*; and, in Hardy's essay 'The Dorsetshire Labourer' (1883), represented as so well-established that it was not uncommon for a labourer to change his farm and master each year.[4] It is this, not as it may or may not have been common in Dorset, but as it occurs in the Wessex of the novels, that is crucial to the different representations of space I am concerned with. It is an experience which produces a change from the sense of space that Hardy describes in *Tess*, where he writes that 'to persons of limited spheres, miles are as geographical degrees, parishes as counties, counties as provinces and kingdoms' – a change from that sense, which can hardly have survived as unadulterated in Dorset as it survives in Wessex, to the geography of those whom he describes, in 'The Dorsetshire Labourer', as the new 'inter-social citizens' of the county.

> Dorset labourers now look upon an annual removal as the most natural thing in the world, and it becomes with the younger families a pleasant excitement. Change is also a certain sort of education. Many advantages accrue to the labourers from the varied experience it brings, apart from the discovery of the best market for their abilities. They have become shrewder and sharper men of the world, and have learned how to hold their own with firmness and judgment. Whenever the habitually-removing man comes into contact with one of the old-fashioned stationary sort, who are still to be found, it is impossible not to perceive that the former is much more wide awake than his fellow-worker, astonishing him with stories of the wide world comprised in a twenty-mile radius from their homes.[5]

As long as Hardy is talking primarily, as here, about the expansion of mental, consequent on that of geographical horizons, he clearly welcomes it; the fact of the labourers becoming less 'local in feeling', however – the essential condition for the development of sharpness, of judgement – is presented with rather less equanimity, and especially in the novels. For it involves, in *Tess* particularly, not so much the exchange of one, 'local', for another, 'regional' sense of space, as the destruction of a local sense and the substitution of nothing in its place; for the new, regional geography of the migrant labourer, at ease with a knowledge of the world comprised 'in a twenty-mile radius from his home', can be acquired, it seems, only on terms that Tess herself cannot manage. In 'The Dorsetshire Labourer', the 'migration' of labour suggests to Hardy the image of the labourers as 'birds of passage', a phrase used to indicate that 'nobody thinks whence or whither' they come and go, but which still serves to remind us that, in moving from place to place, they are searching for the environment most congenial to them.[6] But the phrase occurs again, in *Tess*, to put an entirely negative valuation, as we shall see, on Tess's migrations.

. . .

If Clym [in *The Return of the Native*] willingly allows his shortsightedness to contract the horizons of his mind as well as of his vision, Tess's experience might, in the terms of 'The Dorsetshire Labourer', invite itself to be understood as an expansion, as she becomes after her marriage to Angel Clare an itinerant farm-worker. This is how Hardy describes the geography that she constructs as a child, or that is constructed for her by the limits of the horizons of her childhood:

> The Vale of Blackmoor was to her the world, and its inhabitants the races thereof. From the gates and stiles of Marlott she had looked down its length in the wondering days of infancy, and what had been mystery to her then was not much less than mystery to her now . . . only a small tract even of the Vale and its environs being known to her by close inspection. Much less had she been far outside the valley. Every contour of the surrounding hills was as personal to her as that of her relatives' faces; but for what lay beyond her judgment was dependent on the teaching of the village school . . . [7]

Tess, it seems, had not at sixteen progressed far beyond a child's sense of place, as we might put it: 'what had been mystery to her then was not much less than mystery to her now'. She knows only a small portion of the vale, and the hills that surround it she has seen only from below, only from Marlott, so that, familiar as their contours are from there, the hills have as it were only two dimensions, they are a flat wall on her world beyond which she knows only what she has learned at school.

In her early excursions from Marlott – to Trantridge, and, after the death of her child, to Talbothays in the Vale of Froom – she is represented as apprehending those places entirely in terms of the differences they exhibit from the one place she knows well, her portion of the Vale of Blackmoor. For her, the Vale of Froom

> was intrinsically different from the Vale of Little Dairies, Blackmoor Vale, which, save during her disastrous sojourn at Trantridge, she had exclusively known till now. The world was drawn to a larger pattern here. The enclosures numbered fifty acres instead of ten, the farmsteads were more extended, the groups of cattle formed tribes hereabout; there only families. These myriads of cows stretching under her eyes from the far east to the far west outnumbered any she had ever seen at one glance before ... The bird's-eye perspective before her was not so luxuriantly beautiful, perhaps, as that other one which she knew so well; yet it was more cheering. It lacked the intensely blue atmosphere of the rival vale, and its heavy soils and scents; the new air was clear, bracing, ethereal. The river itself, which nourished the grass and cows of these renowned dairies, flowed not like the streams in Blackmoor.[8]

The experience of elsewhere, then, is constructed in terms of its difference from the constant in Tess's system of geography, Blackmoor Vale as seen from Marlott; and as long as she can still believe she has some geographical centre, some home, the experience of being elsewhere, at some point on the circumference of the circle whose centre is known, can be managed. It does not threaten her identity, whatever else does, for the habit of contrasting what she does not know, with what she does, is a mode of cognition by which she can adapt to the unknown as well – an adaptation facilitated at Talbothays by Hardy's extravagant representation of the life there as one so sustaining that it is two months before it occurs to Tess to make any excursion beyond the immediate environs of the farm. Tess, says Hardy, was 'physically and mentally suited among these new surroundings'; she re-rooted herself there – had been 'transplanted to a deeper soil';[9] and by her marriage, of course, she seems to have the opportunity of making this vale her new home, the new constant by which other places will be known in the future – so that when the marriage collapses, and she can no longer live in the Vale of Froom, she returns to a Marlott which is now strange to her. The turnpike gate on the highway to the village is opened to her by a stranger, not 'by the old man who had kept it for many years', and his reassurance that 'Marlott is Marlott still' serves only to remind that for Tess this is no longer home, which should be, but is not, with her husband in the vale she has been obliged to leave.[10] 'Where do we d'Urbervilles live?' her father had asked the parson who informed him of his illustrious ancestry, and who had replied, 'You don't live anywhere'.[11]

It is this loss of a home, of a centre by which Tess might come to apprehend her migrations as movements along the radii and circumference of a circle, which makes her subsequent travelling, from Marlott to Port Bredy to Flintcomb-Ash to Emminster and back to Flintcomb-Ash, and then again to Marlott, not 'a sort of education', but a destruction of her way of knowing and of her identity alike. To some extent, of course, this loss of identity is willed, or at least an acceptance of necessity: at Marlott and Talbothays, Tess had always been distinguishable, from other women and from the landscape alike, by articles of clothing – a red ribbon, a pink jacket, a white collar – which did not allow her to be assimilated into the mass of either.[12] But on the road to Flintcomb-Ash, to discourage the attentions of the men she meets, she dresses herself as 'a fieldswoman pure and simple', in the grey, buff and whitey-brown of the chalk upland itself, and she becomes 'a thing scarcely percipient, almost inorganic', 'part of the landscape'.[13]

The monotony of this new landscape, its 'blank agricultural brownness', facilitates Tess's disguise: the 'long and unvaried road' from Port Bredy to Flintcomb-Ash, or the road from Long-Ash Lane, whose 'dry pale surface stretched severely onward, unbroken by a single figure, vehicle, or mark'.[14] At Flintcomb-Ash, there is 'nothing but fallow and turnips everywhere; in large fields divided by hedges plashed to unrelieved levels'[15] – the trees and shrubs, which were born to rise vertically from the landscape, cut down and flattened until there is, almost literally, 'no relief' in the landscape. Its anonymous character, and its power of conferring anonymity on those who work it, is perhaps best evoked in this extraordinary paragraph which describes the field in which Tess and Marian are set to hack swedes: it was

> a complexion without features, as if a face, from chin to brow, should be only an expanse of skin. The sky wore, in another colour, the same likeness; a white vacuity of countenance with the lineaments gone. So these two upper and nether visages confronted each other all day long, the white face looking down on the brown face, and the brown face

looking up at the white face, without anything standing between them but the two girls crawling over the surface of the former like flies.[16]

The absolute, unrelieved featurelessness of the landscape, insisted upon by the reminder that when we speak of the 'features' of a landscape we think of it as a face, contrasts quite evidently with the hills at Marlott, 'as personal to her as . . . her relatives' faces' – hills which, as if by confirming their personal relation with her, confirmed her identity in the vale they surrounded. But in these featureless fields on the chalk upland, where even the rain 'had no occasion to fall, but raced along horizontally upon the yelling wind',[17] Tess and Marian cannot make the simple act of self-assertion involved in standing upright – or they appear, briefly, as 'standing' between earth and sky, only to be crushed between the two 'visages' and to be set 'crawling' over the field 'like flies'.

The mechanisation, too, of the modern farm at Flintcomb-Ash contributes to deny identity: Marlott had only a 'rickety' reaper, but to Flintcomb-Ash comes an itinerant steam threshing-machine, the identity of whose operator has been consumed by the engine he serves: 'if any of the autochthonous idlers asked him what he called himself he replied shortly, "an engineer"'. But it is not simply that he serves a machine, that he is 'in the agricultural world, but not of it', that has left him with no name and with no identity beyond his occupation.[18] It is also the fact that he must be, for the engine *is*, itinerant; and his travelling has bred out of him the habit of noticing, so that he hardly perceives the scenes around him, or distinguishes one from another. The idlers who ask his name are distinguished from him, not simply by being idle, and thus not, for the moment, involved, as he is, in the industrialisation of agriculture; they are also *autochthonous* – and to be so, the implication is, is to expect people to have names, which those who are itinerant, as we shall see, may not have.

For beyond the conspiracy of Tess and of the blank landscape to deny her identity, is the fact that it has been destroyed by her new habit of travelling without reference to a constant centre in Marlott or Talbothays, so that she and the landscape merge and disappear: the landscape, existing in no relation to her knowledge of place, is no longer seen by Tess in terms of similarity and difference, and so no longer seen at all. Now all roads are long, unvaried, undifferentiated: this is the account of Tess's journey from Flintcomb-Ash towards Emminster:

> Keeping the Vale on her right she steered steadily westward; passing above the Hintocks, crossing at right-angles the high road from Sherton-Abbas to Casterbridge, and skirting Dogbury Hill and High-Stoy, with the dell between them called 'The Devil's Kitchen'. Still following the elevated way she reached Cross-in-Hand . . . Three miles further she cut across the straight and deserted Roman road called Long Ash Lane; leaving which as soon as she reached it she dipped down a hill by a transverse lane into the small town or village of Evershead, being now about half-way over the distance.[19]

There seems almost nothing to notice, here, but distances and directions, the intersection of one straight road with another: none of the features, the colours, the *differences* that marked the accounts of Tess's apprehension of places earlier in the novel. And yet, what has replaced that earlier mode of cognition is not the extended, educated, inquisitive geography of the tourist or traveller – the point is best made, perhaps, in a passage I referred to at the start of this essay.

> After this season of congealed dampness came a spell of dry frost, when strange birds from behind the North Pole began to arrive silently on the upland of Flintcomb-Ash; gaunt spectral creatures with tragical eyes – eyes which had witnessed scenes of cataclysmal horror in inaccessible polar regions of a magnitude such as no human being had ever conceived . . . [they] retained the expression of feature that such scenes had engendered. These nameless birds came quite near to Tess and Marian, but of all they had seen which humanity would never see, they brought no account. The traveller's ambition to tell was not theirs, and, with dumb impassivity, they dismissed experiences which they did not value for the immediate incidents of this homely upland . . . [20]

Enough has been done, earlier in the novel, to identify Tess, by a series of images, as a bird, for us to see now in this passage a close relation between what Tess has suffered and what has been suffered by these 'birds of passage, whose expressions reveal that they have survived journeys of which they will not speak, and which, not valuing, they dismiss'.[21] The process of moving, of migration, has left them 'nameless', so little time do they spend in one place, as efficiently as Tess's identity has been destroyed, and her name made doubtful, by her homelessness. For the birds, change has not been 'a sort of education' as it had been for the 'birds of passage' in 'The Dorsetshire Labourer': if they have not lost the capacity to learn, they have lost the will to do so, and to tell what they may have learned. They do not have the traveller's sense of geography which

Hardy recognised, in the essay, from the eagerness of the migrant labourers to 'astonish' their fellow-workers 'with stories of the wide world comprised in a twenty-mile radius from their homes'; and simply to quote that sentence is to indicate why. For those migrant labourers still think of themselves as having homes: they experience other places, as did Tess once, as points at the ends of lines radiating outward from that constant centre. Tess, and these nameless birds, 'don't live anywhere'; and Tess, in becoming less 'local in feeling',[22] has become more nothing. The best that she and Marian can do, working at Flintcomb-Ash, is look over to where on clear days, if there were any, 'you can see a gleam of a hill within a few miles o'Froom Valley'; but that centre, made ever absent, invisible, by the 'cloaking grey mist',[23] is not home for her, but only where home should be, and where her name should be clear, and Clare.

\* \* \*

I want to conclude, by turning back from the process by which in Tess the local, circular and self-centred sense of space is destroyed, to look at the ways in which Hardy attempts to communicate to his readers a notion of that primitive geography as it inheres in its purest form in the consciousness he attributed to Tess before her marriage. The geography of the reader that Hardy constructs is regional, pictorial and linear; and to that consciousness of space as it might have been acquired by such a reader, from books and by the opportunity to travel, Hardy appeals with a language rich in cartographical, geological and pictorial reference. Here is his description of the Vale of Blackmoor in the second chapter of Tess:

> The traveller from the coast, who, after plodding northward for a score of miles over calcareous downs and corn-lands, suddenly reaches the verge of one of these escarpments, is surprised and delighted to behold, extended like a map beneath him, a country differing absolutely from that which he has passed through. Behind him the hills are open, the sun blazes down upon fields so large as to give an unenclosed character to the landscape, the lanes are white, the hedges low and plashed, the atmosphere colourless. Here, in the valley, the world seems to be constructed upon a smaller and more delicate scale; the fields are mere paddocks, so reduced that from this height their hedgerows appear a network of dark green threads overspreading the paler green of the grass. The atmosphere beneath is languorous, and is so tinged with azure that what artists call the middle distance partakes also of that hue, while the horizon beyond is of the deepest ultramarine.[24]

'Calcareous downs', 'escarpments', a 'map', a landscape that has 'a character', the 'atmosphere', 'azure', 'what artists call the middle distance', 'hue', 'ultramarine': words and phrases such as these identify the reader as a literate traveller whom Hardy is to introduce to the consciousness of those who do not read about, who do not travel over, the various landscapes of Wessex, but who inhabit just one of them. This language constructs the reader as an Angel Clare, who first encounters Marlott, and Tess, on a walking tour through Blackmoor. The invitation the novels extend is that he should stop, observe, penetrate and 'read the secrets'[25] of a place he would usually pass through; but the secrets of the Vale of Blackmoor cannot be 'read', or certainly not by such a reader as this language constructs, one whose knowledge is customarily derived from reading. It is not *what* but *how* we learn that is at issue, and how we learn determines absolutely what we learn. If the vocabulary of the reader contains such words and phrases as I have just picked out, and by which he is able to understand the Vale of Blackmoor as occupying a place in a broad, regional geography, and among a wide range of possible landscapes, which he has encountered in books, pictures and by travelling, he will not be able to suspend that knowledge, but will understand the local only as a more detailed form of general knowledge – he will fail, if you will forgive the cliché, to grasp its absolute otherness. He will be able, indeed, only to characterise it *as* 'local', which is all I can do – and not as a knowledge which is, for those who have it, so inherent in their living in *this* place and no other, that it is not knowledge elsewhere, or for anyone whose knowledge is not so completely *of* that place, and so completely learned *in* it, that the local is all they know. The reader can certainly grasp from *Tess* that there is such a local knowledge, in Hardy's Wessex if not in nineteenth-century Dorset; but he can grasp only the notion of its existence, not the knowledge itself.

And so the opposition, between a local, and a wider geography and consciousness – between 'the old-fashioned stationary sort' of labourer and 'the habitually-removing man', between what Tess learns by living in Marlott and what she learns at school, between Tess and Angel – that opposition appears in the novel not simply as a *theme*, but as a problem of epistemology which must question the terms on which the novel can be written at all. As it constructs a reader who has to be invited to suspend his general knowledge to discover the local – but for whom, however willing he is to make it, that suspension is impossible – it constructs also a narrator who must claim, if he is somehow to mediate between the general and the local, that he is capable of performing that act of suspension that the reader cannot perform. He must appear capable of knowing what the heathfolk [in *The Return of the Native*] know, and what the reader knows, and of representing the local in the language of the novel without appropriating it to the general. He must be able to write the local in the language of the local, the general in the language of the reader, while performing the same act of separation that Tess performs, in speaking dialect at home and a version of standard English abroad;[26] but not only must these languages co-exist, neither appropriating the objects of knowledge that properly belong to the other, but the transitions from one language to the other must enable the reader to cross over from the sort of knowledge he has to the sort of knowledge he has not, and which, I have suggested, he *cannot* have.

I have defined the problem of knowledge in the novels, it may seem, too hastily, by announcing it as impossible of resolution as soon as I announced what it was; that happened, I suppose, because re-reading *The Return of the Native* and *Tess* before writing this essay, it was the grand impossibility of the narrator's task that struck me most forcibly. For the transitions I have spoken of, which, properly concealed (the fiction is) should enable the reader to step innocently over into the consciousness of the characters, seem quite impossible to conceal, and so work only to insist upon the disjunction between the two sorts of knowledge. The act of concealment that the narrator must try to pull off requires him to call no attention to the most obvious fact about the local, that of its nature it cannot be *written*; but he calls attention to that fact continually, as he represents the speech of the locals in a language which hovers between one degree or another of dialect, their thoughts in a language which hovers no less uncertainly between what we might imagine as appropriate to their thoughts, and one appropriate only to the thoughts of the reader the novels construct. . . .

Take the description of the Vale of Froom as it appeared to Tess on her journey from Blackmoor to Talbothays – in which she was represented as learning the geography of the new vale by comparing it with the old. When I quoted this before, I omitted a couple of sentences which I will now restore, and I will introduce them with the sentence that precedes them, to give an idea of the disjunction of the different modes of knowing they offer:

These myriads of cows stretching under her eyes from the far east to the far west outnumbered any she had ever seen at one glance before. The green lea was speckled as thickly with them as a canvas by Van Alsloot or Sallaert with burghers. The ripe hues of the red and dun kine absorbed the evening sunlight, which the white-coated animals returned to the eye in rays almost dazzling, even at the distant elevation on which she stood.

There is perhaps no need for any very lengthy analysis of this – the disjunction could not be more evident. For whoever it could be to whom the cows appeared like burghers in a Flemish townscape, it is evidently not Tess, and it is evidently not her sophisticated picturesque knowledge which distinguishes the tones of the cattle in terms of whether their skins absorb or reflect the light. And the pretence that it is – that this effect was noticeable 'even at the distant elevation on which she stood', just as evidently calls attention to the disjunction by the elaborate attempt to conceal it.

The chapter continues, a few pages later:

Tess Durbeyfield, then, in good heart, and full of zest for life, descended the Egdon slopes lower and lower towards the dairy of her pilgrimage.

The marked difference, in the final particular, between the rival vales now showed itself. The secret of Blackmoor was best discovered from the heights around; to read aright the valley before her it was necessary to descend into its midst.[27]

It is apparently only when Tess descends into the Vale of Froom that the marked difference between the two vales – the difference that will finally enable her to grasp what she does not know, here, in terms of what she does know, in Blackmoor – now 'showed itself' to her. This descent enables her to 'read aright' the new landscape – and if that phrase 'to read aright' manages to remain just about appropriate to Tess's mode of knowing, by a reflection that she is now outside Marlott, in a space she previously could have known only from the teachings of the village school, we must still ask, of Blackmoor Vale, for *whom* it contained secrets, and by *whom* they were best discovered 'from the heights around'? Apparently, the answer is Tess, for the tense – 'the secret of Blackmoor *was* best discovered – must indicate that this is her internal *oratio obliqua*; but, equally apparently, the answer cannot be Tess, who learned the geography of the Vale from within its depths, and who had access to knowledge of the vale which are secrets only to the traveller. It seems that the traveller who, in the description of Blackmoor I quoted earlier, comes north-ward over the calcareous downs to discover the vale 'extended like a map beneath him' – the traveller whom the novel constructs as its own inquisitive, alienated reader – has here attempted to penetrate Tess's consciousness of place, and to imprint upon it his own.

We can perhaps interpret such attempts at appropriation accord-ing to Hardy's account in 'The Dorsetshire Labourer', as embodying the process in real history whereby the consciousness of the traveller imprints itself on that of the 'locals', and obliterates the local know-ledge; and if we are disposed to believe in the existence of that local knowledge as a matter of historical fact, not fiction, so perhaps they are. But if we are more disposed to believe that primal, local know-ledge to have been a myth deployed by the novel to describe us, its readers, as alienated by the process of the differentiation of a primal unity, what will strike us most is not that such moments of appro-priation occur, but that they occur so *evidently*. They jut out of the narrative as awkwardly as do those, in *The Return of the Native*, where the narrator searches so painstakingly for a viewpoint, with such an evident attempt to do the impossible, that it is evidently impossible for us, too, to cross the space between what we see and what the locals know. The striking incongruity between Tess's view of the Vale of Blackmoor and the traveller's, between her perspective on the Vale of Frome and his, and the obviousness of the attempt to imprint his knowledge on hers, also emphasise the impossibility of the traveller's crossing the space that separates him from Tess, and preserve, on either side of that space, the twin myths of an original, unified sense of place, and of an alienated geography. The traveller can certainly attempt to print his consciousness on Tess, so that Blackmoor, 'an engirdled and secluded region' at the start of the novel, 'for the most part untrodden as yet by the tourist and the landscape-painter'[28] will be trodden, penetrated (as Tess, the bird, is 'trodden'[29] and penetrated by Alec D'Urberville) and inscribed in the list of the traveller's other conquests, Mellstock, Egdon, Little Hintock; and so that Tess will be violated again, by a smart tourist who knows about landscape-painting. But the attempt to do so will establish that she, and the Vale, if they can be violated, must certainly once have been intact; and if they can't be, still are.[30]

From *Journal of Historical Geography*, 8 (1982), 347–61.

# NOTES

[John Barrell is the author of a number of books on related themes: *The Idea of Landscape and the Sense of Place* (1972); *The Dark Side of the Landscape* (1980); *An Equal, Wide Survey* (1983); *The Political Theory of Painting from Reynolds to Hazlitt* (1986); *Poetry, Language and Politics* (1988). The common factors of his work, aside from a primary interest in the late eighteenth and early nineteenth centuries, are a concern with politics (and especially the politics figured in discourse), notions of history (especially as articulated in literature) and forms of representation both visual and linguistic (especially painting and poetry). Whilst not overtly theory-based or ostensibly marxist, John Barrell's criticism is properly seen as politicised, materialist and historically conscious; it is also acutely textual. In the essay reproduced here – from which have been cut two or three passages that draw for evidence on *The Return of the Native* – he shows how characters in *Tess*, and the herione in particular, perceive, and are partly defined by their perception of, their personal 'geographies'. But he also shows how the narrative deploys, and cannot resolve, two contradictory ways of seeing the Wessex landscape – itself then representing a particular static or mythic conception of an historical past from which the 'reader' must of necessity be alienated. In pointing to the contradictions in the narrative voice, this essay once again exposes – although not from within deconstruction – the riven and unstable textual ideology of the novel. Ed.]

1. Denys Kay-Robinson, *Hardy's Wessex Reappraised* (Newton Abbot, 1972); Andrew Enstice, *Thomas Hardy: Landscapes of the Mind* (London, 1979). Earlier studies include B. C. A. Windle, *The Wessex of Thomas Hardy* (London, 1902); Hermann Lea, *Thomas Hardy's Wessex* (London, 1913); R. T. Hopkins, *Thomas Hardy's Dorset* (London, 1922); D. Maxwell, *The Landscape of Thomas Hardy* (London, 1928). Also relevant are F. B. Pinion, *A Hardy Companion* (London, 1968); Robert Gittings, *Young Thomas Hardy* (London, 1975). References to other studies of the 'real' settings of Hardy's novels will be found in the bibliography to Enstice, *Thomas Hardy* (above).

2. H. C. Darby, 'The Regional Geography of Thomas Hardy's Wessex', *Geographical Review*, 38 (1948), 426–43.

3. David Lodge, *Language of Fiction: Essays in Criticism and Verbal Analysis of the English Novel* (London, 1966), ch. 4.

4. Thomas Hardy, *Tess of the d'Urbervilles*, ed. P. N. Furbank, New Wessex edition (London, 1974), p. 400 (all subsequent references are to this edition); Thomas Hardy, 'The Dorsetshire Labourer', *Longman's Magazine* (July 1883), 252–69, rpt. H. Orel (ed.), *Thomas Hardy's Personal Writings: Prefaces, Literary Opinions, Reminscences* (London, 1967), pp. 168–91. An informative and meticulously argued study of

the accuracy of Hardy's representation of the migration of labour and of other aspects of the social history of nineteenth-century Dorset, is Keith Snell, 'Thomas Hardy, Rural Dorset, and the Family', in his *Annals of the Labouring Poor: Social Change and Agrarian England, 1660–1900* (Cambridge 1985).

5. *Tess*, p. 136; *Personal Writings*, p. 180.

6. *Personal Writings*, p. 181.

7. *Tess*, p. 65.

8. *Tess*, p. 139–40.

9. *Tess*, p. 168.

10. *Tess*, p. 299.

11. *Tess*, p. 36. For an illuminating discussion of this passage, see Tony Tanner, 'Colour and Movement in *Tess of the d'Urbervilles*, *Critical Quarterly*, 10 (1968), 219–39, rpt. R. P. Draper (ed.), *Hardy: The Tragic Novels* (London, 1975), pp. 182–208. Tanner's essay remains by far the best discussion of Tess that I am aware of.

12. *Tess*, pp. 42, 124, 328; for a valuable discussion of this topic, see Tanner's essay, section iii.

13. *Tess*, p. 326.

14. *Tess*, pp. 361, 322, 354.

15. *Tess*, p. 329.

16. *Tess*, p. 331.

17. *Tess*, p. 322.

18. *Tess*, pp. 123, 373. It may be worth pointing out that if Denys Kay-Robinson is right in his suggestion that the most likely original for Flintcomb-Ash is the village of Plush in the parish of Alton Pancras, *Hardy's Wessex Reappraised*, pp. 126–7, then Flintcomb-Ash may be appropriately represented by Hardy as a farm on which mechanisation was unusually far advanced; for Christopher Taylor, *Dorset* (London, 1970), p. 153, notes that in 1866 'one of the first steam ploughing-engines in the county was used to break up the downland at Alton Pancras'.

19. *Tess*, p. 343.

20. *Tess*, p. 334.

21. Passages in which Tess, with varying degrees of directness, is compared with a bird, will be found on pp. 105, 138, 161, 183, 238, 263, 332 and 337.

22. *Personal Writings*, p. 180.

23. *Tess*, pp. 332, 333.

24. *Tess*, p. 39.

25. *Tess*, p. 141.

26. *Tess*, p. 48.

27. *Tess*, p. 141.

28. *Tess*, p. 39.

29. *OED*, 'tread', B: 8.

30. I would like to acknowledge the help and advice given to me in the preparation of this essay by Stephen Daniels, Harriet Guest, Adrian Poole, Hugh Prince and Keith Snell.

# 12

# Creating Tess, 1892

*SIMON GATRELL*

Of all of the printed texts of Hardy's novels the first one-volume edition of each is perhaps the most neglected by textual and literary critics; and yet it was potentially an important step in the development of all the novels. It was the first time that the novel had been reset after the first edition – after, that is, the reviewers had had their say about it, and Hardy always took the opportunity to revise, to a greater or lesser degree.

. . .

The one-volume edition that rewards attention most liberally is that of *Tess of the d'Urbervilles,* called by the publishers the 'fifth edition' because there were four impressions (though only three have been identified) of the three-volume first edition; it marks a somewhat different stage in the development of the novel from the other one-volume texts.

When the novel was serialised in the *Graphic* Hardy split off two episodes and published them separately, and made many other temporary revisions; this well-known history is important here because the work needed to restore (for the most part, though not entirely) the manuscript version for the first book-edition meant that he had less energy, and perhaps less time, than usual for fresh considerations of character and theme. Most of this energy he expended on developing Tess herself and themes directly associated with her. That is not to say that in the very large number of alterations made for the first edition there were no reworkings of other aspects of the novel; but it did mean that when, a year later, Hardy was able to revise freely for a reset edition, the novel had still not become a stable text in his mind, and that as a result his creative engagement with it was of a different order from that in the other novels at this stage; in each of them, he was altering details in a text that he chose to think of as established (almost fixed), whereas in the one-volume edition of *Tess*, concepts and characters in the novel were still being worked out.

Two other factors may have contributed to this sense that in 1892 the novel was still growing: once Hardy knew he was going to publish *Tess* in the *Graphic* (with whose editorial board he was about to tangle over *A Group of Noble Dames*), he may well not only have excised material from the earlier part already written, but also have felt unable to make revisions as he would have liked at that stage; more significantly, he must have written the second half of the novel, from Tess's confession to Angel onwards, with the *Graphic's* sensibilities in mind. The first edition would then have been the place to introduce the different tone or incident; but, as I have already said, there was so much to do to the text at that time that he would hardly have felt happy that he had even got (not everything right, because Hardy never felt that) most things more or less right. Hence the extra attention that he had to pay to this next resetting of the novel. His intense commitment to the novel and its heroine must also have made it hard for him to accept that they had finished growing in a substantial way. However, the plates of this edition were also used for the Osgood collected edition and for Macmillan's 1902 Uniform edition, making it inevitable that the one-volume issue was the stage at which the novel became to all intents and purposes fixed – at which the creative umbilical was cut.

It is one of the most noticeable features of *Tess* that the narratorial tone is not homogeneous, that it is split into two voices, which may, in a simplified way, be defined as detached and engaged. Quite a large number of changes in this edition are made in the distanced authorial narrative voice, as if Hardy was only beginning to realise in one or two areas exactly what it was that his novel meant to him personally and what he was saying through it to the world (what one might call the manifesto aspect of the novel). An example of this is the rewriting of a paragraph in chapter 5. It occurs at a place where the manuscript folio is lacking, so the first witness is the serial version:

> As Tess grew older, and began to see how matters stood, she felt
> somewhat vexed with her mother for thoughtlessly giving her so many

little sisters and brothers. Her mother's intelligence was that of a happy child: Joan Durbeyfield was simply an additional one, and that not the eldest, to her own long family of seven.[1]

For the first edition Hardy introduced into this simple mixture of Tess's and the engaged narrator's perception something that could only belong to the distanced narratorial voice, replacing 'she felt somewhat vexed with her mother' with 'she felt Malthusian vexation with her mother'. He also added, 'when it was such a trouble to nurse those that had already come' after 'brothers', and altered 'seven' to 'nine when all were living'.

When he came to the paragraph again a year later for the one-volume text it was with these three already revised details that Hardy was concerned. The first change was an attempt to integrate the apparently alien idea from political economy more closely into the engaged fabric of the novel; the phrase became 'she felt quite Malthusian towards her mother'. The economic motif was also intensified in the other two passages: 'those that had already come' was changed to 'and provide for them'; but more significantly the number of the family, suggesting a large but finite problem, was removed, and in its place Hardy added an outsider's view of their socio-economic position while leaving the family indefinitely large: 'nine when all were living' became 'waiters on Providence'. It cannot be a coincidence that Hardy thus linked the ideas of 'Providence' and 'provide':

> As Tess grew older, and began to see how matters stood, she felt quite Malthusian towards their mother for thoughtlessly giving her so many little sisters and brothers, when it was such a trouble to nurse and provide for them. Her mother's intelligence was that of a happy child: Joan Durbeyfield was simply an additional one, and that not the eldest, to her own long family of waiters on Providence.

And so the paragraph remains, with one exception: in 1895, for the Osgood edition, (though it meant a little plate alteration), Hardy added 'a' before 'Malthusian', subtly increasing the strength of the inference that Tess herself might know what it is to be a Malthusian.

Of all these changes, it is the last one made in the one-volume text that reverberates longest through the novel. That the Durbeyfields are a 'long family of waiters on Providence' is one of Hardy's chief accusations against them, one indeed that Tess herself does not escape; and the phrase gathers force as the crucial events of Tess's life are enacted. Though a small change it has a disproportionately large significance, and this might equally well be said of the whole revision undertaken for the one-volume text.

There are one or two other places where Hardy's concern for the economics of rural life surfaces in one-volume changes, changes expressed also through the distanced narrative voice. One of these suggests that Hardy had done a little research between the first edition and this revision, or else that someone had told him something. It occurs at the beginning of chapter 10, in a narratorial aside explaining why so many of Tess's contemporaries at Trantridge were married; previously the passage read: 'marriage before means was the rule here as elsewhere'. This generalised sententious comment of the superficial moralist was replaced in 1892 by an adequate economic motivation: 'a field-man's wages being as high at twenty-one as at forty, marriage was early here' (p. 65). This informed and concerned perception comes from the same sector of Hardy's interests as that which had stimulated him to write his essay, 'The Dorsetshire Labourer' (some of which is incorporated into chapter 51 of *Tess*). In reviewing in 1892 the role of 'cottagers who were not directly employed upon the land', in the relevant passage at the beginning of chapter 51, Hardy felt the need to add that they 'had formed the backbone of the village life in the past', and that they 'were the depositories of the village traditions' (p. 339). This is his own class that he is writing about, and it is as if it took until the one-volume edition for Hardy to figure out the crucial role with which he wanted to invest that class. In a sense this is a definitive statement of the finally established concern in Hardy which led directly to the revisions made in the two great collected editions that followed. Though it is not exactly a 'village tradition' that field-men were paid the same wage whatever their age and experience, the motivation that caused Hardy to register this fact as a reason for early marriages is very much that of the village historian.

A change in chapter 33 is also worth considering in this context: where the narrator describes the peal of bells rung from the church in which Angel and Tess are married, the passage has been considerably revised. In the manuscript's first version 'a modest peal of four notes broke forth'; later, still in the manuscript, 'a modest peal of three bells broke forth – the limited expression of the small tower ranging no further'. In the serial, 'tower' was altered to 'parish', which transferred the sense of limitation from building to people. This distinction was taken up and further refined in the first edition, when the passage after the dash was altered to 'the power of expressing joy in such a small parish ranging no further', suggesting perhaps a financial connection between the smallness of the parish and the paucity of bells. But the crucial change in emphasis came only in the one-volume edition – the fifth time the description had been revised – when the passage became: 'a modest peal of three bells broke forth – that limited amount of expression having been deemed sufficient for the joys of such a small parish' (p 211). At once, the meanness of the carillon is the responsibility of some agency superior to the parish and the parishioners, and class and authority have become factors; at the same time the irony is considerably sharpened. That the identity of those who have made the decision is left vague only increases the scope for suspicion – vicar? lord of the manor? church commissioners? Whoever it is, the decision is made outside the community. The final changes to the passage partially remove this ambiguity, by adding 'by the church builders' after 'sufficient'; both the paperback edition of 1900 and the Wessex edition of 1912 have this. Ambiguity still remains, since the narrator does not say who was responsible for building the church, but even more clearly it is not the folk who worship, or who get married, or christened, there.

Again it is Hardy's aligning himself with his class that stimulates the 1892 change. But *Tess* is a curious novel; I have used the terms detached and engaged narrator to distinguish between the primary voices that can be heard attempting to direct a path through events and introducing states of mind. I want now to suggest that there are contradictions within the detached narrator. I am not claiming that it was in this one-volume edition that Hardy *first* embodied in his narrator the representative of his class; what does seem to be true is that at this time something about this novel in particular, and his perception of his own fiction in general, was clarified, and stimulated the revisions I have been looking at and others like them. The 'Dorsetshire Labourer' borrowings, though lamenting, at times angrily, the decline of the artisan-craftsman class in rural areas, are written from the point of view of one who has escaped from that class-destruction into middle-class celebrity as a writer; the change to the bell-passage is made from a different point of view, that of a displaced and oppressed craftsman. And these two facets of Hardy's writing coexist uneasily in *Tess*, though driven far into the background for most readers by the power of the personal history that the novel enacts, the conduct of which is substantially the business of the engaged narrative voice.

In part, this distinction might be defined by the characters of Angel and Tess, and Hardy recognised that he had a problem in the presentation of Angel (one that he thought about carefully during the revision for the one-volume edition), especially in his relation to Tess. For instance, when Angel's harp is first introduced it is simply 'an old harp which he had bought at a sale'. We are given a fresh insight into Angel's nature by the addition to this, in 1892, of 'saying when in a bitter humour that he might have to get his living by it in the streets some day'. We hardly get a glimpse of this bitterness during his time at Talbothays, and the added detail here prepares us in a very small way for what comes at Wellbridge (p. 122).

There are changes made to every aspect of Angel's sense of his relationship with Tess, changes to his thoughts of her, to his physical sense of her, to his conversation with her. One of the most memorable sentences in Angel's unspoken response to Tess was only added at this stage of the novel's development: his naïve and rather priggish 'what a fresh and virginal daughter of Nature' (p. 124) was until the one-volume edition the more down-to-earth 'what a genuine daughter of nature'. The reader is, of course, aware of the ironic significance of 'virginal' at the moment that the thought passes through Angel's mind, but the irony becomes more powerful and poignant when the truth is also revealed to Angel. The capitalisation of 'Nature' is significant too, in that it reflects accurately the tendency in Angel to abstraction and idealisation, and thus helps to make his seduction by 'nature' at Talbothays more ironically effective.

Hardy was unsure how far Angel should be physically aware of Tess. In earlier revised texts the tendency had been towards emphasising Angel's asceticism at the expense of his capacity for sensuous perception, but in 1892 Hardy felt that the balance needed readjusting. Thus, for example, to a fragment of observation: 'Clare, regarding for a moment the wave-like curl of her lashes as they dropped with her bent gaze, lingeringly went away', Hardy added 'on her soft cheek' after 'lashes', registering more fully the impact of Tess on Angel's senses.

It is in particular during the terrible days at Wellbridge that Hardy uses revisions to dialogue to modify the reader's perception of Angel. Soon after Tess's narration of her experience with Alec, Angel proposes that she is out of her mind, and then answers himself:

> 'Yet you are not. I see nothing in you to warrant such a supposition as that.' He stopped to resume sharply, 'Why didn't you tell me before?'

So it is in the first edition, harsh and apparently without feeling; it becomes quite different in the one-volume edition:

> 'Yet you are not . . . My wife, my Tess – nothing in you warrants such a supposition as that?'
> 'I am not out of my mind,' she said.
> 'And yet – ' He looked vacantly at her, to resume with dazed senses: 'Why didn't you tell me before?'
>
> (pp. 225–6)

Here, instead of a secure assertion it becomes an agonised question, and instead of being sharply self-possessed he is bewildered.

We also see Angel differently through the narrator's commentary. To Tess's perception – 'She was awestricken to discover such determination under such apparent flexibility' – Hardy added a narratorial view, this time directly engaged with the character, as if it were only now that he felt fully the force of the character he had created: 'His consistency was, indeed, too cruel' (p. 238). On the other hand there is the addition a few pages later of: 'Some might risk the odd paradox that with more animalism he would have been the nobler man. We do not say it' (p. 240). The second sentence is Hardy's narrator at the height of evasiveness, and the plural pronoun, the characteristic note of the reviewer, is quite remarkably out of place. Furthermore Hardy *does*, of course, 'say it'. The 'odd' is so clearly ironical that it ensures the reader's disbelief of the narrator's denial, and encourages the reader to see in the word 'Some' Hardy himself separating himself still further from the text that has proceeded from his pen into print.

There are more engaged narratorial comments, though, and that one of these occurs in the same paragraph as that just considered points yet again to the remarkable flexibility of the narrative voice in *Tess*. As if to remind the reader of Angel's claim that he had not married the Tess before him but another woman in her shape, in the first edition the paragraph ends: 'The figurative phrase was true: she was another woman than the one he had desired.' This was an addition in the first edition; a year later Hardy felt that this put the matter too actively, and altered the last phrase to read 'the one who had excited his desire', which puts the primary onus on Tess; here is more evidence that Hardy has been thinking closely about the relationship between the two characters.

A second example is of a change to the summary of the couple's situation at Bramshurst Court; it is a moment that provides some interest. Tess says, 'looking through the shutter chink':

'All is trouble outside there: inside here content.'

He peeped out also. It was quite true: within was affection, pity, error forgiven: outside was the inexorable.

(p. 376)

This is the first-edition version, holding subtly in balance the three voices of Tess, Angel, and the narrator. There is a carefully managed contrast between Tess's perception and the second, which is Angel's mediated by the narrator and uses vocabulary that could not, despite her education, ever be Tess's. And in particular it is the word 'pity' that distances Angel from Tess; however selfless the pity, it is necessarily the emotion of one in happy and superior circumstances towards one in sad and distressed. As Meredith saw in the 44th section of *Modern Love*, when the lover feels pity he knows that he has left love behind. Hardy too saw this in 1892, and altered 'pity' to 'union', transforming the effect, giving authority to the reader's sense that in these few days there is an intensity of emotion which is in its way satisfying to the lovers reunited, remembering the earlier contention that 'experience is as to intensity, and not as to duration' (p. 129).

It is not only in his relationship with Tess that Hardy alters the way that the reader is enabled to see Angel; when he meets with Izz Huett at Wellbridge Hardy reshapes a number of Angel's speeches, making him less patronising, less priggish, more aware of the implications of what he asks Izz to do, and more aware of the pain he causes her by his withdrawal.

One of the revisions is to the central question itself; Angel reveals that he has parted from Tess: 'I have separated from my wife for personal, not voyaging, reasons. I may never live with her again. Will you go with me instead of her?' (p. 263). The middle sentence was an addition to the first-edition text, but Hardy was not satisfied with the simple proposal, and a year later he gave to Angel a piece of honesty deriving from self-knowledge, amending the last sentence to read: 'I may not be able to love you; but – will you go with me instead of her?'

Besides these and similar changes to aspects of Angel, there is a wide range of other facets of the novel that attracts Hardy's attention during this revision. Both of the other central characters, Tess and Alec d'Urberville, are refocused in small ways. The effect of the revisions to aspects of Tess is to make her more aware of what she is doing and feeling, and to make her slightly less immature; they might be taken as a pattern for the general direction of all the revisions that were made to her role in the novel from the first edition onwards. In the one-volume version almost all of the changes that relate to her are made to the three crisis-points in her life; her violation, her confession, and the murder of Alec – and their surrounding prefigurings and consequences. Laird has detailed the most important ways that the violation is altered:[2] the removal of the 'cordial' that Alec forced Tess to take before laying her in the leaves; the addition of 'succumbed to a cruel advantage he took of her helplessness; then, temporarily blinded by his flash manners, had been stirred to confused surrender awhile: had suddenly despised and disliked him, and had run away' (p. 87) to the narratorial summary of her life after that night; and the addition of a reference to her child that looks backward to that night: 'A little more than persuading had to do wi' the coming o't, I reckon' (p. 95).

I have already looked at many of the changes to the confession, but there is a further point worth mentioning: as Tess is preparing to match Angel's confession, Hardy decided in 1892 to make the most important feature of the whole episode more explicit for the reader, ensuring, as elsewhere in revision for one-volume editions, that the significance of the moment for his argument about Tess will not be missed. To Tess's 'No, it cannot be more serious, certainly' he added 'because 'tis just the same!' (pp. 221–2).

It was at this time that Hardy added what in isolation seems the most important single sentence in the narratorial voice that helps the reader to understand the events surrounding the murder of Alec. As Tess leaves him on the doorstep of The Herons, Angel has an insight into her state of being, which illuminates all that has preceded and all that follows – another of those passages of crucial clarification in which Hardy the faithful presenter of Tess recognises for the first time precisely the implications of the character he has created through three successive revisions: 'But he had a vague consciousness of one thing, though it was not clear to him till later; that his original Tess had spiritually ceased to recognise the body before him as hers – allowing it to drift, like a corpse upon the current, in a direction dissociated from its living will' (p. 366). It seems possible that another addition slightly earlier provided the hint that stimulates Angel's insight into Tess's state of mind. It comes in Tess's explanation of how it is that she is with Alec again: 'These clothes are what he's put upon me: I didn't care what he did wi' me!' (p. 366).

It is in this edition also that the first tentative steps are taken towards the reconsideration of Alec d'Urberville's conversion, which is completed in the paperback edition of 1900 and the Wessex edition of 1912. At this stage in the transformation from sincerity to hypocrisy the motivation is not the criticism of reviewers concerning the probability of the conversion but rather Hardy's deeper penetration into Alec's response to the sight of Tess again after a number of years and in such a role. Hence the addition (p. 299) to Alec's first words to Tess: 'Of course . . . there is something of the ridiculous to your eyes in seeing me like this. But – I must put up with that.'

Similarly, to his second speech (p. 299) Hardy adds: 'though perhaps you think me a humbug for saying it' and to his third (p. 300) the comment: 'Well, it is a strange story; believe it or not'. The strangeness of the story was the subject of some comment, and in the later editions Hardy went much further.

Finally, there is a good example of Hardy rethinking his attitude to a fundamental idea within the narrative. It is at the end of chapter 5 that his narrator analyses the implications of the first meeting between Alec and Tess:

> Tess Durbeyfield did not divine . . . that there behind the blue narcotic haze was the 'tragic mischief' of her drama – he who was the blood-red ray in the spectrum of her young life.

And further:

> she might have asked why she was doomed to be seen, and marked, and coveted that day by the wrong man, and not by a certain other man, the exact and true one in all respects – as nearly as human mutuality can be exact and true; yet to him at this time she was but a transient impression half-forgotten.
>
> (pp. 45–6)

There is a certainty about these passages that amounts to determinism, suggesting both that Tess's life is pre-ordained, and that the fiction in which the narrative is conducted is leading to already previsioned ends. In 1892 Hardy altered both, so that they now read:

> Tess Durbeyfield did not divine . . . that there behind the blue narcotic haze was potentially the 'tragic mischief' of her drama – one who stood fair to be the blood-red ray in the spectrum of her young life.

and

> she might have asked why she was doomed to be seen and coveted that

day by the wrong man, and not by some other man, the right and
desired one in all respects – as nearly as humanity can supply the right
and desired; yet to him who amongst her acquaintance might have
approximated to this kind, she was but a transient impression half-
forgotten.

Thus, Alec is only potentially the tragic event, and Angel 'might have
approximated' to the 'right and desired' lover of Tess. When looked
at in isolation this change seems significant and, even when
reintegrated into the continuous fabric of the novel, the reverberative
effect felt is quite different in the second version. We can no longer
rest comfortable on the narrator's authoritative statement which
implied that if Angel and Tess had come together before she met
Alec, all would have been well in their relationship; there is now
room for doubt whether the two would ever have found the basis for
a lasting and satisfying relationship in marriage or out of it. In the
end Hardy is giving both his narrator and his reader more freedom.

  There may be a good case for choosing as a favoured version of a
much-revised novel the one where it can first be suggested that the
writer's sense of it became established. With most novels, that is
likely to be its first appearance in book form, and with Hardy too
this is so for most of his novels. With *Tess*, though, I have argued
that this one-volume edition represents, with one quite important
exception, Hardy's first final version of the novel. That exception,
the way in which Alec's conversion is vulgarised and trivialised,
might be the subject of some debate – to what degree was it forced
upon him by critical comment? But, in any case, that is a narrow area
of concern; and it is the feature of the one-volume edition of *Tess*, as
it is not of any other of Hardy's novels, that the revisions range
widely throughout the text, and are in many cases of the first importance in understanding the ideas or characters that they touch.

From Simon Gatrell, *Hardy the Creator: A Textual Biography* (Oxford, 1988), pp. 99–110.

## NOTES

[Simon Gatrell is a well-known textual scholar and critic of Hardy. In
addition to the major Clarendon Edition of *Tess of the d'Urbervilles* that he
edited with Juliet Grindle, he has also edited the World's Classics edition
(again with Juliet Grindle), as well as *Under the Greenwood Tree* and *The
Return of the Native* for the same series. He is responsible for the Thomas

Hardy Archive volumes on both *Tess* and *The Return of the Native*, and has recently completed a further book on Hardy's fiction, *The Proper Study of Mankind* (London, 1992), in which there is additional discussion of the developments and material detailed in the excerpt reproduced here – in particular an account of the novel from Angel Clare's point of view. The present essay, taken from a longer chapter entitled 'From *Tess* to *Jude*: 1892–1894', is a good illustration, as implied in the Introduction (p. 7), of Simon Gatrell's conception of 'textual biography', in which a writer's development is charted by way of the revisions he or she makes to sequential editions of their work. Taking the 1892 one-volume edition of *Tess*, which offers a unique occasion in Hardy's writing career because he was for once able to substantially revise a novel which 'had still not become a stable text in his mind, [where] concepts and characters in the novel were still being worked out' (pp. 172–3), the essay details the subtle and highly self-conscious emendations Hardy made to the text at that point and the effects these have on our understanding of the whole, leaving us with an even stronger sense of just how unstable, uncertain and 'unfinished' a text *Tess* is. It seems clear that Hardy himself did not fully understand the novel he was trying to write or what he wanted to say. Ed.]

1.  Thomas Hardy, *Tess of the d'Urbervilles*, ed. Juliet Grindle and Simon Gatrell, with an Introduction by Simon Gatrell, The World's Classics edition (Oxford, 1988), p. 49. All further references are to this edition and appear as bracketed numbers in the text.

2.  J. T. Laird, *The Shaping of 'Tess of the d'Urbervilles'* (Oxford, 1975), pp. 176–9.

# 13

# The Offensive Truth: 'Tess of the d'Urbervilles'

*JOHN GOODE*

## I  PURITY AND FAITHFULNESS

*Tess of the d'Urbervilles* is one of the most discussed novels in the language. It was clearly intended to be. Everything about the presentation of the text calls on the reader to participate in its production: the subtitle, a *pure* woman *faithfully* presented, offers a double challenge, first to the moral values it expects to encounter and contest, and secondly to an aesthetic judgement – what is 'pure', what is 'faithful'? The division into 'phases' spatialises temporal change so that, at the moment of crisis, between 'The Consequence' and 'The Woman Pays' a decisive progression is made between the moment of speaking and the silence which follows, and makes it a deterministic growth so that 'pure' cannot be ascribed to a state of being 'untinctured by experience' (since the first 'phase' is not that of a 'woman' at all but of a 'maiden'), but most effectively to the moment of death ('fulfilment'). 'Untinctured' clearly differentiates itself from the moralistic 'untainted', but as clearly brings that possibility shamefully to mind. And the Preface confirms this dislocation of prevailing assumptions. Quoting St Jerome, the most unlikely defender of sexual growth, it links truth with offence.[1] Even its textual history confirms our sense of its designs upon us – there is no freezable text, only a constant exchange of revisions, particularly polemical sharpenings. It is possible that Hardy sent the novel to publishers certain to refuse it in order to generate an atmosphere of controversy before its publication.[2]

This discussability is resisted in various ways in order to inscribe the text within the institution of literature. In order to ascribe *meaning*, liberal analysts of the late 1960s and the 1970s met the disjunctions of the text as a confusion arising from a prior ideological commitment and an insurgent humanist identification with the protagonist.[3] They discarded the polemic altogether, so that what remains is a naturalised Tess, as though she is more than the words of the text, to be mourned, loved or otherwise possessed in the sacred refuge of the (usually male) reader's good nature. A later generation, seeing the danger of this, reconstructs the text as discontinuity or endless repetition of forms, and this is closer to my own analysis, but I think it reaches the impasse of Hillis Miller, by which the text is trapped in an infinite plurality of decipherings which are no more than the ruins of human song that blow about Egdon Heath.[4] And even P. Boumelha ends with a strangely despairing pluralism that does not question the gleeful appropriation of J. Bayley.[5] At least those readers who look in vain for coherence retain a sense of the novel's impact, which does not cease to be unified in the double anger of the subtitle – pure/faithful.

We should try to become the reader the book demands. If there is no comfort in coherence (we cannot put the book down, and say amen) it is no more merely an exhilarating exercise. We must acknowledge the novel's disjunctions as a particular strategy. On the one hand there is no form which is not discontinuous since signs only identify themselves as difference, but discontinuity cannot be a function of 'form' at all since the opposite to their differentiation is amorphic/amorphous (formless). I will stress a polemical design in which the discontinuities are seen as properties of the ideological discourses the text articulates. It is heteroglossic, in Bakhtin's real sense which is not the revisitation of polysemic ghosts as it is often treated, but the evaluation of verbal interactions.[6]

At the centre of critical debate is the correlation of two discourses, that of 'nature' and that of 'gender'. There is a third, that of the social relations of production. They form an ideological hierarchy which can be formed in the primary model of superstructure and base. The discourse of nature is effectively about 'reality' that is 'wisdom', the free play of concepts within the role of uncontaminated ideology. Gender too is ideological – it takes its origin from the assumptions about reality which are marshalled by ideology but it is not pure as nature is, for gender relations subserve a specific economic need – specifically marriage is a form to facilitate the production of surplus value, and organise its distribution. It mediates the 'natural' and the 'social', which are respectively the concerns of ideology (the super-structure) and the relations of production (the base). The presence of these discourses is not in doubt. What I want to establish is that they open out into one another. Or rather as the look such discourses bestow on life is returned from the contradiction within them, their intended foreclosure is subverted, not endlessly, but ending on a question. For each discourse is manifest as a way of looking which is at the same time looking at looking. Although the ideological discourse of nature and the discourse of the social relations of production correspond to the opposed metonymies of the return and the gesture (as being aligned with the repeated 'rhythms' of life and the 'march' of history respectively) and the discovery of gender constructing the object of love as symptom with the metaphor of human making, so that it manifests itself finally on the sacrificial stone, the identifying signal is the gaze, either appropriated or at last returned.

. . .


## II  JUSTICE WAS DONE

The gaze of wisdom is the double gaze, the gaze of sexual oppression is the appropriated gaze, the gaze of the social relations of production is reciprocated – the gaze in exchange. It appears most dramatically when Tess and Angel take the milk to the trains:

> The light of the engine flashed for a second upon Tess Durbyfield's figure, motionless under the great holly-tree. No object could have looked more foreign to the gleaming cranks and wheels than this unsophisticated girl, with the round bare arms, the rainy face and hair, the suspended attitude of a friendly leopard at pause, the print gown of no date or fashion, and the cotton bonnet drooping on her brow.
>
> (ch. 30)

Like the fly on the billiard table, and the girl in the pink cotton jacket, this is an image of Tess which momentarily turns the novel inside out so that we gain a certain determined distancing from the experiential narrative. But it is very different from these. For our intimacy with Tess at this point is much greater since it is mediated through Angel's company, so that the change in perspective is not merely from her to an opposing gaze, but her visibility to the opposing gaze of something outside the novel (and therefore outside the illusion in which it holds us). Moreover it is not the eye of the painter who picks out a girl from a landscape, or of a god, but the eye of the gleaming cranks and wheels of a locomotive. This estrangement of Tess involves therefore the construction of the reader's eye in terms of a specific social and cultural medium. We have to transpose ourselves to an unspecified passenger seeing Tess as an image lit only by the form of transport in which we are carried. Our vision in other words does not liberate the viewer in the manner to which he is accustomed in the construction of images. 'Foreign' also discards any possibility of an absolute possessing assessment – she is not simple or beautiful but only different (and 'unsophisticated' doesn't give a positive purchase). The moment is further troubled by the simile 'the suspended attitude of a friendly leopard at pause'. Again it is redolent of a strange paradox – it is a moment which returns the gaze we try to hold it in.

In terms of the novel's structure, the function of this passage is to remind us of the social specificity of the story that is being told. And it is not the image taken away by the train that is developed (the reader is whisked away by it and has to be returned to the text); it is a moment whose meaning is *voiced* by the 'receptive Tess'. What follows is her observation of the immensity of the social gap specifically in relation to the Ruskin–Morris critique of the division of labour: 'Londoners will drink it at their breakfasts tomorrow won't they . . . Strange people that we have never seen.' Angel who, as we know, reduces social experience to cultural choices (the ache of modernism is something that may be learnt by rote) vaguely comments on the adulteration of milk (note that his response is on behalf of the consumer), but is totally unable to grasp the social relations which Tess is defining. As she insists and elaborates, *he* takes refuge in the humorous potential of her unsophistication ('particularly centurions') and as she continues, he tries to silence her by reminding her of the private function of their presence at the station. We have seen this before as well when Angel, 'privateering' at the garlic picking, singles out Tess. But what is different here is that he is not artificially selecting Tess but suppressing the real social relationship by which she relates, and thinks of herself as relating, to the world as a whole. More specifically, since the relationship is defined in the reciprocal gaze (the train watching Tess watching the train), I mean *our* world, the world of the consuming reader who will not only drink milk without ever having seen a cow but consumes Tess's story without having to undergo it.

The process recurs – at the climax of what for Tess is an epoch of letting things be. Moving in a photosphere (of her 'excess of honour' for Angel) and knowing that her past sorrows 'were waiting like wolves just outside the circumscribing light', she desires 'perpetual betrothal' so as not to tie time to an institutional structure. Angel presses her for a date in the presence of gnats knowing nothing of their brief glorification. It is another image of dualistic possibility of Darwinian nature since, although it includes the wisdom that knows of their coming extinction, it does not diminish their ecological identity ('irradiated as if they bore fire within them'). At the same time, the transition in the cows lying-in hospital reminds us of the actual economics of Talbothays, and it is in the context of her coming redundancy that Angel presses his hint: 'I don't think you ought to have felt good, Angel.' Note also in this chapter how Angel plans to stay with her to continue the process whereby she learns to talk like him. In other words there is a process of socialisation going on which looks like chivalry to her and is actually a form of possession for him.

Significantly again Tess, off her guard, is responsive to the social world as a whole. Listening to the waters of the vale forces on their fancy that a great city lies below them. But it is she who speaks: 'It seems like tens of thousands of them . . . holding public meetings in their market places, arguing, preaching, quarrelling, sobbing, groaning, praying and cursing.' Again Tess reaches out through her imagination to the populous world from which she is held apart by her fictionality and we note how that reaching out is by her own linguistic awareness. For not only is this a novel in which ways of speaking define relationships but one in which, too, the *potential awareness* of its protagonist is in terms of linguistic interaction. It links her to the world of the reader, the communal and the linguistic. But again it is repressed: 'Clare was not particularly heeding' – and he reminds her that she is about to be made redundant.

Now obviously the vision of the train does not inaugurate the discourse of the social relations of production. It has been present from the beginning and it motivates in the last instance both the discourse of nature and the discourse of gender. But what is important about this passage is the reciprocity of the gaze, and this may seem an odd thing to insist on in a context in which the determinations exercise a non-self-contradictory control. But just as the privileging of the voice over the eyes is a token of the evolution of the discourse of gender, so this return of the gaze across the social divide indicates the whole strategy of the novel. For the discourse of the social relations of production is present at first as the one-way gaze of the anthropologist and sociologist, Parson Tringham's thoughtless genealogy, or 'the yellow melancholy of this one-candled spectacle'. But the attack on nature's holy plan is an anger that arises from a securely distant cliché, 'All these young souls were passengers in the Durbeyfield ship.' And, at its most dislocating, the 'picture' of the Durbeyfields merely switches from the flippant to the serious: thus the lurching of the drunken John Durbeyfield between his wife and his daughter 'produced a comical effect, frequent enough in families on nocturnal homegoings: and, like most comical effects, not quite so comic after all'. We only get *into* this world with the controlled terms of Tess's selection from it. Her emergence, and her consequent availability to the less determined ideologies of wisdom and love is the condition of the reader's involvement. But what happens during the passage from Tess's acquiescence in Angel's courtship and his rejection of her is that her mind is developed and her voice *audibly repressed*, so that we can no longer revert to the comfortably distanced realism of the opening. And yet that is precisely and explicitly what Hardy does – he sends Tess back into the world of the social structure from which both Alec and Angel have temporarily, and violatingly, separated her.

Thus when Tess re-enters the novel in chapter 41, she is both a solitary and a social phenomenon: 'We see her a lonely woman with a basket and a bundle in her own porterage.' Later, of course, when the already disastrous consequences of her selectability become a general danger she has deliberately to violate her beauty to survive and become, in a savagely ironic transformation of the title, 'a fieldwoman pure and simple'. It is the more ironic because it picks up and confirms in a bitter way the 'improvement' Clare has made to Tess by decking her with jewels and lowering her neckline: 'The beauty of the midnight crush would often cut but a sorry figure if placed inside the fieldwoman's wrapper upon a monstrous acreage of turnips on a dull day.'

But what we have is a double movement. In the first place, of course, there is a vividly realised sequence of contexts in which Tess is made to pay as a working-class woman for the desire of the middle-class males. Feeling 'hunted', she takes refuge in a copse where wounded partridges take refuge and she has to kill them to put them out of their misery. From then on we have the totally realised starveacre Flintcomb Farm, which produces the most extreme alienation in the woman forced to work there (Marian tells Tess that they can see 'the gleam of a hill' to remind them of Talbothays). Then follows the journey to Emminster, the battle with Alec, and the threshing machine which reduces Tess from the selected object in the pink coat in the previous threshing episode to a mere vibration. Finally the whole episode of the death of the father and the Lady Day eviction reduces her to a sociological phenomenon. (Hardy actually, of course, quotes from his own essay.) I don't need to spell out the vivid realism of this narrative – unlike some of its contemporary naturalistic representations of how the poor live, it is fully presented from the inside as a realm of experience. We only need to read ten pages of George Moore's *Esther Waters*, which Bayley amazingly considers to be superior in some ways to Hardy's novel, to understand the difference between a writer who can present working-class reality and one who relies on 'local colour'. But at the same time, it picks up and modifies the range of perspectives offered. To begin with, it puts Tess in her class again. She may be Mrs Clare but she is one of the girls who are trying to survive on casual labour and dreams. This is not only true of Flintcomb–Ash but also, in a more significant way, at Marlott, when she works the vegetable plot in the twilight. 'She was oddly dressed tonight, and presented a somewhat *staring aspect*, her attire being a gown bleached by many washings . . . The women further back more white aprons . . . ' (ch. 50; my italics, stressing the gaze returned). The focus on Tess dissolves into the group. So much, Hardy had commented earlier, for Norman blood unaided by Victorian lucre. Selection is a condition of the economic structure. Of course here she is about to be selected again by Alec working alongside her, but it will be a selection whose condition is solely economic.

Secondly, the process explicitly revalues the discourse of nature. When the Durbeyfields are exposed to the Lady Day eviction it is broached with that evolutionary wisdom that has tried to place the oppression of Marian and Tess within 'the two forces'. But just as that is undermined by the immediate comment that Marian's will to enjoy has to be aided with drink, so this is openly contradicted. 'So do flux and reflux – the rhythm of change – alternate and persist in everything under the sky' (ch. 50). The Lady Day migrations are part of the life of the countryside. But, he recalls, 'a depopulation was also going on'. This is a historical and not merely a sociological event. Flux and reflux do not account for the irreversible change. This refocusing of gender, from almost standard woman to fieldwoman, and of nature, from the rhythms of life to the history of agriculture is half of the process by which ideological discourses open up into the discourse of the base.

The other dialectically contradicts the generalising tendency of the first. As she is absorbed more and more into the landscape, becoming a documentary case, as she becomes more and more the object of a text whose concern is less 'with' her than with the social process she represents, she emerges contradictorily as a woman capable of telling her story in her own voice, more than by her eloquent eyes. The 'somewhat staring aspect' responds to her historical placing as a question about the just and the unjust. There is a powerful transition to this return when a little earlier in the chapter she is watched by Alec in the barn. She appears on his altar as a 'Cyprian image' which well nigh extinguishes the fire of the priest. The reconstruction of Tess as *femme fatale* at this stage is a reminder of how far away we have moved from that appropriation, since there is no way, having seen Tess bent double over a field of stones, and hobbling back from Emminster because Mercy had taken her boots, that we can identify with Alec's idealisation. But it also leads to an astonishing passage in which the erotic gaze is assimilated into her consciousness as an act of exploitation: 'She went on without turning her head. Her back seemed to be endowed with a sensitiveness to ocular beams – even her clothing – so alive was she to a fancied gaze that might be resting on her from the outside of the barn' (ch. 45). It takes her hunger for affection and replaces it with an 'almost physical sense of an implacable past'. The gaze that is returned is the gaze of the victim who knows that victimisation is the law, who knows that the question she asks about justice is not going to be answered.

This has two consequences. In the first place, precisely insofar as she is absorbed into a social setting which silences her as one of many in a long line of many changes, she acquires a voice for the reader. Thus, after she has spent the night in the copse, she kills the birds 'tenderly' and feels ashamed of her 'gloom of the night, based on nothing more tangible than a sense of condemnation under an arbitrary law of society which had no foundation in Nature'. We should obviously compare this with the end of chapter 11 – what is said there by the author against Tess's erroneous consciousness is now her consciousness. Later it becomes impossible to tell whether Hardy is echoing her consciousness or commenting on it: 'Then she grieved for the beloved man whose conventional standard of judgement had caused her all these latter sorrows.' The disconversion of Alec, the letters to Angel, the complaints about being a victim, the comment that life is vanity – these are not isolated outbursts but aspects of a structured development of a voice which does not accept the socialisation which is inevitable. So that we are both presented with a picture of Tess's life and times, and made to hear the voice that the picture silences. Obviously the fact that she has to speak through *writing* has its own kind of resonance and this is confirmed by the fact that Hardy reprints the second letter at its arrival. The only *voice* she is allowed is the imitation of Angel but nothing stops her from making a text. And, of course, this is exactly what is happening in relation to the reader. For we no more hear Tess than we see her: what we have is a textualisation which offers us (in theory) the choice. Clearly we only make the choice that is made necessary by the event but what is important is that Tess is a heroine for the writing age. She is 'fulfilled' in the space between the social rubric and the offensive truth.

This dialectical movement is intensified and it means that the novel has no satisfying end. But it does not mean that it has no end. What the reader is forced to do is to take on the inexorable logic of the socialisation of Tess in the context of her increased articulateness. Thus, for example, the way in which she talks to Alec – not the arguments learnt from Clare, but the comments she makes in terms of her own experience ('and then it is a fine thing, when you have had enough of that, to think of securing your pleasure in heaven by becoming converted', 'He won't hurt me. *He's* not in love with me'; 'Why, you can have the religion of loving kindness at least.') – have a very different effect on the reader from what is actually happening. That is, she is allowed to reach a certain kind of wisdom based on her experience which promises to reconstruct her as a voice rather than as eyes for the reader. Above all, the voice textualised in the letters to Angel makes a stand against his values, so that they effectively for the first time 'faithfully' represent the affirmed integrity of the sub-title: 'I am the same woman, Angel, who you fell in love with.' The second thus recognises the cruelty of his rejection, and labels it with a word which casts a radical ironic shadow over the end as injustice. The last gives up on justice altogether and calls out that term which we have already seen constitutes the collective gesture in response to the reproach of the law: 'please, please, not to be just; only a little kind to me' (ch. 53). The more authority she gains with the reader, the more she is deleted by oppressive forces: as Tess 'learns' by experience, the lessons serve no purpose except to make her aware of what will happen to her anyway.

The action of the text *puts the reader through* the primary work-ing-class experience: the truth does not make you free, it simply exposes your chains. There are other novels which show this. But I know of none that actually thrusts it on the reader. This is strengthened by the fact that her two decisions – to go with Alec and to murder him, which each in their turn trap her into the system whose conse-quences they attempt to subvert – echo Angel's 'truth': 'Yet a con-sciousness that in a physical sense this man alone was her husband seemed to weigh on her more and more.' We want to ascribe this to the ideology which her whole development has denied. But in the end it is what is left her. Prostitution is the ultimate capitalist relationship for the woman. Her whole economic being is the sale of her body – the violation of the threshing machine is clearly coherent with the occupation of her body. In this perspective the murder is not an escape from this closure. 'How can we live together,' Angel had asked, 'while that man lives?' (ch. 36). The rational answer is obvi-ous as Tess's first letter makes clear. Rationality, however, is not that she has an answer but the same as power to rule the world – the only way it is possible to live together is to end Alec's life. Again the effect on the reader is to make him (yes) protest. She doesn't have to go that far! 'What bodily? Is he dead?'

Angel's silly question here echoes one dimension of the reader's response – that is the desire to naturalise the situation, to reserve it in terms of a personal survival. His consequent reflections spell out the other dimension of his logic, the inscription of the reciprocated gaze:

> His horror at her impulse was mixed with amazement at the strength of her affection for himself; and at the strangeness of its quality, which had apparently extinguished the moral sense altogether. Unable to realise the gravity of her conduct she seemed at last content; and he looked at her . . . and wondered what obscure strain in the d'Urberville blood had led to this aberration – if it were an aberration.
>
> (ch. 57)

'Amazement', 'obscure strain', 'aberration – if it were an aberration', 'nothing could be more foreign': Angel's trip to Brazil has taught him relativity but it is not enough to take him over to her. And this applies to us as well, since he is the reader's main agent in the last phase, the narrative centrality of Tess having been brought to an end with the unexplained decision to go off with Alec. That is why, in spite of the dialectic of experience and circumstance by which the reader is increasingly frustrated as the novel progresses, what we have to acknowledge in the end is the reciprocation of the gaze. From that reciprocation grows, however, not some privatised privileging of experience (by which we could possess 'Tess' as an act of love) but the unviolated signifier of the returned gaze as question and dream.

First let us look at the moment of recognition itself and then try to pick up its reverberations in the text.

> They stood, fixed, their baffled hearts looking out of their eyes with a joylessness pitiful to see. Both seemed to implore something to shelter them from reality.
> 'Ah – it is my fault!' said Clare.
> But he could not get on. Speech was as inexpressive as silence. But he had a vague consciousness of one thing, though it was not clear to him till later; that his original Tess had spiritually ceased to recognise the body before him as hers – allowing it to drift, like a corpse upon the current, in a direction dissociate from its living will.
>
> (ch. 55)

On one level, the reciprocation of the gaze here is the recognition of how the truth is a form of bondage: they stand *fixed*, their hearts look out of their eyes (as though out of a cell), and the joylessness (the negative of the recognition after absence, the very reverse of what should be) is effecting a positive force (like the later 'existlessness'). Seeking 'shelter' (the word is proleptic) from 'realms', Angel tries to resolve it by *language*, but is unable to continue. Note that Hardy says not what one would expect, 'go on', but 'get on' – it is as though language would be a way of progress, but it is devoid of its power now. (This may have something to do with the expressive power of Tess's own 'realism' – 'he bought me', 'these clothes are what he's put on me. The step back to him was not so great as it seems. He had been as husband to me: you never had.') What remains to him is 'a vague consciousness' of the implications of the reciprocated gaze. Note how carefully Hardy sets up this sentence (an addition of 1892; he must have felt it necessary to establish Tess's specific presence). She ceases to recognise (see) her body, which is the body in his gaze, her body before him, as hers. Throughout what we have seen is her body – here at the moment of epiphany (which is what it ironically is). It is on offer as a property of someone else. He *bought* me. This confirms the imprisoned look which they exchange, but leaves two openings. In the first place, the new Angel is *conscious* that the look makes this separation, and secondly it is like a corpse to a current (Ophelia) dissociated from *its living will*. So that there is an other that has vacated this purchased body clothed by its owner. An other that the new Angel is forced to recognise.

The terms of this recognition are worked out in such detail that we have for the moment merely to follow the text. Of course Angel, for whose ideology the murder is done, thinks she has gone mad: 'As well as his confused and excited ideas could reason, he supposed that in the moment of mad grief of which she spoke her mind had *lost its balance*, and plunged her into this abyss' (my italics). It reminds us of 'you are ill; and it is natural'. The gesture Tess makes which embodies the full force of her emancipation from Alec and her commitments to Angel is bound to appear like an act of insanity. There is a point beyond which the eloquence of woman, in her own voice, is always *insane*. Obviously you don't need to go around killing the men who possess you. That is going too far. 'What, bodily? Is he dead?' But just as Angel is able to stop speaking and be vaguely conscious, so here his ideas are confused and excited and are inadequate ideas (in Spinoza's sense). And a remarkable transition takes place, prepared for by the relativism of Brazil, foreseen in the gentle way he carried her across the streams:

> It was very terrible [read tragic] if true: if a temporary hallucination [women are hysterical. He never meant bodily dead!], sad [I'll look after her till we get her to a hospital]. But, anyhow [this is confusing] here was this [here, no other but this one, not a constructed generality] deserted wife of his, this passionately fond [she terrifies me] woman, clinging to him without suspicion that he would be anything but her protector [poor thing has forgotten that there is a law. She seeks shelter from reality!].

Angel is still the old ineffectual Angel beating in his void. But also new. Thus:

> He saw that for him to be otherwise was not, in her mind, within the region of the possible. Tenderness was absolutely dominant in Clare at last.

After all those confused ideas and shifting responses, HE SAW. But what he sees is not that she is mad or sad or any other objectifiable predicate. He sees what in her mind is the region of the possible. He sees her as subject of her own sentence. And the word that Hardy reaches for in this context is, of course, 'tenderness'. It is a word that has previously occurred in the sleepwalking sequence: 'The revelation of his tenderness by the incident of the night raised dreams of a *possible future* with him.'

This last is, of course, a private thought of Tess. In fact she has deliberately suppressed it because it might imply that she was laughing at this compromised dignity, and she is not sure that he won't think her calculating. That privacy, that silence, however, constitute a trace in the novel that is not the novel for the novel is the law. But there is also a not-the-law, *'dreams of a possible future'*. Two moments at Talbothays indicate this. The first is the negative, silent response Tess makes to the story of Jack Dollop: 'This question of a woman telling her story – the heaviest of crosses to herself – seemed but amusement to others.' Almost immediately after, she varies that other in response to his individuation and selectivity:

> 'Our tremulous lives are so different from theirs, are they not?' . . .
> 'No so very different, I think . . . There are very few women's lives
> that are not tremulous.'

The significance of these statements becomes clear in the last but two chapters of the novel. Ideologically what is important is that they reach out to other subjectivities. There are instants of tenderness, but which go against the uttered phrase. However, they are important because they are of the text as well as in it. This question of a woman telling her story is precisely the question of the novel which is compelled by the silence of her oppression to tell it for her, and tell it as an amusement, since that is what novels are, for others. Moreover her process of selection – this is Tess's story and not anybody else's – is part of the condition of the novel too. But, as we are constantly reminded, the distance between Tess and the other girls is not always so very great. There are other stories. Other women's lives are just as tremulous. The whole pragmatic effect of the novel is called by this into question. Boumelha says that Hardy cannot make up his mind whether Tess is exceptional or representative. But we must try to distinguish the effect of the text from its commodity value. For the process of representativeness itself is a process of exceptionalising. To write a novel is always to lift the single story out of the social picture and for precisely that reason it is bound by its very nature to lure the reader towards the private solution. In other words we ought to be feeling very strongly that Tess needn't have actually murdered Alec and that she and Angel could have worked it out. And maybe if they had been actual living human beings they could have worked at some kind of private solution to the contradictions with which they engage. But it is precisely this kind of confusion that Ellen in Morris's *News from Nowhere* objects to in the novel and which Hardy, motivating Tess at the end as *actress* (in both senses of the word) avoids. He opens out the book not in the sense of leaving it available but in a sense that pushes it back into life, into the general. So that if we do feel very strongly that Tess didn't need to murder Alec, we ought in the end to understand that to feel that way is irrelevant.

It is irrelevant because Tess has understood what constructs her and the murder makes possible a parenthesis within the sentence (in both senses) in which she is inscribed. For actually, like Sancho Panza, she is given an island, not in space but in time, during which she is allowed to learn from her experience.

We have to return to this running commentary on the text; it is so necessary to be careful. She has killed Alec because it has come to her as a shining light that she 'will get you back that way' (ch. 57). Her response to Angel's decentring of love (not for its own sweet sake but for the sake of the species and the institution) is to turn him into a god (she mistakes his lack of fervour for chivalry, remember?): 'I was unable to bear your not loving me.' 'I will not desert you' (whatever you have done!). She, however, takes possession of the novel's campaign key word: 'the one man on earth who had loved her purely, and who had believed in her as pure'. (Note she has told Alec that it is possible to retain *loving kindness* and '*purity*'.) There is, however, an unalienated version of this worship: 'the thought of going through the world with him as her own familiar friend . . . the laugh of a woman in company with the man she loves'. Out of this she creates Utopia. We note now that for this space, it is *Tess who looks at him* (he was still her Antinous, her Apollo even) and he is no longer at the service of his own consciousness but of hers. They move not to the station but into the woods. Briefly they recover a natural rhythm: 'They promenaded over the dry bed of fir needles, thrown into a vague intoxicating atmosphere at the consciousness of being together at last, with no living soul between them; ignoring that there was a corpse.' I call it 'natural' here simply because the only significance of the corpse is the law – in 'nature' there is no reason why you should take any notice of a corpse. (Utopias are by their nature natural.) Moreover it is a journey into the 'interior' (Angel's word), which makes us forget for a while that we are actually talking about England.

They follow 'obscure paths' – it is to a new terrain, a new life they tread. And yet the journey is not fugitive but innocent: 'Their every idea was temporary and unforefending, like the plans of two children.' The perspective created by these phrases gives them a parenthesis. They are in movement rather than flight. Later, coming to an abandoned house, Tess interprets it socially: 'All these rooms empty, and we without a roof over our heads.' So it is her comment as much as Angel's decision that takes them back. Hardy, of course, reminds us of the actual state of affairs by having the housekeeper leave them alone because of the fine quality of the clothes Tess has been wearing – which, were, of course given her by Alec. In case we miss the point, she thinks of it as a genteel elopement – that is, she inserts it into a romantic love story. 'Rest at last' – an epoch of rest – news from nowhere. 'Why should one put an end to all that's sweet and lovely? . . . All is trouble outside there; inside here content' (ch. 58). She is looking out and he looks out *after* her. Later, when she hears the *music* of Stonehenge, he will listen – in contrast with his unheeding responses earlier. Moreover, he finds what she says is true – 'Within was affection, union, error forgiven: outside was inexorable.' The happy house, a dream of rest, of union, which cannot last for really it is not just there but part of a social system – a property, like Tess herself. The contrast between what is and what might be.

The utopian interval makes the novel's end completely uncathartic. Passing through the intercepting medieval city to the heathen temple of Stonehenge they reach a theatre of containment. Stonehenge is clearly the monument but it is full of problems. Angel thinks it monstrous but she hears there the music of a gigantic harp. She asks to stay, but he says it is too *visible*. She replies that it is an ancestral home (through the mother). She asks whether it has been used as a sacrifice to God and he replies no, 'I believe to the Sun.' So that it is a heathen and matrilinear, and it is also the site of her question about Liza Lu. Neither Boumelha nor Bayley find this acceptable. But it is neither fantasy nor childish. What Tess is asking Angel to do is marry his deceased wife's sister, which is not merely blasphemous but specifically is the occasion of Matthew Arnold's most vituperative attack on modern liberalism in *Culture and Anarchy*. Tess is once again challenging the hegemony, this time in terms of the customs of her country. So although it is right for the site of sacrifice it is not the sacrifice of the present order. She is too fit, as one of my undergraduates pointed out, to die at Stonehenge. Hardy stresses her capacity for walking and effort. What we have instead is a line of policemen crossing a plain to take her back into her sentence.

I have read and reread *Tess of the d'Urbervilles* many times during twenty years, and I still find the end impossible to read. Throughout I have warned against naturalising Tess, but, of course, it is part of the strategy of the novel that we should do so. The novelist aims at an illusion. But this novelist aiming at it and succeeding only does so to punish us for our complacency. How many other English novels end with the execution of the female protagonist, who has already been raped? To have her die would enable us to say amen – terrible and sad but so be it. But she is hanged by the neck until she is dead. 'Justice' is in inverted commas, both because it is a legal term carried over into aesthetic discourse (hence the savagely ironic invocation of the Aeschylean phrase). We know what average human nature thinks of divine morality, and we know that Tess understands the meaning of sport: 'she had occasionally caught glimpses of these men in girlhood . . . strangely accoutred, a bloodthirsty look in their eyes'. Our ruling classes, like gods, administering justice as sport. But notice how it continues – gaze and speech again – 'the two speechless gazers bent themselves down to earth, as if in prayer, and remained thus in prayer absolutely motionless.' But the flag, the only signifier of narrative left, continues like some distant friend to 'wave silently'. Invocations of *Paradise Lost* are not adequate here (though they are relevant). Hardy is making us read about the response to the *hanging* of a loved one. As soon as they had strength they arose. Nothing, of course, is left to reciprocate their gaze. They are not silent, but speechless. The only language is the flag's. But it is also the novelist's. 'Justice' is torn between legal action and poetic fitness, but, as we know Hardy sent *Tess* to Morris, and the original newspaper of the Social Democratic Federation was called *Justice*. Justice is more than the prevailing law. It is something that is fought for, a truth that is on the offensive.

From John Goode, *Thomas Hardy: The Offensive Truth* (Oxford, 1988), pp. 110–12, 125–37.

## NOTES

[John Goode is a critic whose work, while passionately and unremittingly materialist in nature, incorporates but was not formed by the theoretical debates of the past two decades. It is based on 'the premise that historically informed and politically committed readings of poems, plays and novels can help us expose, understand and deplore all forms of oppression and exploitation, and celebrate the necessity of justice' (letter to the editor). As I have acknowledged John Goode's earlier contribution to the remaking of Hardy's fiction more extensively in the Introduction (see pp. 7–8, 10). I will not repeat myself here. However, the present essay (which has had cut from it two sections, 'Nature's Holy Plan' and 'An Almost Standard Woman', in which conventional discourses of 'Nature' and 'the natural' are shown to be, in effect, agents of patriachy used to repress and dispossess women) catches up many of the themes which structure this New Casebook: the unstable text of *Tess*, the naturalisation of the novel by the 'liberal analysts of the late 1960s and the 1970s' (p. 185), its finally unresolvable 'incoherence', and its own, self-reflexive, obsession with representation ('looking' and 'speaking') – especially in relation to the patriarchal imaging and silencing of women. But the essay, while implicitly underwriting the novel as a heteroglossic postmodern text, refuses to accept it as an 'infinite plurality' of meanings. Rather John Goode proposes that the novel's disjunctions and discontinuities are reflexes of its challenge to the ideological discourses it confronts, and that, in this sense, *Tess* enacts its own anger at them: an offensive truth is also a truth on the offensive. Ed.]

1.   St Jerome was, of course, notorious for his violent adherence to chastity. Hardy could have read an account of St Jerome in F. W. Farrar, *Lives of the Fathers: Sketches of Church History and Biography* (London, 1889), II, pp. 203–402.

2.   J. Grindle and S. Gatrell (eds), *Tess of the d'Urbervilles* (London, 1983), p. 10. This is now the standard edition of the novel, and the kind of plurilingual text Hardy deserves. On the shaping of the novel and its entry into the public domain, see also J. T. Laird, *The Shaping of 'Tess of the d'Urbervilles'* (Oxford, 1975); and N. N. Feltes, *Modes of Production of Victorian Novels* (London, 1986), pp. 57–75.

3.   The best is B. Paris, '"A Confusion of Many Standards": Conflicting Value Systems in *Tess of the d'Urbervilles*', *Nineteenth-Century Fiction*, 24 (1969–70), 116–46.

4.   J. Hillis Miller, *Fiction and Repetition* (Cambridge, 1982), pp. 116–46.

5.   Penny Boumelha, *Thomas Hardy and Women: Sexual Ideology and Narrative Form* (Brighton, 1982), p. 132.

6.   Mikhail Bakhtin, *The Dialogic Imagination: Four Essays*, ed. Michael Holquist, trans. Caroline Emerson and Michael Holquist (Austin, 1981). See also V. N. Volosinov, *Marxism and the Philosophy of Language*, trans. V. I. Titunek (1926; New York, 1973), pp. 40–1.

# Further Reading

There is, of course, a daunting mass of critical writing on Hardy's fiction in general (not to mention his poetry) and on *Tess of the d'Urbervilles* in particular, but I have restricted myself here to about thirty-five further works of criticism related to *Tess*, from about 1970 onwards, which might have found themselves represented in the present collection if space or my preference had not ruled them out. The list of suggested reading which follows, therefore, is heavily selective, and should be used in conjunction with the synoptic analysis of recent tendencies in criticism and their impact on the study of Hardy's fiction outlined in the Introduction (pp. 3–11): while not being strictly sectionalised, the list is broadly governed by the categories of Hardy criticism identified there. I offer, then, further representative collections of essays on Hardy and on *Tess*; significant earlier instances of what I have called 'humanistic formalism'; and additional examples of work relating to the critical approaches which this New Casebook promotes: materialist criticism, feminism, poststructuralism and so on. I have not included editions of Hardy's work or 'further writings', or biographies, letters, 'Companions' or any other examples of the scholarly underpinning of Hardy Studies; neither have I listed again the works which comprise the present volume – except in the case of a collection of essays from which only one piece appears here. I have, however, in some cases repeated reference to influential works mentioned in passing in the Introduction or in the Notes to it. Where it seemed helpful to do so, I have offered a brief comment on the works listed below.

## I

Further collections of essays on Hardy, or specifically on *Tess*, would include:

Albert J. LaValley (ed.), *Twentieth-Century Interpretations of Tess of the d'Urbervilles* (Englewood Cliffs, NJ: Prentice-Hall, 1969).
R. P. Draper (ed.), *Hardy: the Tragic Novels*, the 'Casebook' series (London: Macmillan, 1975). Contains influential 'humanist-formalist' essays on *Tess* by David Lodge and Tony Tanner (revised edn, 1991).
Dale Kramer (ed.), *Critical Approaches to the Fiction of Thomas Hardy* (London: Macmillan, 1975).
Anne Smith (ed.), *The Novels of Thomas Hardy* (London: Vision Press, 1979).
Norman Page (ed.), *Thomas Hardy: The Writer and His Background* (London: Bell & Hyman, 1980).
Harold Bloom (ed.), *Modern Critical Interpretations of Thomas Hardy* (New York: Chelsea, 1987). Reprints influential sexual/textual essays on *Tess* by J. Hillis Miller and Mary Jacobus – see below – as well as a further excellent piece by Kathleen Blake – see below.
Lance St John Butler (ed.), *Alternative Hardy* (London: Macmillan, 1989).

## II

Well-regarded examples of an earlier, more formalistic interpretation of Hardy's fiction are:

Jean Brooks, *Thomas Hardy: The Poetic Structure* (London: Elek Books, 1971).

Ian Gregor, *The Great Web: The Form of Hardy's Major Fiction* (London: Faber, 1974).

J. T. Laird, *The Shaping of Tess of the d'Urbervilles* (Oxford: Oxford University Press, 1975). This is the pioneering study of the textual evolution of *Tess*, and is referred to in the Introduction to the present volume at p. 6 and Note 12.

John Bayley, *An Essay on Hardy* (Cambridge: Cambridge University Press, 1978). See section vii, especially, on *Tess*, but the whole book is a classic literary-critical reading of Hardy's work.

Peter Casagrande, *Unity in Hardy's Novels: 'Repetitive Symmetries'* (London: Macmillan, 1982).

J. B. Bullen, *The Expressive Eye: Fiction and Perception in the Work of Thomas Hardy* (Oxford: Oxford University Press, 1986). Especially useful, as noted in the Introduction to the present volume, on Hardy's use of the visual arts in his novels.

Two helpful 'study-guides', specifically on *Tess*, are also worth noting:

Arnold Kettle, '*Tess of the d'Urbervilles*', 'The nineteenth-century novel and its legacy', units 17–18 (Milton Keynes: Open University Press, 1982).

Graham Handley, *Thomas Hardy: Tess of the d'Urbervilles*, 'Penguin Critical Studies' (London: Penguin Books, 1991).

Terence Wright's *Tess of the d'Urbervilles*, The Critics Debate series (London: Macmillan, 1987), unfortunately concerns itself with older Hardy criticism for the most part, and so limits its usefulness.

## III

Good 'sociological' or 'materialist' criticism of Hardy, and more particularly of *Tess*, is hard to find, and apart from that represented in the present volume, all I can securely recommend is:

Raymond Williams, *The English Novel from Dickens to Lawrence* (London: Chatto & Windus, 1970). See the Introduction to the present volume, Note 19, and the introductory note to essay 1 for further brief comment on this.

Merryn Williams, *Thomas Hardy and Rural England* (London: Macmillan, 1972).

Judith Weissman, 'The Deceased Wife's Sister Marriage Act and the Ending of *Tess of the d'Urbervilles*', *American Notes and Queries*, 14 (May 1976), 132–4. No more than a note on a very specific matter, but a telling point which problematises many historically illiterate literary-critical readings.

Patricia Alden, *Social Mobility in the English Bildungsroman* (Ann Arbor: UMI Research Press, 1986). The chapter on Hardy explores the way his own complex social position shapes, and is refracted by, his fiction.

## IV

Two further interesting reviews of Polanski's film, *Tess*, are:

Nell Kozak Waldman, '"All that she is": Hardy's *Tess* and Polanski's', *Queen's Quarterly*, 88: 3 (Autumn 1981), 429–36.

Margaret Harris, 'Thomas Hardy's *Tess of the d'Urbervilles*: faithfully presented by Roman Polanski?', *Sydney Studies in English*, 7 (1981/2), 115–22.

Both these brief essays attempt to compare book and film.

## V

The following books and essays are not in every case strongly recommended, but in different ways they all relate to the issues and approaches the present New Casebook has foregrounded: in these respects they are, exactly and only, suggested 'further reading'. By and large they appear in date order, and are roughly clustered by topic.

J. Hillis Miller, *Thomas Hardy: Distance and Desire* (Oxford: Oxford University Press), 1970.

J. Hillis Miller, *Fiction and Repetition: Seven English Novels* (Cambridge: Harvard University Press, 1982). The chapter, '*Tess of the d'Urbervilles*: Repetition as Immanent Design', a long, displayful, deconstructionist reading, is reprinted in Harold Bloom (ed.) above; for further detail on the essay's history, see the Introduction to the present volume, Note 16.

John Lucas, *The Literature of Change* (Brighton: Harvester, 1977). Contains a long, opinionated but lively reflection on 'Hardy's Women'.

Mary Jacobus, 'Tess: The Making of a Pure Woman', in Susan Lipshitz (ed.), *Tearing the Veil: Essays on Femininity* (London: Routledge & Kegan Paul, 1978). This influential essay, which is reprinted in Harold Bloom (ed.), above, analyses the way Hardy seems progressively to intensify Tess's 'purity' in the course of composing the novel. For further publication details of the essay, see the Introduction to the present volume, Note 16.

Rosalind Miles, 'The Women of Wessex', in Anne Smith (ed.), *The Novels of Thomas Hardy* (London: Vision, 1979). A 'positive', non-feminist, account of Hardy's presentation of his female characters.

Patricia Stubbs, *Women and Fiction: Feminism and the Novel, 1880–1920* (Brighton: Harvester Press, 1979). The whole book is excellent general contextual reading, but in particular, chapter 4, 'Thomas Hardy, A Study in Contradiction', is a persuasive account of what its title proposes.

Adrian Poole, '"Men's Words" and Hardy's Women', *Essays in Criticism*, 31: 4 (October 1981), 328–45. Tries to deal sensitively with sexuality and language in Hardy's fiction, but its own endemic and unself-consciously sexist discourse hampers its effect.

Kathleen Blake, 'Pure Tess: Hardy on Knowing a Woman', *Studies in English Literature*, 22: 4 (Autumn 1982), 689–705. This illuminating and perceptive essay is reprinted in Harold Bloom (ed.) above.

Rosemarie Morgan, *Women and Sexuality in the Novels of Thomas Hardy* (London: Routledge, 1988). There is a long chapter on Tess as 'Passive Victim?' The whole book represents an odd grafting of deconstruction-influenced textual analysis onto a rather ingenuous upbeat celebration of Hardy's treatment of female sexuality.

T. R. Wright, *Hardy and the Erotic* (London: Macmillan, 1989). Contains a complete chapter on Tess as 'A Pure Woman?' Despite its interesting and potentially rich topic, however, the book as a whole is disabled by its rather gestural deployment of French theorists such as Foucault and Kristeva, and by its otherwise overly descriptive analysis of the novels.

Four other works, less concerned with sexuality and gender than the above, are finally worth mentioning in so far as they relate to those issues of language, perception and structure which the present volume has also focused on:

Peter Grundy, 'Linguistics and Literary Criticism: A Marriage of Convenience: a reply to Peter Barry's article in "English" Summer 1980', *English*, 30: 137 (Summer 1981), 151–69. An exhaustive, professional linguist's analysis of one passage from *Tess* – the 'rape/seduction' scene at the end of 'Phase the First'.

Suzanne Hunter Brown, '"Tess" and *Tess*: An Experiment in Genre', *Modern Fiction Studies*, 28:1 (Spring 1982), 25–44. A 'reader-response'-influenced essay, which interestingly, if slightly perversely, takes a piece of the novel (the journey on which Prince the horse is killed) and reads it as though it were a free-standing short story in order to see how our perception of structure influences our reading.

Janet Freeman, 'Ways of Looking at Tess', *Studies in Philology*, 79: 3 (Summer 1982), 311–23. Detailed account of the incidence of this aspect of the novel.

Joe Fisher, *The Hidden Hardy* (London: Macmillan, 1992). A fascinating reading – too recent to be incorporated in the present volume – which analyses the subversive subtexts beneath the 'impostures' which are the acceptable surfaces of Hardy's fiction.

# Notes on Contributors

**John Barrell** is Professor of English at the University of Sussex. His most recent books are *The Infection of Thomas De Quincey* (New York/ London, 1991) and *The Birth of Pandora* (Basingstoke, 1991). He is currently working on a study of politics in Britain in the 1790s.

**Penny Boumelha** holds the Jury Chair of English Language and Literature at the University of Adelaide. She is the author of *Thomas Hardy and Women* (Brighton, 1982) and has written the volume on Charlotte Brontë for the Key Women Writers series (Brighton, 1990). She is currently working on the colonial metaphor in *fin de siècle* feminism and on theories of realism, and is editor of the volume on *Jude the Obscure* in the New Casebook series.

**Laura Claridge**, an Associate Professor of English Literature at the United States Naval Academy in Annapolis, Maryland, is co-editor of *Out of Bounds: Male Writers and Gender(ed) Criticism* (Amherst, 1991) and author of *Romantic Potency: The Paradox of Desire* (Ithaca, 1992). She is currently working on a study of 'the beautiful' as the neglected supplement to the dominant aesthetic of 'the Sublime' in late-eighteenth-century literature.

**John Goode** is Professor of English at Keele University. He has published works on politics and culture in the nineteenth century, on George Gissing and Henry James, and is at present working on a study of the changing public role of the writer in the late-nineteenth century.

**Simon Gatrell** is Professor of English at the University of Georgia. He has published extensively on Hardy, and also written *A Bibliography of George Crabbe* (Folkestone, 1978), edited *The Ends of the Earth* (vol. 4: 1876–1918) of *English Literature and the Wider World* (London, 1991), and is working on a critical study of the Irish novelist Jennifer Johnston and a biography of the poet William Allingham.

**Patricia Ingham** is a Fellow and Senior Tutor in English at St Anne's College, Oxford, where she is Times Lecturer in English Language. She has written the Introduction to the Everyman edition of *Tess of the d'Urbervilles* (London, 1991) and is the author of *Dickens, Women and Language* (Hemel Hempstead, 1992).

**Jean Jacques Lecercle** is Professor of English at the University of Nanterre. He has written *Philosophy Through the Looking Glass* (London, 1985), *Frankenstein: mythe et philosophie* (Paris, 1988) and *The Violence of Language* (London, 1991). He is currently writing a book called *Philosophy of Nonsense*.

**Jane Marcus** is Distinguished Professor at the City University of New York Graduate School and the City College of New York, and also co-ordinator of the Women's Studies Programme there. One of her more recent works is *Art and Anger: Reading Like a Woman* (Columbus, 1988). Amongst other projects, she is currently working on a volume called *Britannia Ruled the Waves*, about colonialism, Virginia Woolf and others.

**Kaja Silverman** is Professor of Rhetoric at the University of California, Berkeley. She is the author of *The Subject of Semiotics* (New York/ Oxford, 1983), *The Acoustic Mirror: The Female Voice in Psychoanalysis and Cinema* (Bloomington, 1988) and *Male Subjectivity at the Margins* (London, 1992).

**Charlotte Thompson** is Adjunct Scholar in the Faculty of Humanities at the University of Arizona where she teaches medieval and early renaissance literature. She is the author of a number of articles on medieval topics, and is currently writing a book on Chaucer's *The Knight's Tale* and a further substantial essay on *The Manciple's Tale*.

**Peter Widdowson** is Professor of Literature at the University of Brighton. He has edited the Longman's Critical Reader on D. H. Lawrence (London/ New York, 1992), is preparing a selection of Hardy's poems and non-fictional prose for the Routledge English Texts series, and is planning a book, *Newstories*, on contemporary British fiction.

**Merryn Williams** is a poet and translator of Lorca. She has written *Thomas Hardy and Rural England* (London, 1972) and *A Preface to Hardy* (London, [1976], 1992).

**Raymond Williams** was, from 1974 to 1983, Professor of Drama at the University of Cambridge. His many books include *Culture and Society, 1780–1950* (London, 1958), *The Long Revolution* (London, 1961), *Modern Tragedy* (London, 1966), *The English Novel from Dickens to Lawrence* (London, 1971), *The Country and the City* (St Albans, 1973), *Marxism and Literature* (Oxford, 1977) and *Culture* (London, 1981).

**George Wotton** is Senior Lecturer in Modern English at the University of Hertfordshire. He is the author of *Thomas Hardy: Towards a Materialist Criticism* (Goldenbridge, 1985).

# Index